Sextus Julius Frontinus and the Roman Empire

Sextus Julius Frontinus and the Roman Empire

Author of *Stratagems*, Advisor to Emperors, Governor of Britain, Pacifier of Wales

John D. Grainger

Pen & Sword
MILITARY

First published in Great Britain in 2023 by
Pen & Sword Military
An imprint of Pen & Sword Books Limited
Yorkshire – Philadelphia

Copyright © John D. Grainger 2023

ISBN 978 1 39905 122 4

The right of John D. Grainger to be identified as
Author of this Work has been asserted by him in accordance
with the Copyright, Designs and Patents Act 1988.

A CIP catalogue record for this book is
available from the British Library

All rights reserved. No part of this book may be reproduced or
transmitted in any form or by any means, electronic or mechanical
including photocopying, recording or by any information storage and
retrieval system, without permission from the Publisher in writing.

Typeset by Mac Style
Printed in the UK by CPI Group (UK) Ltd, Croydon, CR0 4YY.

Pen & Sword Books Limited incorporates the imprints of After
the Battle, Atlas, Archaeology, Aviation, Discovery, Family History,
Fiction, History, Maritime, Military, Military Classics, Politics,
Select, Transport, True Crime, Air World, Frontline Publishing, Leo
Cooper, Remember When, Seaforth Publishing, The Praetorian Press,
Wharncliffe Local History, Wharncliffe Transport, Wharncliffe True
Crime and White Owl.

For a complete list of Pen & Sword titles please contact

PEN & SWORD BOOKS LIMITED
47 Church Street, Barnsley, South Yorkshire, S70 2AS, England
E-mail: enquiries@pen-and-sword.co.uk
Website: www.pen-and-sword.co.uk
or
PEN AND SWORD BOOKS
1950 Lawrence Rd, Havertown, PA 19083, USA
E-mail: Uspen-and-sword@casematepublishers.com
Website: www.penandswordbooks.com

Contents

Maps		vii
Introduction		xii
Chapter 1	Early Life: An Exercise in Speculation	1
Chapter 2	Frontinus on Surveying	20
Chapter 3	Rise to Consul	31
Chapter 4	Governor of Britannia, I: The West	53
Chapter 5	Governor of Britannia, II: The North	79
Chapter 6	Frontinus on War	100
Chapter 7	*Comes* in Germania	113
Chapter 8	Asia	130
Chapter 9	Nerva	144
Chapter 10	The New Regime at Work	160
Chapter 11	Traianus Imperator	173
Chapter 12	Water, and Another Book	183
Chapter 13	The Narbonensian and Other Connections	191
Chapter 14	The Man	204
Chapter 15	Frontinus and the Roman Empire	216
Notes		226
Bibliography		239
Index		243

Maps

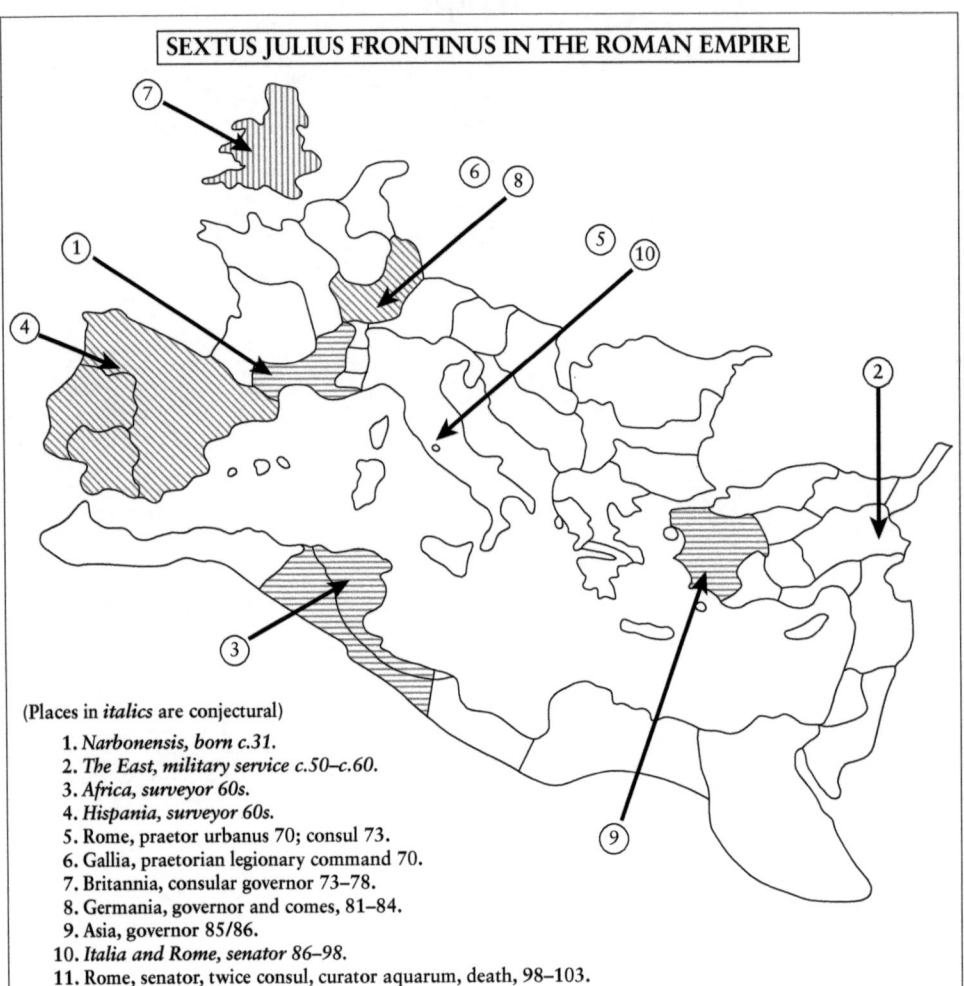

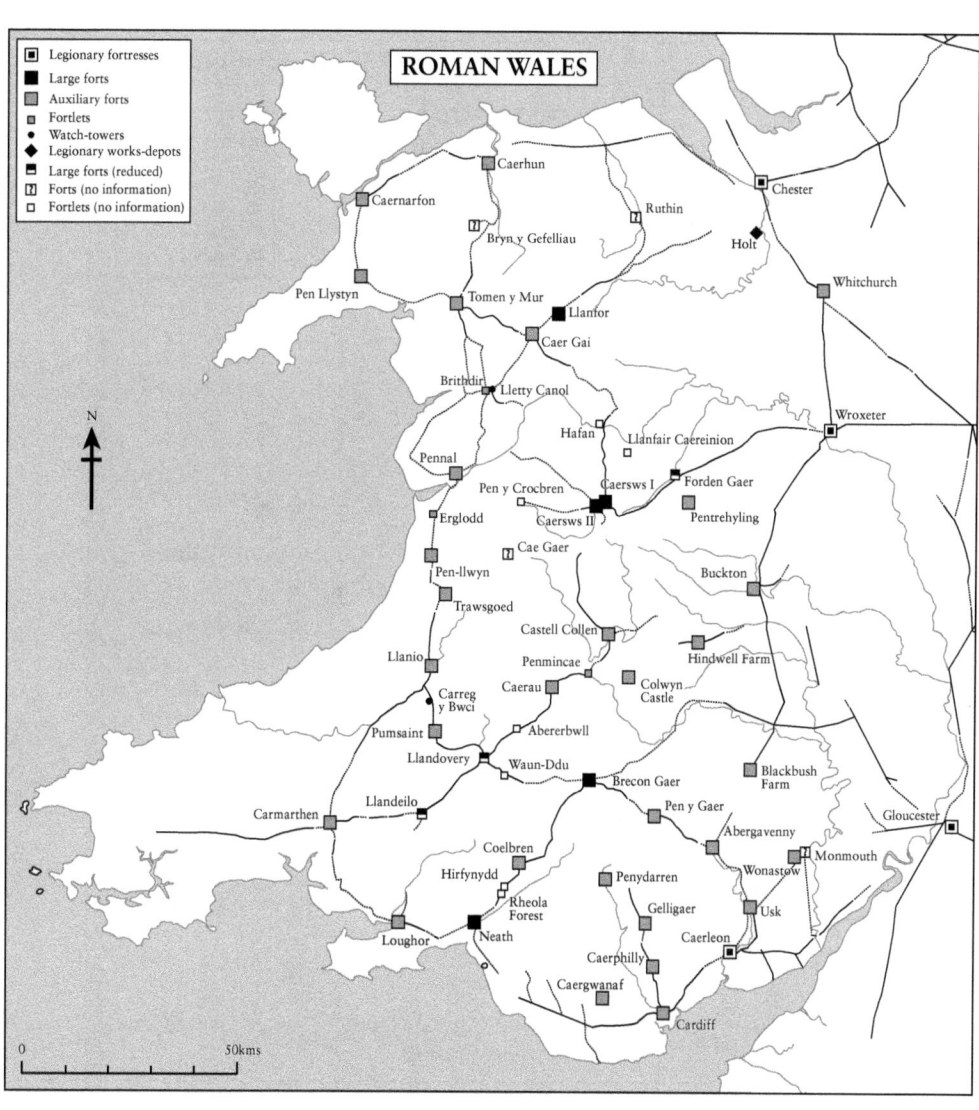

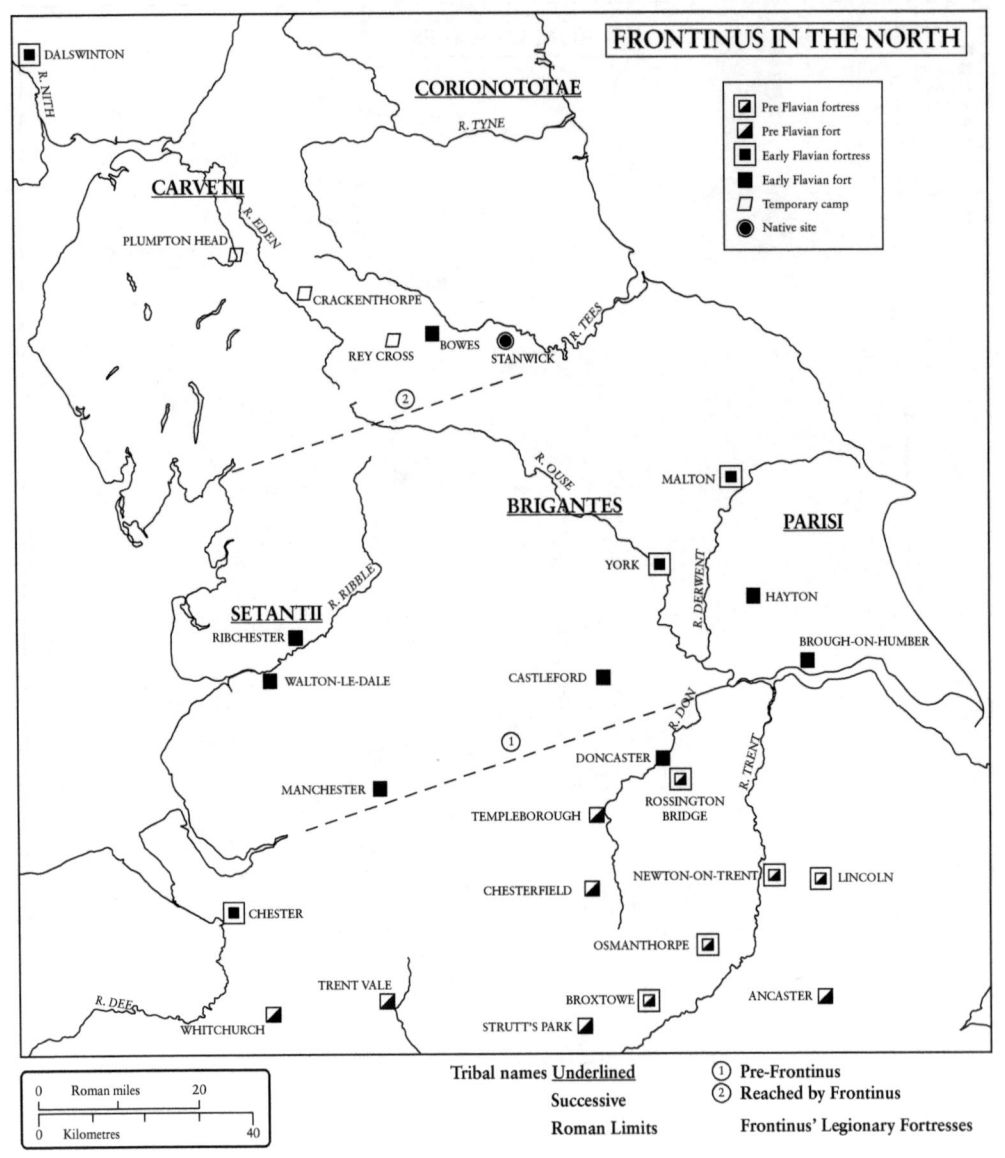

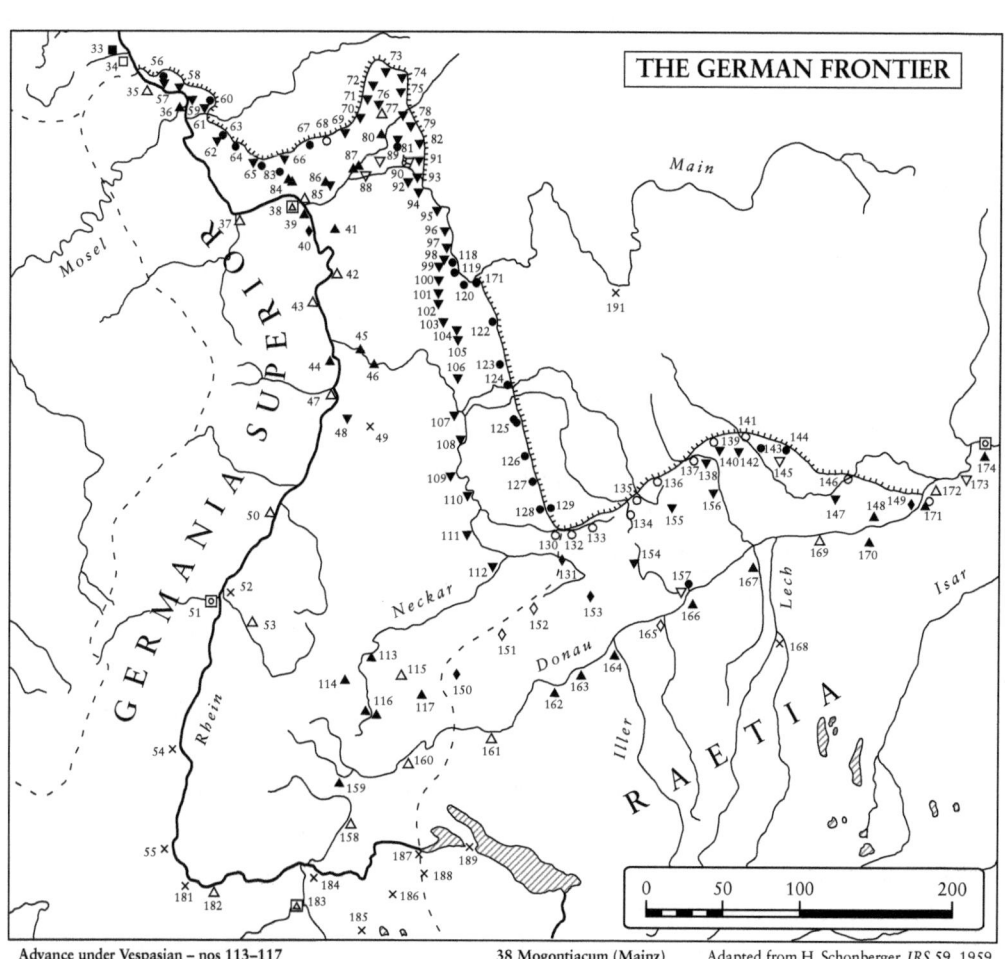

Advance under Vespasian – nos 113–117
Forts of Domitian – nos 56–112 (i.e., probably planned by Frontinus)
Legionary fortresses:
  34 Bonna (Bonn)

38 Mogontiacum (Mainz)
51 Argentorate (Strasbourg)
183 Vindonissa (Windisch)
174 Reginum (Regensburg)

Adapted from H. Schonberger, *JRS* 59, 1959.

Introduction

The Roman Empire was ruled, it is usually explained, by the will and decisions of the emperors. These men were, however, a very varied group, from the dilettante Nero to the stern Trajan and the half-mad Caligula, to note only some of those who ruled while my subject was alive. The emperors are, of course, the most easily studied people of imperial Rome, and were the most effective in directing affairs, but the size of the empire constantly limited their ability to do so. Many other men were instrumental in guiding the fortunes and events of the empire – senators, governors, army commanders, legionary and auxiliary officers – but on a distinctly lesser scale. Of course, this is a banal observation, which any historian cannot but agree with, but there were a few men, not emperors, who can be singled out as such instruments and whose lives can be studied.[1] This is apart, of course, from those who went on, sometimes unexpectedly (as with at least three of our subject's emperors), to become emperors themselves.

Sextus Julius Frontinus, my subject, was one of those influencers and non-emperor effectors. He catches the eye for a variety of reasons and from a variety of aspects. He was an author, not a particularly common achievement in Rome, with its largely oral culture; three of his books survive and are still read and consulted; as many others have perished. He was consul no less than three times, which was something very rarely achieved outside the ranks of the imperial rulers in his lifetime and for a century and more later, and particularly among men of his social rank. He rose to importance from relatively lowly origins, probably of the equestrian class – though even this means his family was wealthy. He was a conqueror of territory and an expander of the empire; he governed no less than three provinces; he commanded two major armies; he was an adviser to a succession of emperors, and at one point he was a sort of deputy emperor; he was also a 'Vicar of Bray' character, capable of, if not supporting, then at least counselling, a series of emperors of opposing and discordant views, aims and policies. He was constantly energetic, capable of taking up a major task at the age of well over sixty. And lastly, his descendants, even though he had fathered only two daughters, eventually married into the Roman imperial family; two other families were related, one rose even higher, royally, the other failed after a single generation.

For all these reasons and accomplishments, Frontinus is worth studying. It is my contention also that he was able at more than one point in his life to influence the outcome of wider events. His praetorship in 70, his proconsulship in Britannia in the 70s, his activity in Germania in the 80s, and his second and third consulships in 98 and 100, all gave him scope to exert decisive influence where it mattered. His other offices, some of which can only be conjectured, were perhaps less decisive, but they took him to almost every corner of the empire, from northern Britain to Armenia, from Germania to Asia and Africa. It is doubtful that we can find any other Roman citizen of his time of whom that can be said, who did not become emperor.

A warning is needed right at the start. Frontinus' life is not as well recorded as one would like, and certainly not for the first forty years of his life. Even in the years of his greatness and renown, from 70 to 100, there are large gaps, though some of these were clearly filled by his work as an author. A good deal of this account therefore has to be, shall we say, less than well sourced; it is, that is, in parts conjectural and in others, speculative. Nevertheless, I believe it is possible to tease out from the inadequate sources enough to attempt his biography. Or so it seems to me. But let the reader beware.

Note

There is no biography of any length of Frontinus, and none seems ever to have been written in the ancient world. There are brief biographies in the introductions to editions of his works,[2] and in Birley's series of biographies of governors of Britannia,[3] and in his Wikipedia entry. None of these spread over more than half a dozen pages at the most. They are nevertheless useful and are based on the same sources which I am using here. The length of this book is in part due to my dissatisfaction with the brief biographies, which tend to confine themselves to the sources and nothing else, whereas the imperial context requires to be included to bring out Frontinus' own importance – and also the necessary speculations surrounding the sources which exist to expand this text.

Chapter 1

Early Life: An Exercise in Speculation

The *Praetor Urbanus*, AD 70

The first datable event in Frontinus' life is in AD 70, when he became *praetor urbanus* in Rome. He was, as it happened, the ranking magistrate of the city at the time, second to the consuls. These were the new emperors Vespasian and Titus, but they were out of the city, finishing off the recent war. He therefore presided on 1 January 70 at the opening of the new session of the Senate. He resigned his post a day or two afterwards, so that Vespasian's other son, Domitian, who was in Rome, could take office as suffect praetor.[1]

This sequence of events tells us a good deal about our man. First, there is no evidence, nor any clear indication, that he had held any of the normal earlier offices – in the vigintivirate, as aedile, or quaestor, and so on – though his prominence later is such that we might expect such a record to survive. So if he held none of these posts, his achievement of the praetorship was at the gift of the new emperor, and he had been adlected to that rank and office, and so he had been installed by imperial fiat. Further, his resignation was clearly pre-arranged with the emperor. Domitian, his replacement, was still a teenager in 70, well below the legal age to hold this office, and the praetor's task on that day was to preside over the reopening of the Senate on the first day of the year; Vespasian, a conservative type, was not the man to force the Senate to see a teenage boy installed as its presiding officer at one of its more ceremonial moments. Frontinus, a fully mature man of some notable achievements already, was a much more acceptable president.

However, there is more to the situation than that, for Vespasian was not even in Italy at the time, but was still in Alexandria-by-Egypt, where he had remained all through the preceding civil war. Titus, his elder son, was also out of the city, busy in Syria with the expiring Jewish War (Jerusalem was finally taken later in 70) and with the possible threat of a Parthian war. The question, therefore, is who was it that chose Frontinus for this task? For, as will be discussed later in this chapter, Frontinus was probably not even a senator until he was adlected and appointed praetor. Such a decision was one which only the emperor could make, and Vespasian was absent. We know he wrote to the Senate a little earlier,[2] and his colleague C. Licinius Mucianus had arrived in the city not long before the Senate session, at the conquest of the city on 20–21 December. Mucianus may have made the decision, but it is more likely Vespasian had done so since only he had the power to appoint a new praetor. Whichever man had chosen Frontinus, it had been done some time before January 70, even though it was only in late December that the successful Flavian forces gained control of Rome.

This, of course, then raises a further question. How did Vespasian (or Mucianus) come to choose Frontinus? He must have been known to the new emperor well before the Senate meeting, or perhaps to Mucianus, if it was his recommendation. There is no clear answer to these questions, except to assume that Vespasian had made the decision to appoint him praetor some time before, for he did not leave Alexandria until the spring of 70. There must have been other men in the city who could have been nominated, so we have to assume that Frontinus was a deliberate and personal choice of the emperor and his advisers, notably Mucianus.

The assumption must be that Vespasian knew Frontinus from earlier in their careers. This would suggest they had been acting as colleagues in some work, and the two obvious places for this would be, if not actually in Rome (as will be seen later, Frontinus seems to have spent little time in Rome before 70), then during Vespasian's governorship in Africa in 63, or during Vespasian's command in the east from 66. Vespasian would hardly choose Frontinus if he did not know him and trust him to do as the new emperor wished.[3]

For Frontinus to be trusted with such a post, and to be rewarded by the new emperor in such a public way is also to raise the question of what Frontinus could have done to earn such approval. We have no precise or datable information, as noted in the Introduction, about his life or his work before his brief praetorship in 70, though to have been selected for that post, most likely by the new emperor, his work must have been noteworthy. Plenty of other men were rewarded, however, or promoted, in the last days of the Civil War – Plotius Grypus, for example, was adlected to praetorian status and given command of a legion,[4] and others are listed by Tacitus.[5] No clear account of Frontinus' earlier career has survived, but, on the other hand, there are a number of hints and plausible assumptions which can be added up to provide an outline of it which may be reasonably acceptable.

An eques

Frontinus appears in two references in a collection of the works of Roman surveyors – the *Corpus Agrimensorum* – compiled in the fifth century AD, and surviving in an illuminated manuscript.[6] The references to Frontinus are in his own text in that collection, and connect him with surveying work in Spain and in Africa – though the evidence is the inclusion of what seemed to be personal experiences, and which stand out from the rest of the text of that account.[7] This was not the task of a man of senatorial rank, which Frontinus would have been had he held any of the pre-praetor magistracies. So, if he was in those provinces working as a surveyor, he was not a senator but an *eques*, a member of the layer of Roman society between the citizens and senators, but still wealthy.[8]

The opportunities for advancement for men of equestrian rank had been gradually expanding under the imperial regime, as men of ability were recruited to serve in various administrative offices, to supplement the limited number of senators. The offices they could hold ran parallel to the senatorial *cursus*, and included at least three at the very highest administrative levels, as praetorian prefect, governor of Egypt, or *praefectus annonae* (supervisor of the grain supply) in Rome. But the two most likely to have been arrived at by a man such as Frontinus in his youth (he was born about AD 30) were command of an auxiliary regiment in the army, or procurator, a post which could cover a multitude of positions: tax collector, financial investigator, governor of a minor province – the expanding Roman imperial bureaucracy was good at inventing such posts. As an *eques*, Frontinus, clearly a man of ability, could have hoped to hold any or all of them. The only clear evidence, however, is that he was a supervising surveyor, in command of a group of experts, and before that it can be conjectured that he held some military command or commands, either in a legion as a military tribune, or in command of an auxiliary regiment;

such a command would be a very appropriate preliminary to command of a surveying group, many of whose men were soldiers or ex-soldiers.

The limited number of senators, not all of whom were prepared to work, or attend regularly, or to leave Rome or Italy to reside for a time in a province, meant that an increasing number of tasks had to be done by *equites;* similarly the expanding nature of the Roman imperial government created posts at a level to be filled by *equites*. The survey work of Frontinus is suggested to have taken place in Spain and Africa, and possibly elsewhere; it provided the basis for one of Frontinus' books and the *Commentum*, which were clearly based on the acquisition of specialist knowledge. This would strongly suggest that he was in charge of the work. And since he was apparently employed in at least two provinces, probably successively, he will have earned a reputation as an expert.

The evidence for his surveying career is indirect, based on his book on surveying. In Spain, Frontinus mentions three widely separated cities – Salmantica (Salamanca) in northern Lusitania, Pallantia (Palancia) in Tarraconensis, and Emerita Augusta (Merida) in southern Lusitania, in connection with survey.[9] These are well spread examples, in two different provinces, which would suggest some personal experience of these issues. The evidence of his presence in Africa is especially poor, consisting of two references to Africa in the *Agrennius Urbicus* text, which is based at this point entirely on Frontinus' earlier text; one reference is to a temple dispute between two cities, Hadrumetum and Thysdrus, which was probably solved in Trajan's time but had gone on for half a century of legal disputes; the other is a remark about large estates in Africa. Both of these references suggest Frontinus' familiarity with Africa, but perhaps only the temple dispute would suggest a close acquaintance; it was surely common knowledge that there were large estates in Africa.[10] The comment about the temple dispute includes information that the dispute had been going on for some years; it was resolved in Trajan's reign, so this makes it clear that the text dates from before then.

Frontinus would not, of course, have done the survey work himself, which was the work of the men recruited as experts: soldiers seconded to the task, slaves, free men, all of whom had gathered the requisite skills. Frontinus himself clearly had acquired some expert knowledge, which would not necessarily have been gained by other men in his position; he was primarily in command to see that the work was done and to give orders. This was, of course, the usual Roman acceptance that a well-born man was a natural commander. The assumption was that all that was needed was his assured manner; technical expertise was not required in such men. In this, as will be seen, Frontinus was different.[11]

Corbulo and Military Service

It is time to consider his life before he worked in the survey. In his book of military anecdotes, *Stratagems*, a dozen of the items which are included stand out from the rest. Most of the items he included were historical in origin, mainly from Greek history, culled from such historians as Xenophon or Thucydides or Polybios, or from the Roman Republican period or the early part of the empire, above all from Livy. (See Chapter 6.)

There are few from the imperial period, but there are a dozen which are contemporary with Frontinus' own life, and can best be seen to be a result of his own experience of war. Five of these are ascribed to the Emperor Domitian in his German campaign of 83 (to be considered in Chapter 7) and one of Gaul in 70 (which will be of interest later in this chapter), and two are ascribed to Vespasian. But the other five are ascribed to Domitius Corbulo's Parthian War in the 50s and 60s. We know that Frontinus was a close associate of both Vespasian and Domitian when they were emperors, in Britannia and in the German war, and this was evidently the source for his Flavian anecdotes. It was also Vespasian who must have agreed to install him as praetor – or even promoted him for the post - in 70, and later as consul and provincial governor in Britannia, so it is quite possible that he was recalling events in Vespasian's and Corbulo's commands in the East because he was similarly a participant, or, in Vespasian's case, included them as compliments to the emperor. If so, as an *eques*, he was probably serving as a military tribune, an officer in a legion or in an auxiliary regiment. The nature of the Corbulo items also suggests they were personal reminiscences.

The war with Parthia developed from a diplomatic contretemps which began in 54 and developed into open warfare by 58, when the commander Cn. Domitius Corbulo attacked and destroyed the Armenian capital of Artaxata.[12] (The dispute was over who should nominate a king for Armenia; Parthia had done so in the past and so the target was the Armenian capital to remove the Parthian nominee.) Corbulo then moved onto the city of

Tigranocerta, which was captured after a siege in the summer of 60. This is the scene of one of Frontinus' items about Corbulo in his *Stratagems*. He describes an incident which he claims brought about the surrender of Tigranocerta. Corbulo was exasperated at the length of the siege, which had gone on at least six months. He captured a leading Armenian, Vadandrus, who had been involved in an assassination plot aimed at Corbulo himself. He had him beheaded, and then slung his head into the city from a ballista. It is said to have landed in the midst of a council of commanders, and so disconcerted them that they resolved to surrender the city thereupon.[13]

In fact, of course, such an incident would scarcely so disconcert a group of commanders who had already endured a siege of six months as to induce them to give up the fight. One might suspect that, if it actually happened that way, the council was already discussing the surrender of the city. Also, it seems fairly unlikely that a severed head fired from a ballista would land in their midst, since it is most likely that they would have been meeting indoors. Nevertheless, it sounds a good story, one that would be handed round in a soldiers' camp, being expanded and exaggerated with each repetition; there is, however, no reason to doubt that the head was actually fired into the city. (It was also a story told of earlier commanders, including Crassus, also in a war against the Parthians, and in the Hannibalic War, but that is no reason to disbelieve Corbulo's role as a perpetrator, though it might suggest that Corbulo was well versed in such military methods, and could readily select items from the past – this was Frontinus' purpose, after all, in compiling his *Stratagems*; the example of a commanding general who was well versed in the history of his profession could have been a strong influence on the young Frontinus.)

This is not an item recorded elsewhere about Corbulo's campaigns, though Tacitus has a fairly detailed account of the war in the *Annals*, and would probably not have been able to resist such an item, had he known of it. The other anecdotes of Corbulo's war that Frontinus records are much more personal both to Frontinus and to Corbulo, and have the air of recollections by the author of small incidents he had witnessed. The capture of Tigranocerta and then Legenda were followed by several years of manoeuvring, partly military, partly bluff, always with diplomatic aspects, each move by each side aimed at securing minor improvements in their local position, either geographically or diplomatically. In the end it was agreed that the Romans would abandon their own puppet king (an

Armenian), and would reinstate the Parthian Tiridates (the brother of the Parthian King Vologaeses), who would travel, at Roman expense, to Rome for his ceremonial installation as king; he did so, slowly and very extravagantly, at great cost to the Roman treasury.[14]

None of this is noted in Frontinus' book, but he does include a set of items which emphasize Corbulo's methods and conduct in command. Corbulo was notorious for his imposition of strict discipline during his command of the first expedition against Artaxata and Tigranocerta. He took two legions, III Gallica and VI Ferrata, and associated auxiliary regiments, out of the Syrian province. These were legions whose men had relaxed into a comfortable, overfed, under-exercised, and very pleasant existence for the previous peaceful half-century. Corbulo marched them into the Armenian mountains in winter. There they became fit and soldierly, or died, or were crippled by frostbite.[15]

This is the atmosphere of Frontinus' other Corbulo items. In a fight at 'Initia' (not a place otherwise known) a Roman detachment retreated when attacked. Corbulo decided that it was the fault of the troops and made the men – two squadrons of cavalry and three cohorts of infantry – presumably *auxilia*, and up to 2,000 men – form a separate camp outside the shelter of the siege works, and from there go on raids against the enemy 'until they should atone for their disgrace'.[16] (No doubt they were expended in particularly difficult and dangerous assignments.) A second incident, when a cavalry unit gave way under attack, was blamed on the commander, Aemilius Rufus, who had neglected to equip the men with adequate weaponry, and so it was Rufus who was punished.[17] The result of all this, and other measures of a similar sort, so Frontinus claims in a third item, was a great improvement in the discipline of the Roman forces. As a result, the army was able to withstand a much larger Parthian attack when it came.[18] The final item is that Corbulo was said to have remarked that a pick was an especially useful, battle-winning weapon, a remark no doubt made when surveying trenches dug by the soldiers as a means of persuading them to work harder. Frontinus twists this into claiming that the pick was a decisive weapon, but surely Corbulo's remark was off-the-cuff and without the heavy meaning given to it by our man.[19] But he did make use of the usual temporary fortifications which was normal to the Roman forces on the march.

None of these items is recorded elsewhere, so it is reasonable to assume that they were collected, or perhaps recollected, by Frontinus personally, either from the general himself, or from the general gossip in the army. Their minor, near-inconsequential nature is therefore useful evidence that Frontinus himself was present in Corbulo's army. In so far as they can be dated, three of them refer to the captures of Artaxata and Tigranocerta which took place in 58–60. These events took place in the early part of the war, which went on until 64, and with his final item, a general remark about the value of discipline which allowed Corbulo to defeat the Parthian attack, he makes an assumption without any context, and this could well be the conclusion drawn from less personal experiences, but one which was also a popular remark.

Given his presence in Corbulo's army, which these anecdotes strongly suggest, we have to decide what was his role and status in that army. He was, as the work he did as a surveyor, an *eques*, so he will have possibly served in an auxiliary regiment as an officer. An early appointment would be as a military tribune in a legion, from which he could be promoted to command an auxiliary regiment – this would be expected if he showed real promise in command (as he certainly did later in his life). There is no way of deciding between these possibilities, though since his abilities were hardly hidden – no Roman with any ambition would be reticent – the route of promotion to command of an auxiliary regiment seems most likely. None of the anecdotes can be read to imply personal acquaintance with the general, but such would not be unlikely if he reached a position of command – Corbulo was the sort of commander who made it his business to know his officers. At such a level, he would need to deploy his command qualities very clearly – or to put it another way, command of an auxiliary regiment might well have afforded him the chance for gaining renown and acting independently, which service in a legion might not provide. (The anecdote about Aemilius Rufus suggests that such commanders had a certain freedom of action.) This campaign in the mountains, which continued throughout every season of the year, was, as many men serving in the Syrian legions in this war discovered, a hard service; those who survived were tough and resourceful and skilled soldiers. And Frontinus later showed just such qualities and abilities in warfare and command.

His Early Career – a Likely Outline

The outline of Frontinus' career before 70 is thus emerging. He was born the son of an *eques* in about AD 30 to 35, and so was by no means poor. (His precise origins will be discussed in Chapters 13 and 14, in connection with his family's links.) He took up an equestrian career which began with service in, and eventually command of, an auxiliary regiment in the Eastern war, though probably not until he was above the normal age for a military tribune, which was eighteen or so – though maturity would no doubt assist his promotion. (He would not have served in the East until the war developed, that is, not before the later 50s.)

He may have been active in both Spain and Africa in connection with administrative duties suitable to an *eques*, probably as a procurator of some rank. There he was involved in surveying work in both provinces, though no doubt his activities were not restricted to surveying. All this would presuppose other work as well, including possible service as a military tribune in a legion, or as a junior officer in an auxiliary regiment, or indeed both, before promotion to command an auxiliary regiment. It seems his service in the eastern army lasted at least two years at the minimum (58–60), according to the anecdotes, but may have been longer, since able junior officers are unlikely to have been easily released while the war was on, and he may have joined at the start of the war, in 56. He could even have taken up such a post at about the age of eighteen, as a military tribune, which would be in about 50 or later, but he was probably older when he joined. To have been put in command of an auxiliary regiment he will have served with sufficient ability in more junior positions for some time to earn his promotion. Corbulo was a severe commander who would not accept inefficiency and laziness in his officers – not that Frontinus would ever have been accused of such failings at any point in his career – and a commander like Corbulo was always on the lookout for military talent, so that to be promoted by such a man would have been distinction indeed.

The evidence for his military service with Corbulo is indirect, to say the least; on the other hand, it is necessary to accept that he must have had some sort of experience of the army and war to have succeeded in his commands so quickly during Vespasian's reign, when he commanded in Gaul and in Britain, in both places successfully. It was always possible for a young man of his equestrian rank to gain military experience by enlisting as a junior officer, learning the routine of the camp and the march and even in police work, but it was fairly rare to gain such experience in a major war – the Roman Empire only rarely indulged in wars of any length of time. This is what the anecdotes he recorded later about Corbulo suggest. It might imply that he volunteered to gain such experience when the war began, in 54–56. This in turn meant that he was above the normal age for military tribunes when he enlisted; starting a few years above the normal would probably commend him to a general like Corbulo as being promotion material. He might, that is, have been fast-tracked because he had some experience of life beyond that of a schoolboy and an adolescent.

He was consul in 73, for which the earliest permitted age was 42; this would put his birth in about 31, so he would have been about eighteen years of age in 50. (The date of his birth is often stated at 'c.35', but this is far too late for his consulship.[20] The suggestion that he was of patrician rank has not been accepted, even by its originator.[21]) To be sure, his first consulship came at a disturbed time; yet it was unlikely that Vespasian would so obviously violate the rules of the Senate in his first years; his choice of consuls in the first five years was confined to a small group of old friends, proven supporters and colleagues; he was at the same time endeavouring to return Roman society to normality, and breaking the rules would spoil his purpose. Therefore, Frontinus' service as a military tribune could have begun in the early 50s, perhaps at the beginning of Corbulo's eastern campaign, which started in 54; in that case he will have served in that army for six years, assuming he left the army in 60, as his anecdotes might suggest. This length of service is more convincing for his further career than a mere two years, given that he showed plenty of military skill and ability later. He certainly had a strong interest in, and experience of, war, as his writings and his later experiences imply.

Corbulo's military and personal reputation remained high, especially after his enforced suicide in 66, so that his officers remained loyal to him and to his memory. Vespasian was, in effect, Corbulo's successor, having taken command of the eastern army in the Judaean War not long after Corbulo died. Many of Corbulo's former officers turned out to support Vespasian, another eastern general, when he made a play for the empire in 69.

This set of speculations and conclusions can take Frontinus' career up to the late 50s or early 60s, after which he will have occupied other equestrian posts, and those postulated procuratorial posts in Spain and Africa. One may assume that there were two successive posts, and that they each lasted perhaps three years, the normal Roman period of office; this would fill the gap between his military service and the succession crisis which began in 68. There would probably be a break between his military and civil employments, and possibly another break between his two posts as a civil employee.

Exactly what he will have been employed at in the 60s is as opaque as the rest of his early life, but it seems clear that he had been successful enough in his earlier military posts to become noticed where it was useful to be noticed, at the imperial court and administration. He also built up his personal wealth. A man who went in for a senatorial career, as Frontinus eventually did from 70 onwards, was required to be rich, to possess land and a large income; we know that he had an estate at Terracina later; his origin in Narbonensis would clearly also suggest his family had estates in that region, which he no doubt inherited. He married at some point in the 60s; estates in Italy and Narbonensis, purchased or inherited, plus a dowry, were his means towards the proper qualification for membership of the Senate, which he clearly possessed by 70. It was possible to become wealthy as a procurator or in other equestrian careers, indeed it was a requisite to have a certain degree of wealth to qualify as an *eques* in the first place, but only at the highest levels could one accumulate sufficient wealth to qualify as a senator. So we may assume that Frontinus had reached these levels of notice and wealth before beginning his second, senatorial, public career amid the Civil War of 69.

The career he embarked on after his military service, that is, during the 60s, was probably in command of a set of surveyors. How he gained his preliminary experience in surveying will be discussed in the next chapter, but it may be emphasized here that he did so as a commander-cum-manager, and probably while on his military service. His corps of surveyors was comprised of a disparate group of men, soldiers, ex-soldiers, freedmen, slaves, but all of them experts with experience as surveyors.[22] His military experience in command would thus be useful. If, as supposed from the remarks in his book, he spent the time in surveying in Spain and Africa, presumably it had been at the direction of the emperor, or at least of the imperial government. One might top this speculation by suggesting that he had two terms of three years each, one in Africa, one in Spain.

Galba

Frontinus' time in Spain will have coincided with the governorship of Servius Sulpicius Galba (59/60–68) who struck out for the empire as Nero's rule collapsed in 68. If he was in Spain at any time in the 60s, this was inevitable, since Galba was such a long-lasting governor. Nero had pushed him into the governorship of Tarraconensis to get him away from Rome, where his presence was a standing rebuke to the emperor's lifestyle and frivolity. But this was only to discover, too late, that the grand old republican-style martinet was a dab hand also at intrigue. He had persuaded a reasonable number of his Spanish subjects to support him when he made a play for the empire (he organized them as a provincial senate in a flattering move, and recruited enough men to form a new legion). He had the support of one of the other governors in Spain, M. Salvius Otho in Lusitania, who had similarly been exiled to the province because Nero was in love with Otho's former wife, Poppaea – and Otho was also a long-stay governor, from 58 to 68. A procurator, or other official, in Spain at the time of Galba's rising would need to decide on the direction of his loyalties when Galba came out against Nero. If Frontinus was in Spain in 68, it is probable that he would have elected to support Galba. Another governor in Spain at the time was M. Ulpius Traianus, Trajan's father, governor of Baetica, though the precise date is not certain.[23] Ulpius was promoted to command Legio X Fretensis in the East by 67; his governorship of Baetica could well have coincided with Frontinus' time there. If Trajan was with his father in this post, it meant that there were three future emperors in Spain at the time; it is quite possible, stretching it a little, that Frontinus in Spain met all of them.

Nero was widely despised, whereas Galba, for the moment, was a man who could command the admiration of old-fashioned conservative types. Frontinus exhibits all through his life the dislike of corruption of any conservative gentleman, though he was not necessarily old-fashioned, and his conservatism, as will be argued, was of a particular sort. But to support a rebel such as Galba was certainly a gamble. At first he had only a single legion under his command, VI Victrix, though he drummed up enough support in Spain to enlist sufficient men for another legion. (It came under the command of Antonius Primus, but Frontinus would have been an asset as an officer in that legion.[24]) Previous rebellions against the emperors had generally failed (including one which Galba had helped suppress), with the result that dire vengeance was inflicted on the rebels, so to come out in support of one of these rebels was dangerous, even brave, especially if, like Frontinus, one was reasonably prominent.

Alternatives

Several alternatives to the preceding assumptions about Frontinus' early life can be suggested. Frontinus might have been still in the East at the time of Galba's putsch, but there he will have been faced with the same political dilemma. His later loyalty to the Flavian emperors would suggest he came out in support of Vespasian, if he was in the East. Another alternative would put him in the other province in which he is thought to have been employed as surveyor: Africa. (In Africa he could have come into contact with Vespasian, who had been African governor in 63/64; this would have been an extra mark for him when Vespasian emerged as the major imperial contender in 69.) If he was in Africa in 68, the choice would have been to support a rebel, though in this case it was Lucius Calpurnius Piso, who made no more than a feeble attempt before being murdered, or the existing emperor. Wherever one was in the empire in AD 68, a political man was faced with exactly the same problem, though there were a variety of pretenders. Finally, Frontinus might have been in his home province of Narbonensis, where no doubt he had estates, but where he would have been faced, as a prominent local figure, with the same choice as everywhere – and everyone – else. But even more likely than anywhere else, he would be faced with the rebellion of Julius Vindex, the march of Galba through the province, the failed proclamation of Verginius Rufus, and later fighting. Choosing who to support was difficult, and possibly fatal.

Origin

This, of course, raises the issue of where Frontinus came from. The direct answer, as usual, is that we do not know. It is generally assumed he came from Gallia Narbonensis, the province which lay along the Mediterranean coast of France, from the Alps to the Pyrenees. The evidence for this is, once more, extremely indirect, since Frontinus himself gives no indication of his homeland, nor does anyone else. There were a number of other men with the name Sextus Iulius on record in that province, and also a number of Frontini, the evidence of which is usually found in inscriptions; this makes the possibility of his origin there seem plausible, if hardly certain.[25] This was the time when men from that province were beginning to make a powerful mark in Rome, no doubt because the development of Gaul in peacetime (since the widespread devastation of Julius Caesar's conquest a century before) had allowed the rich to expand their wealth, and had begun to reach for political power within the empire (see Chapter 13); it was a local rebellion in another part of Gaul which began the Civil War; the rebellion was partly suppressed by Galba. It was the province of Julius Agricola, Frontinus' successor in the governorship of Britain, and of Trajan's wife, his emperor and benefactor at the end of his life, though neither of these suggestions is in any way more than indicative for his origin. Cn. Domitius Corbulo was probably also from Narbonensis.[26] Let us say that Gaul was his homeland, for this is as good an assumption as any, and better than most. Narbonensis had been a province of the empire for the last 190 years by the time of the Civil War, so that Roman citizenship had time to percolate through the wealthy classes, even if his name is not distinctive. As a place from which an *eques* could launch his career in the Roman Empire in the latter years of its first dynasty it was better than most of the provinces.[27]

Narbonensis

The number of Roman citizens who could attempt to enter the Senate from any part of Gaul other than Narbonensis was minimal. That province had begun to produce senators in the 30s, when some of the inhabitants had accumulated enough wealth to qualify for the Senate, had acquired estates in Italy, and were ambitious enough to go through the *cursus* of offices in Rome. There were prominent Gallic senators in the reign of Claudius, and a steadily increasing number in every decade after that. One was probably Cn. Domitius Corbulo, and another was the father of Plotina, the wife of Trajan the future emperor. There were a dozen or more such men in the Senate by the time of the Civil War. These men did not come from the old Republican or Augustan colonies, but from the wealthy layer of men of Gallic descent who owned large country estates – the colonists' descendants were well off, but their allocated lands were not a basis for large wealth.²⁸ Some of these senators were undoubtedly descended from Gallic chieftains who had retained their lands and converted them into possessions, and this may be Frontinus' origin also.

Narbonensis was a province which had been affected strongly by Greek settlement along the coast from the seventh century BC onwards, well before Roman intervention. Massalia was a Greek-speaking university town as well as a busy port, and several other coastal towns were Greek in origin and language. The interior had been Celtic country, and one of the effects of the Greek-Celtic interaction had been an incipient urbanization among the Celts, to add to the Greek *poleis* on the coast, of which Massalia was the chief. The region had seen Hannibal pass through in 218 BC, with no obvious effects – though he had been resisted by a Gallic army at the Pyrenees; the Scipio brothers marched through the other way, and Hannibal's brother Hasdrubal came through ten years later, again with no obvious effect locally (on his way to having his head thrown into his brother's camp). In the 120s BC it had been converted into a Roman province by Cn. Domitius Ahenobarbus (one of whose descendants was the Emperor Nero). He had organized one of the first Roman colonies outside Italy at Narbo Martius (Narbonne), which gave its name to the province.

The region, therefore, had a long association with first Greek, then Roman, civilization. There were a considerable number of Domitii (like Corbulo) in the province, as well as many Iulii (like Frontinus). The citizenship of these people dated from either the time of Ahenobarbus, or that of Julius Caesar, who had Narbonensis as one of his provinces in his Gallic campaigns, or from Augustus, who lived for a time at Lugdunum as he reorganized the whole of Gaul; Valerius was also a frequent *nomen* in the province.²⁹

If Frontinus, as seems likely, came from Narbonensis, he came from a region which had been steeped first in Greek influence, and then in Roman culture, for the past seven centuries, and yet still maintained a strong Celtic presence. It was a good place to originate for a man with an ambition to succeed, in part because a number of pioneers had already made their way through the Roman political jungle and would be likely to assist others from the province who were on the rise. It was also, therefore, where he was educated, where he certainly spoke Latin and the local

Celtic language from childhood; Greek was available in the schools of Massilia and probably elsewhere. All these languages were current in the first century AD, though Celtic was declining, as was Greek. Massalia still counted as a Greek city and was a centre for a Greek-style education. This was, as noted, a most suitable region, cosmopolitan in its population and languages, for a man intent on progressing in the Roman Empire – his Latin useful in Rome and Italy and the West, his Greek in Asia and the East, his Celtic in parts of Spain, in the rest of Gaul and in Britannia.[30]

Vespasian

To return to Spain. If Frontinus was in that country in 68, as seems possible, he will in all likelihood have supported Galba and Otho in the anti-Nero expedition. This follows in a sense from his later association with Vespasian, who at first welcomed Galba's accession in place of Nero, and had only come out against Otho when the latter contrived Galba's murder, and would have nothing to do with Vitellius. Vespasian thus set himself as Galba's political successor, appealing to the old emperor's supporters to boost his own support. In the East he had a similar source of support among those who were Corbulo's former officers; they had also supported Galba against Nero, and then Vespasian against Otho and Vitellius. But, again, there is virtually no evidence for Frontinus' preferences in 68–69, though the fact that he was promoted by Vespasian in late 69 to be praetor in 70, and was therefore trusted by him in a difficult time, is a strong indication that he was one of the new emperor's early supporters, and that his transfer of his allegiance to Vespasian can be taken as evidence of his attachment previously to Galba, if his presence in Spain in 68 is accepted. Their earlier relations in Africa are very possible, just as Galba's and Frontinus' acquaintance when in Spain was likely. And if he was in Spain in 68, Galba would surely have employed his military skills.

Once again, that praetorship in 70 implies Frontinus' early support for Vespasian, based on joint acquaintance and mutual support for Galba. Opposition to Otho and Vitellius, the first because he was the murderer of Galba, and the second because of his Nero-like voluptuous lifestyle, may be assumed for one who cleaved to Galba first, and then to Vespasian. But we do not know of any action taken by Frontinus between his possible presence in Spain in 68 and his assumption of the praetorship on the first day of 70. Guesses would suggest he travelled from Spain to Rome with, or in the wake of, Galba, possibly as an officer in the new Legio VII Galbiana, which had been raised in Spain. Galba, of course, travelled through Narbonensis, where Frontinus' local expertise and connections could be useful. When Vespasian's forces reached Italy, Frontinus would no doubt have been available to assist. Vespasian, of course, did not leave Alexandria until after the beginning of 70, though one must assume that Frontinus was contacted at some point in 69, to be appointed praetor.

If he was appointed to Legio VII Galbiana, he had an adventurous time. After moving to Italy, Galba sent the legion to be stationed at Carnuntum in Pannonia. When Galba was murdered (on 15 January 69) the legion was bereft of its founder. It marched to support Otho – Galba's murderer, but also a former Spanish governor – but failed to join him in time to fight at the first Battle of Bedriacum. Vitellius sent it back to Pannonia. It was now commanded by M. Antonius Primus, one of the more dubious politicians of the Civil War period. Under him, the legion played a crucial role in events. He declared for Vespasian when he heard of his declaration against Vitellius (and perhaps before, if one of Vespasian's agents had reached him). He gathered support from neighbouring legions and governors, and marched against Vitellius. The Galbiana suffered heavy casualties in the second Battle of Bedriacum, but the news of this battle convinced the legions in Spain, Gaul, and Britain to join Vespasian's side. The legion then took part in the march on Rome and fought against Vitellius' last stand, and suffered more casualties. Primus was soon relieved of his assumed authority by the arrival of Lucianus Mucianus from the East. Mucianus separated Primus and the Galbiana as a precaution, and sent the legion back to Pannonia once more.

These movements and fights therefore finally brought Frontinus, if he was with the Galbiana, to a position alongside Mucianus, with whom he was to go on expedition the following year to Gaul, and to the notice, probably once more, of Vespasian. It is a plausible linkage – so long as he was with the Galbiana, which cannot be proved. If he had made his mark in the legion and in the fighting, promotion may well have come quickly, to fill up vacant posts caused by the heavy casualties at Second Bedriacum, and if so, he could well have been further promoted, by adlection and appointment as praetor by an emperor who clearly knew him.

Frontinus included two anecdotes concerning Vespasian in his *Stratagems*. However, by contrast with the personalized anecdotes concerning Corbulo (or indeed later items about the wars in Gaul and Germany) these two anecdotes about Vespasian carry no air of reminiscence. One is a general comment that he, Vespasian, attacked the Jews (he does not say where or when) on the sabbath, since they were forbidden to fight on that day. This was, no doubt, common knowledge and normal practice amongst the Roman soldiers, since it was an obvious ploy to use when fighting a devout group of Jews – and is recorded of Ptolemy I four centuries earlier. By Frontinus' time it had become a commonplace in recounting Jewish wars. It is unlikely to be accurate, since the Jews had abandoned the prohibition long before; it probably did not apply in the new Vespasianic fighting.[31] The other anecdote is a story of his generosity and common sense – a typical Vespasianic virtue – by which he gave a monetary gift to an impoverished and incompetent junior officer – a case where birth and education was not sufficient to provide him with command ability – and so both got rid of him as a military liability and put him back on his financial feet.[32] Neither of these stories seems to have any relevance to Frontinus' own life; both of them could be simply general knowledge and common gossip.

Summary

Abandoning the inhibitions of speculation, the following conclusions for Frontinus' first forty years of life may be suggested. As an adult Frontinus had been a minor Roman functionary, of provincial origin. In pursuit of his career, he had spent several years in the East, that is in Syria and the Asian provinces as part of Corbulo's army, and had visited and worked in Spain, Italy, and Africa. He knew Narbonensis, his homeland, where he had grown up, and where he had learned Latin, Greek, and the local Celtic language. As a Galba supporter in Legio VII Galbiana in 68, he saw Pannonia. This mixture of professional participation and provincial experience is typical of men who took up a Roman imperial administrative career, whether as an *eques* or as a senator, or indeed as a soldier or a merchant. Until the upheaval of life in the Civil War of 69, he could have expected to spend a few more years doing the same work, as a military commander of an auxiliary regiment, or as a procurator, possibly rising to the governor of a small province, until retirement at about the age of fifty, which would come in about the year 80; instead, from 70, thanks to the Civil War and his adlection to the Senate, he embarked on a completely new career. This began the second half of his life, and about that we have rather more, and more-certain, information.

Chapter 2

Frontinus on Surveying

Frontinus' book on surveying is probably the earliest book produced by him. It survives as part of a collection of manuals and other items referred to as the *Corpus Agrimensorum Romanorum*, which describe in various ways the uses, practices and results of surveying. The text in the edition I am using, by Brian Campbell, is 275 pages long, half text and half translation, in which Frontinus' part is 15 pages - 7 pages of printed Latin.[1]

The arrangement of the book is complicated. After an introduction to all the sections and the authors, the contents, in Latin and English on facing pages, follow in sequence. Included is a *commentum*, a commentary on types of land, discussing a series of quotations from Frontinus' text. After the texts is Campbell's own commentary, in effect explicating and providing context. Reference therefore requires three parts: 1 to the original text; 2 to the (original) *commentum*; 3 to Campbell's notes. This makes awkward referencing. In my notes I shall provide page numbers to these three, separated by oblique lines. I may have to include comments of my own. The collection also includes eight appendices, and illustrations and diagrams extracted from all the several contents which are grouped together; those from Frontinus' text, which were probably added much later, are numbers 1 to 33. This makes yet another reference point to turn to. (Added to which the book is heavy; not an easy read.)

The hostages to fortune in my introductory paragraph are many. First, the surviving elements of Frontinus' surveying account are little more than a short pamphlet in length, so 'book' is hardly an accurate classification. Second, whether the document is complete as originally written, or is only a surviving part, is not known, though it is probably less than complete. Third, we do not know when it was written. It is part of a collection of pamphlets copied out in the fifth century, so it may not have been Frontinus' 'first' literary attempt, though it seems likely that, since part of his early career was apparently occupied in surveying, this is very likely;

it may also be the first such surveying text. Fourth, several commentators have cast doubts on Frontinus' authorship, though since this is standard for a discussion of any ancient text, it need not be taken too seriously; his name has been attached to it immovably since the fifth century AD, and perhaps earlier It is part of a set of documents, many of which show that their authors were familiar with Frontinus' text, so that his name is attached to it seems to be quite acceptable; nevertheless, it must be admitted that proof of his authorship is not available, and it may even be, if one wants to be hyper-critical to the point of destruction, that a different Sextus Julius Frontinus might be the author. It is, however, pleasant to note that, despite these textual problems, some of them only apparent, or perhaps invented, the subject of the pamphlet really is surveying.

There are four sections to the text, each of which has a title, though none of these seems to be original. Two were probably awarded by whoever collected the materials into a single volume, that is, probably in the fifth century, and the other two were awarded by C. Thulin, its German editor in the early twentieth century. In order the sections are entitled: 'types of land', 'land disputes', *'limites'* (that is, boundaries and roads), and 'measurement of land'.

The text is a dense technical summary, almost unreadable at times. It was not designed, it would seem, for practical surveyors in the field, who, in the first century AD, were probably functionally illiterate. It is a handbook for managers, the men in command of the surveying squad; it includes enough technical detail to allow a manager to check on the work of the surveyors, and to allow the manager to check what was going on. This would fit well with the assumption that Frontinus was an *eques* and was therefore socially above the men who did the detailed work in the field.

He was, therefore, addressing an educated audience, his successors, essentially, that is, other *equites,* men who were surveying the surveyors. The work of actually measuring land was done, so far as we can understand, by the freedmen, slaves, soldiers, and volunteers in the group. But these were not in command, though there are cases of them becoming so expert that they were seriously in demand for specific tasks.

The task of such men as Frontinus, an *eques* who had evidently developed a particular taste for technical matters and practicalities – something which can be observed in his other works as well – was to organize, supervise, ensure that the task was completed, and report. The man in command was the man responsible, which compelled him to insist on good work by his staff. A major survey, such as laying out the centuriation for a settlement of retiring soldiers, or the foundation of a *colonia*, would be initiated by the emperor's decision, and the person appointed to command would be selected by the emperor's staff and approved by him, so we may assume that Frontinus had already gained considerable knowledge of surveying before his appointment.

He could have acquired this experience and knowledge as an army officer. The first task in making camp was to choose and survey a suitable site. This was done by a designated set of soldiers, who went out in advance to lay out the plan of the camp. This was a task which Frontinus as an officer may well have had to supervise, and probably he had to make a final decision on the camp site.

Frontinus was therefore brought to the attention of the imperial government, in this case Nero's men, by one or more of the officers who had commanded him in his military service, possibly Corbulo himself, and was appointed directly by the emperor to the post of surveying supervisor. The tasks involved would seem to have been essentially civilian, though carried out largely by soldiers and quite possibly for the benefit of retiring soldiers. Centuriation (the division of land into allotments for veterans), the layout of a new city and decisions on boundaries were all part of the task. This was a major imperial task, one for which the commander of the surveyors would necessarily be chosen at the level of the emperor.

The text in Frontinus' name is organized in a competent way. The first section, on types of land, is not a description of the suitability of land for human purposes – marsh, farmland, pasture, waste, and so on – but is a discussion of the types of land in relation to surveying; it is therefore a strictly technical discussion, and is not an exposition of land in a geographical, geological or agricultural sense, though presumably surveyors acquired a good deal of knowledge of these subjects in their work.

Each section works through the subject in a reasonably logical way. It is not clear if Frontinus had an earlier manual on surveying to refer to – or crib from – but he was hardly a pioneer in the subject, except perhaps in the sense that he was writing it down in a formal manner. He refers back to Etruscan practice, and to surveys of lands made in the Roman Republican period, especially when new colonies were being set up, if the territory had to be mapped and divided. Republican-period centuriation is evident throughout Italy and in many other provinces, including Narbonensis – Spain and Africa were territories where a considerable number of *coloniae* were established, and much land even now shows evidence of centuriation.[2] It is probable, however, indeed highly likely, that earlier surveyors had to learn their craft by a type of informal apprenticeship, in the same sort of way that Frontinus acquired his knowledge. The freedmen, soldiers, and slaves who were the work force were unlikely ever to have written anything down on the work they were doing; previous supervisors, who would be expecting to move on to different tasks after a stint in command of the surveyors, would have had little incentive to do so; they may have made some notes but are likely to have destroyed them or to have taken them off with them when they left. But Frontinus was the sort of man who wanted jobs to be done properly, and writing instructions and advice to his successors seems to have been a task which came naturally to him. It is what he did with other subjects in the rest of his life – conducting war, managing the water supply of Rome.

The subjects he wrote about are in fact strictly limited. Under 'types of land' he means land which has been subject to survey, and he lists their types in that context – land which has been 'divided and allotted', land fully surveyed, land with an 'uncertain boundary'. The first refers particularly to colonial allocations of land, so the surveyor's task was to lay out the allotments. The second refers particularly to the land belonging to a particular community, but it might also refer to private land belonging to an individual, that is, generally speaking, sections of a larger area. The third type is land which is unsurveyed but which has traditional or natural bounds, such as 'rivers, ditches, mountains, roads, trees, watersheds', or any other markers which might be used as boundaries, often the natural elements in a landscape; this last is the most difficult to survey, for such boundaries seem to be wandering and were sometimes unclear.

The text gives a series of examples. Some would seem to be stock cases, explaining particular local peculiarities, such as the reference to centuriation at Suessa Aurunca in Campania, which was orientated north-south, whereas east-west was normal.[3] Others may be from his own experience. The latter might include the three cases from Spain he comments on, which rather stand out from the others cited – Salmantica, Pallantia, and Emerita Augusta, none of which were *coloniae*;[4] Emerita

Augusta, however, was a place where veteran soldiers were certainly settled, over a period of time and in a series of events, in which case there were repeated needs to survey their allotments; this may have been part of Frontinus' work.[5] In Africa five separate episodes of centuriation have been detected, with a sixth when the local legion (III Augusta) moved its base further west to Lambaesis in Vespasian's reign. It is clear that the work of the surveyors continued over a long continuous period, like painting the Forth Bridge. Frontinus also notes an example from Gaul, the Ager Uritanus, but which cannot be located.[6]

Of the other examples he refers to, all of them were in Italy, which, given the intense reallocation of Italian lands during the later Republic and by Augustus, is not surprising. He may have investigated these examples when he was writing everything down. The curious example from Suessa Aurunca he could have heard of from the common gossip of his surveyors, as a notorious example. There are no examples from Britannia, or Africa (despite the ubiquity of the land division there), or from the eastern provinces, though Frontinus was probably familiar with the East at least before he wrote, and other indications suggest his presence in Africa.

This may well argue that in the East he was not involved in commanding surveyors, which, since it may be assumed that he was an active soldier, is very possible, except in the case that his camps were surveyed before construction; it also would suggest that he had composed the text before going to Britannia, where there were clearly new *coloniae*, as at Lindum Colonia (Lincoln), and Camulodunum (Colchester), but not necessarily land allocated by centuriation. (There are also no examples in *Stratagems* from Britannia, where he himself conducted campaigns.)

This would make some chronological sense, and furthermore it could be sensible to see this whole text as a working up of notes he made while working with the surveyors. It is technical enough that he might need to check with the experts, and the whole spread of examples would suggest that they might be collected from others, as well as from his own experience. It is likely enough that the records were kept of particular cases of surveys, either locally or, more certainly, in Rome, which he could consult and quote. His work in Wales and the North of England later was such that surveying experience would be very valuable (see Chapters 4 and 5). But one must admit that reading personal experience into any text of Frontinus' is somewhat hazardous, given their generally technical nature.

This preliminary introduction on types of land leads on logically to the problem of disputes about land, which are the sorts of things which would be resolved by a survey, and then to boundaries, which was also a matter of reaching a decision by survey. The whole pamphlet is therefore strictly limited in its application, like all such textbooks. The last section was entitled, by Thulin, rather portentously 'the science of land measurement', and it is this part which is accompanied by a large set of illustrations. Frontinus' text contains thirty-three diagrams illustrating parts of the text. Some of these may have been part of the original manuscript, others were possibly added by copyists, or by later users until they were included in the eventual state of the manuscripts copied out in the fifth century.

Other texts in the collection contain further diagrams and illustrations, those of 'Balbus', for example, being rather mathematical, an aspect which does not appear in Frontinus' work, and they may be seen as an attempted extension of Frontinus' text to deal with parts of the subject which he ignored. Those in the Frontinus section seem to be straightforward enough, which is all in keeping with his text as a whole.

The remaining items in the agrimensorian collection have much the same purpose, sometimes quoting directly from Frontinus or paraphrasing or elaborating on sections of his pamphlet, or expanding on items which he had not dealt with in great detail. All of them, by depending on Frontinus, were clearly later than his work, but also indicate the evident usefulness of his work. Here I am only concerned with Frontinus' text, but it is worth noting that the other texts appeared at intervals after Frontinus' until the whole set of manuscripts was produced as it now exists in the fifth century. Frontinus' text may be dated to circa 70, then 'Hyginus 1' at about the end of the century (Frontinus was still alive, and one wonders if he saw this successor), which was followed by the text already mentioned by 'Balbus', who was clearly a professional surveyor, not a manager type, and who elaborated on the mathematical side of the profession.[7] That of 'Siculus Flaccus' was of the second century, and 'Hyginus 2' was of the second or third century. These texts were thus produced fairly regularly for a period of perhaps a century and a half.

The *Liber Coloniarum* is not a surveyor's text, but a list of *coloniae* in Italy. It, the *Commentum* and 'Agennius Urbicus', are all from the fourth or fifth centuries, and these latter two refer directly to Frontinus' text. The gap in the third century suggests either a lack of surveying in the chaotic conditions of that period – and the practice of founding colonies certainly was suspended in that period - or that the availability of the first set of texts was seen as sufficient. The collection is completed, if that is the correct word, with a series of short extracts from larger works, which are usually otherwise unidentified, and are all late in date.

The *Commentum*, written much later, enlarges on some of the items included, or those which have been missed, in Frontinus' original. It is a feature of these other accounts in the collection that they tend to elaborate on issues Frontinus barely touched on, implying that he had not the detailed knowledge of these aspects which the others could display, or that he had decided that his audience was not likely to be concerned with such detail, or that it was only later that the omissions were realized as people worked from the text and noticed their absence. The heavy concentration he laid on the problems encountered by surveyors also suggests what his audience's concerns were expected to be.

This is the basis for the conclusion that Frontinus' work was effectively the first of its type in the world of surveys; or, of course, it may just have been the best and most useful, and so became the one which men habitually used, and anything earlier was discarded. Frontinus' text is regarded as fragmentary and incomplete, which, for something written as the first of its type in the first century AD, would hardly be surprising, but this conclusion is partly due to an assiduous process of comparison between his surveying text and those of the other writers' texts, which tend to be longer. Yet it is a coherent document, whether or not parts may be missing – most supposed gaps are minor, amounting to sentences or less. There is no sign that it is incomplete, with no indication that he intended to write more sections, and what there is reads without obvious breaks, or *non sequiturs*. It is thus better to accept it as it is, and to take it as complete and as originally written, rather than to deconstruct it and leave it scattered about in fragments and ruins. Many of the suggested quotations from his work are in fact integral parts of other accounts with no obvious reference to Frontinus' work, but can be regarded as customary phrases in the profession; they are only assumed to be from Frontinus by modern guesswork. They are not necessarily to be assumed to be quotations from his work.

On the other hand, we have the text of a man who clearly had experience of managing a company of surveyors. The question then is, how did such a man, an *eques* and a military officer, become involved in such work? Here we may note that his earliest work was in fact not as a surveyor but probably as a junior officer in the army, a military tribune, in which capacity he probably served in the Parthian War in his 20s. Supervising the regiment's or legion's surveyors may well have been a task disliked by other, more socially superior – or lazy – officers, so that the most junior of the officers would be allocated to it, in a fashion normal to every army or hierarchical organization that has ever existed. However, even if he was not detailed to such work, it is likely that, as an officer, his experience of warfare in the East will have brought him into contact with military surveyors, laying out roads, establishing forts, and so on.[8]

This will have been especially the case if, as I have assumed in Chapter 1, he rose to the command of an auxiliary regiment, which would form its own fortified camp whenever it moved. This experience will have given him, as an intelligent and curious man, a grounding for his work as a supervisor in Spain and Africa, which has been conjectured here; he was also an army officer, which will have inculcated in him the habit and method of command, while the surveyors were evidently organized in a quasi-military way, even if they were necessarily expected to work somewhat independently. It may also be that, in an early example of his ability to seize opportunities, he was able to see that a step forward in a career by shifting to surveying after his military service would be advantageous. It is not unknown for non-soldiers to assume that former soldiers are the best people to govern and administer in other activities since they have the ability to sort out the important from the irrelevant and to command (even if they know little or nothing of the task in hand). He clearly gained his information and technical knowledge fairly thoroughly, which would suggest that he was not averse to, as his subordinates might have put it, 'getting his hands dirty'.[9]

But the account he gives in his pamphlet also shows that he investigated the wider context of the work. He knows something about the history of the subject, of the Etruscan methods, and the colonial settlements in Italy, Africa, and Spain, and has a fairly good knowledge of the legal situation of surveyors; he refers to the *lex Mamilia*, the text of which is also quoted in the collection, as the legal basis of surveying. He had a good natural knowledge of the possible problems, such as land disputes, as well as typical cases, but also of anomalous cases. Some of this could have been acquired by personal experience – if he was from a landowning family, which is highly likely since that was the basis of senatorial and equestrian wealth, he would certainly have experienced land disputes and boundary problems – but this would be limited; more will have been learned from discussion and gossip among the surveyors, and still more from systematic study. When he came to write it all down, perhaps from the notes he had made on the job, he had to arrange his material in a presentable fashion, which he did. The account he wrote moves through the basics, from the fundamental types of land survey to the disputes which could arise from that process, to the problem of making and marking boundaries, and finally onto the problems of measuring land.

It is all plausibly and pleasantly systematic, if difficult to read at times because of the technicalities involved. He does not shy away from jargon or from technical terms – how could he? Why should he? This is a technical subject, in which such terms were normal and expected.[10] So Frontinus was evidently writing for the benefit of future surveying supervisors, men such as himself who had been placed in a commanding position with little direct, hands-on experience of the subject, but were assumed, as officers, to be able to command. That is probably one reason why the pamphlet survived in use, and in several copies, to be collated in the fifth century with a whole series of other surveying documents in the *Corpus*. These other items seem to have been written in emulation of, or expansion of, or in correction of, his work, so that the whole collection would be a textbook for the profession. The whole set acts as a symposium of all the usefully written work on the subject of surveying, and that was clearly the collection's function.

Frontinus' work was quite certainly, and deliberately, placed as the first in the set because it was the first to be produced, and so was fundamental for the rest. (The several other inclusions are placed roughly in chronological order of composition with the exception of the *Commentum*.) And possibly it was the most useful and concise. In a sense it was also a general account, where others concentrated on specific aspects. One may imagine copies being made in the imperial bureaucracy and delivered to later supervisors, and copies being retained locally by a group of surveyors, for later supervisors to use, who might arrive without one. It is short enough to be carried unobtrusively in a soldier's or surveyor's pack, or as part of the equipment of a group of surveyors.

The work involved a variety of possible tasks: delimiting areas of land for the settlement of military veterans, the layout of roads, the planting and planning of military forts, planning new towns and colonies, laying out the imperial boundaries – a surveyor was the first on the scene of Hadrian's Wall – all of which were skills required during his governorship of Britannia (see Chapters 4 and 5). It was intricate work, requiring experience and judgment, as the methods used by the men on the ground would normally be learned from another surveyor in a quasi-apprentice system, whereas there may have been nothing in writing until Frontinus' work for the manager; the various gangs may well have varied in their methods, or results, of their work. As a job it required precision, and in the case of land disputes, it required a diplomatic ability, but also some force of character; no doubt this was why an *eques* with experience of command was normally put in charge; he would have a social authority to deal with both ordinary farmers and estate owners. The term used, reasonably enough is usually *mensor*, for the man in command; Plautus used the term *initio*, which may be a playwright's licence. He was presumably subject to the provincial procurator, or possibly the governor. If Frontinus' examples from Spain are anything to go by he was active throughout the peninsula, in all the provinces, which might suggest that he had a fairly high equestrian rank, perhaps that of procurator.

Much of the work was necessarily done, at least preliminarily, by the individual surveyors, the freedmen, slaves, private soldiers, and so on, and was presumably only referred to the man in command when it was needed – as in a dispute over land boundaries, or urban taxation rights, or between individual landowners, or to lay out the bounds of estates which were to be awarded to retired soldiers, or formally viewed at the end as a formal gesture of completion. Plenty of evidence in the form of centuriation, the division of territory, usually fertile plains, into small peasant estates, has survived; each plot for a citizen soldier to cultivate in his retirement. This is normally noted in terms of Augustus' settlement of time-expired soldiers at the end of the civil wars in the first century BC, but epigraphic records show that the practice continued right through Frontinus' time in Spain and Africa, which is where he is thought to have worked.[11] Precision of dating is rarely possible, however, and none of the examples can be ascribed to him, even by guesswork.

If this reconstruction of Frontinus' early life and work – before it enters the realm of our direct documentation in 70 – is anywhere near accurate, he was working as a surveyor-supervisor in the 60s, after learning the ropes – as an officer in command, and as an amateur of surveying – during his military service in the East. There he had made an impression on his superior officers, came to the notice of the emperor, or at least the imperial administration, who will always have been on the lookout for young men of ability, both *eques* and of senatorial rank. He was one of a number of men at the time who came from Narbonensis who were active in various parts of the government service, in the army, in particular, in the Senate, and in administration, and were becoming more and more noticeable as a group. He will perforce, since he was obviously an ambitious man, and a man of his time, have known and used this Narbonensian network of friends and acquaintances to assist in forwarding his own career (see Chapter 13), and he will have assisted others in the same way. But Roman careers often, particularly in the early stages, had gaps in them, years off between appointments, partly presumably so that their previous work could be evaluated, though it is also an aspect of the overall amateur nature of the aristocratic administrative system. We have no knowledge of his actions in 68–69, other than an assumption that he was with Galba (because it is here assumed he was in Spain at the time – a fairly hazardous set of conjectures, see Chapter 1). Also, after 70 and until 73 he is again out of sight (to us at least), but he was now a senator and we may assume he was active in debate and in committee. He was ambitious, and again he will have wished to be constantly in the emperor's eye. This will have been the time when he wrote his account of surveying practice. For another network of men into which he had entered at Rome was that of the *literati*, the poets and historians, Pliny and Martial and others.

Chapter 3

Rise to Consul

The Lingones

The reward for a job well done is to be given another job, probably more difficult than the first. Frontinus' acquiescence to imperial requirements over his brief praetorship had earned him this at least. Later in 70, sometime after resigning his praetorship to Domitian, he was part of the difficult expedition sent to suppress rebellions in Gaul and Germany. It would be very helpful if we could know what Frontinus had been doing during the Civil War of 69, though, since he was in Rome on 1 January 70, it is reasonable to assume that he had been there for some time before that date, and it may be that he had been in the city during all that dangerous year, 69, though my hypothesis is that he came from Spain with Galba, and may have been an officer in Galba's new legion, VII Galbiana, in which he will have moved back and forth between Italy and Pannonia. This would certainly put him in Rome in December 69, when Vitellius was finally destroyed.

The fighting in the city only ended on 20 December. If he arrived with the Flavian army, he would have taken part in the fighting; alternatively he had been in the city since arriving with Galba late in 68. As an *eques* he would not be important enough, nor would he have sufficient political influence, to be hunted down by the supporters of either Otho or Vitellius; on the other hand, he was clearly a Flavian supporter.

The new job he was given was to command a legionary force in an expedition to recover control of Gaul and Germany from an assorted group of rebels. A major expeditionary force of five or six legions was assembled in Italy and marched north, while other legionary forces came in from the Danube garrisons and from Britannia. The main fighting was against the Treveri tribe and its allies in the Moselle and Rhine valleys, and the larger section of the Roman force fought there and along the Rhine, under the command of Q. Petillius Cerialis Caesius Rufus, related by marriage to the new emperor. The Lingones further south are also mentioned as being involved; indeed, at first the Lingones were equal with the Treveri in their attachment to the rebellion. Tacitus strongly concentrates on the Treveri, and this seems to have been the main enemy which the expeditionary commander, Petillius Cerialis, identified and campaigned against.

The Lingones were located in the later Burgundy, in country which contained the headwaters of the Soane River, flowing south, and of the Moselle, flowing north, a high plateau country which was crucial to any power wishing to control Gaul, a land which saw more than one of Julius Caesar's necessary victories during his conquest of Gaul (including Alesia). It was a strategic area, therefore, with the Belfort Gap nearby, linking the Rhine and Rhône Valleys. Eventually it would be attached to the Germania Superior province when it was formed, which had a substantial serving garrison with which to watch and control the area; for the present it was part of the Gallia Belgica province.

The Lingones in rebellion, however, were surrounded by tribes loyal to Rome, and had the unfortunate experience of attacking the neighbouring (loyal) Sequani, only to be soundly defeated. A section of the Lingones joined the Treveri when the Roman counterattack and Cerialis arrived.[1]

We have only one item of information about Frontinus in these events, an item in Book IV of his *Stratagems* in which he claims to have received the surrender of a large number – 70,000 – of the Lingones. The fighting against the Treveri took place well to the north of the Lingones' homeland, and they were separated from it by the Sequani, but a Roman force, including Frontinus, commanded nominally by the Caesar Domitian, with Licinius Mucianus as his mentor, travelled as far as Lugdunum, in Narbonensis, just to the south of Lingonian territory. This was the force which now menaced the Lingones.

Frontinus' Book IV has been attacked as not being by him, on a variety of grounds; above all, he said at the beginning that he would write his account in three books.[2] The fourth book is, however, now regarded as more likely than not to have been compiled by him, an addition to the original. In that case we have here in the Lingones item another example of Frontinus' personal participation in events, for he says explicitly that the Lingones surrendered to him, to the number of 70,000 armed men. This surprising development is put down to the fact that the advancing Roman forces had refrained from ravaging and destroying the land. This would suggest that 70,000 armed men were gathered as a defence force, but were not needed once Roman moderation was seen.³ It helped the Roman cause that news will have arrived that the Treveri had suffered a massive defeat at Cerealis' hands, so that the Lingones were now alone in the fight.⁴ The account is in fact notably unspecific about location, and exactly who was included in the 70,000 – it is probable that this was a population figure, not a force of armed men.

Frontinus' participation was presumably at Mucianus' invitation, though Frontinus has no room for him in his brief account of the expedition to Lugdunum (which might suggest that this item was completed well after Mucianus had faded from the political picture). As a man now of praetorian rank, Frontinus would be eligible to command one of the legions in Mucianus' force. Domitian was also, of course, of praetorian rank (a slightly higher version than Frontinus' since he had consular *imperium* attached). Mucianus' main task in the expedition seems to have been to keep Domitian under restraint, though it had been Mucianus' plan of operations, and he was the overall organizer of the several expeditions. Many stories were told of Domitian's ambition to command in war, often clearly hostile or even invented. This was clearly a means to obliquely criticize his father, but this also meant he could not be allowed to suffer a defeat. Domitian himself, and Mucianus, clearly understood this; no doubt Frontinus took the point as well. In this case, the achievement of the Lingonian surrender makes Frontinus the actual commander in the field, with Domitian and Mucianus exercising overall command behind the line from Lugdunum, since they were both of higher rank, and more obviously political; Domitian and Mucianus presumably remained at headquarters, Mucianus being unwilling to let Domitian, an unstable adolescent, be in command of anything. So Frontinus, the ranking commander, was in charge of the actual campaign; it was also necessary, for the good of the new regime, that he be victorious.

The object of the force which was gathered at Lugdunum was thus to suppress the rebellion of the Lingones. Their participation in the revolt had come early, but they were now divided between those who stayed at home and those who joined the Treveri in the war along the Rhine, and had suffered defeat alongside them. The tribe had originally been on the Roman side in the rebellion of Julius Vindex in 68, whereas their neighbours the Sequani had joined Vindex. In the battle which destroyed that rebellion, the

Lingones had gleefully helped. Now the tables were turned. The Lingones had attempted to repeat the trick, but this time alone, and against an infuriated Sequani, who defended themselves with skill, determination, and success.[5] The detachment which went to join the Treveri was presumably composed of those warriors especially committed to the anti-Roman side, so those remaining at home were less than enthusiastic, hence their ready surrender. The Lingones were already thus much subdued when the Roman expedition approached. They were fearful of punishment, and would fight if necessary, but that would depend on Roman behaviour.

If Frontinus was in field command, as the command structure suggests, as his praetorian rank implies, and as his anecdote states, it is not known which legion he commanded, though guesses have been made. The legions with Mucianus and Domitian at Lugdunum are not noted by Tacitus (there is a gap in his text here), but two possibilities have been suggested, II Adiutrix and XXII Primigenia, though there is nothing in the way of proof either way.[6] It seems likely that Mucianus, who was the overall commander in this part of the reconquest, understood that Frontinus was a capable commander, and therefore employed him. If no legion was available – the two which are suggested had in fact been allotted to other expeditions – he could have commanded a force of *auxilia*, for which his Eastern experience would have fitted him admirably. The object, of course, was not necessarily destruction of the enemy, which would create lasting resentment, but conciliation and subjection of the rebels, who had been beaten once already. This was a civil war, after all – and the conduct of Cerialis' campaign along the Rhine was frightening enough to obviate any need for massacres elsewhere. When the Lingones, beaten already, saw the Roman good behaviour enforced by Frontinus, this was apparently sufficient to bring about their surrender.

This is as far as Frontinus' anecdote takes us, but there was a follow-up by the Roman command. At Mirabaeu-sur-Beze, just across the border of the Lingones in the territory of the Aedui, a new legionary fortress was built, starting in 70, soon after the Lingones' surrender. It was occupied by Legio VIII Augusta, which was not apparently involved in the campaign against the Lingones. The legion stayed there for at least a decade and perhaps some years longer. It was clearly placed there to overawe the Lingones, who would therefore appear to have been less reconciled to Roman rule than Frontinus' story might imply.[7]

Imperial Connections

The fact that Domitian and Frontinus in their later lives were friends and colleagues on another expedition in this area, suggests that Frontinus in 70 was fully capable of getting along with the excitable prince, who developed into a more sober emperor. The Lingones expedition, therefore, links Frontinus with two members of the new imperial family. Domitian, his colleague at Lugdunum, was the younger son of the new emperor, and would become emperor himself ten years later; Petillius Cerialis, the commander on the Rhine campaign, who went on at once to govern Britannia from 71 to 73, had been married to one of Vespasian's daughters, Flavia Domitilla, who had since died.[8] Cerialis was the father of several children, who were, therefore, Vespasian's grandchildren, and clearly would be in line for the succession if the direct line of Vespasian's sons failed.

These connections put Frontinus, the former *eques*, who had already been favoured by being made praetor, right in the heart of the new imperial regime, where he remained for the rest of his life. It was also, so long as he was careful, the key to his future advancement and to personal prosperity. As a result of the Civil War, by what was probably a judicious choice of whom to support in that war (first Galba, then Vespasian), he had leapt from having an obscure but potentially interesting minor career as an *eques* to become a senator of praetorian rank, a victorious commander, and with connections with the imperial house; he was clearly a new man with a major political career in the offing.

This was to be confirmed a little over a year after his successful campaign against the Lingones. Petillius Cerialis was soon appointed governor of Britannia, which required a strong hand after some unfortunate Roman ditherings and disputes during the Civil War, and a member of the imperial family would be just the man, especially one as rough and ready as Cerialis. He had a recent victory in the war in Gaul and Germany to his credit, and so had the prestige and authority to attend to matters in Britannia. The problem there was partly internal to the army, and partly a renewed restlessness amongst the British tribes, both the conquered and the 'free', so it needed a soldier and a man of the highest social position to gain proper control.

It has been suggested that Frontinus, supposedly in command of Legio II Adiutrix in the Lingones campaign, then went to Britannia when it was transferred there in 71, to reinforce Cerialis, but this is piling conjecture on supposition, and going too far. (Not but that any interpretation of Frontinus' career will contain plenty of such suppositions.) In the first place, it is not known which legion took part in the Lingones campaign; also, Frontinus was surely expected to stay in the conquered territory of the Lingones for some time after subduing the tribe, in order to ensure a continuing peace, and to solve any lingering problems. It is thus possible that it was he, with his combined military and surveying experience, and his local victory, who was placed in charge of the founding of the new legionary fortress at Mirabeau-sur-Beze.

Consul – Vespasian's Problem

Frontinus was made consul in, probably, 73, a date arrived at because he was made governor of Britannia, a consular post, later that year. For a man who was still of *eques* rank until 69, and had been praetor only two years before, and only briefly, this was a surprising speed of ascent. It is an even more surprising promotion when one considers the other men who were made consuls in Vespasian's first half-decade as emperor. Almost all of those men were of a small tight-knit set of obvious allies of Vespasian: members of the imperial family, men serving as consuls for the second time, or men who were especially selected friends of Vespasian, but who had supported one of the other contenders in 69.[9]

Vespasian, in the years immediately after the Civil War, had to choose men to be consuls with unusual care. His reign was unsteady. There were many eminent men of higher prestige than him who had supported other candidates and brief emperors. It would not take much to drive him from the throne. He therefore chose consuls for the first five years in order to reward supporters, and to build up his own and his sons' prestige (he, Titus and Domitian were consuls every year) and to shut out his internal enemies from any power position. The Senate was uncontrolled for several months, especially since Vespasian took until October 70 to get to Rome, and Titus was away from the city even longer. Then, for the rest of his reign, Vespasian faced senatorial opposition. It did not emerge into violence or rebellion, partly because Titus acted as his father's security agent and enforcer as praetorian prefect. This was probably only because Vespasian was careful in dealing with his opponents, isolating them, and engaging them in dialogue with him, though he did in the end finally lose his temper with some opponents and resorted to execution. But by then the Senate was much calmer.[10]

One consequence of this uncomfortable political atmosphere was that Vespasian was exceptionally careful and selective in compiling the list of men who became consuls. They would gain prestige by the appointment, and appointing his enemies would be dangerous, not necessarily conciliatory. This is especially noticeable in that first half decade, 70–74. His consular lists were filled with the names of men he could absolutely depend on. The promotion of new men, or those of doubtful loyalty, was not something to be indulged in until they had proved themselves loyal, dependable and competent. These were men who would go out of Rome after their time as consul to govern the provinces and to command the armies, and with their prestige would dominate the Senate.

In the recent civil war, provincial governors from Spain, Germany, and Syria had marched on Rome with their armies. It was now clear that to become emperor the first necessity was to be in command of an army. Ironically, it had been that old advocate of ancient republican virtues, Galba, who had shown the way. In Roman imperial politics the task of commanding armies was one which required absolute loyalty to the emperor – after 69 rebellions always came from men who were already in command of an army. So no man who exhibited animosity towards Vespasian, in the past or the present, or even neutrality, or whose loyalty was in any way doubtful, could be allowed to be consul, or to come near an army. Even a man who was lukewarm in his support would be seen as a problem and denied office or promotion. It would not be necessary to imprison or kill such men, except in extreme cases, only to sideline them – and, of course, keep an eye on them.

Therefore, the men whose names appear on the consular list in the first half of Vespasian's reign must be presumed to be firm Flavian supporters. Later it was possible to relax a little and expand the pool of men selected to be consul, but some were still excluded. An example is Roscius Coelius, who had commanded a legion in Britannia in the late 60s. He was thus of praetorian rank before he took command of the legion, and yet Vespasian never chose him as consul. The reason was that he had led a mutiny against the serving governor in 69, and this showed that he could not be trusted.[11] Under normal conditions he would have become consul by 73 or

74; he had to wait until 81, when he was appointed by Titus. This makes the rapid appointment of Frontinus particularly striking.

The emperor was further constrained in his selection of men as consuls by the need to appoint men who had reached the preceding rank of praetor in the magistral *cursus,* and yet any man of that rank who had reached it under Nero, or even Claudius, might hanker for a return to those days. Vespasian was determined that he and his two sons must accumulate a long list of consulships so as to build up their own prestige. From the beginning he was determined on establishing his family with a hereditary right to the *imperium*, by adopting the methods pioneered by Augustus. He associated Titus with him as, in effect, joint emperor, just as Augustus had with Agrippa and later Tiberius, and by multiplying his and his sons' holdings of, above all, ordinary consulships, so that the sons would have the accumulated authority to succeed him without question. This practice must also, however, automatically limit the number of non-family men who were made consul. During his reign Vespasian himself took eight of these posts in the next ten years, but Titus also held the office on seven occasions and Domitian on six (one ordinary and the rest suffect); no one else could match this concentration of prestige. It was an obsession which was also all too obvious an indication of the new emperor's own political, and even personal, insecurity. A result of these measures was that there were only a few slots available for other men as ordinary consuls, and these few will, of course, have been his most loyal and prominent supporters.

But the constraint noted above had a further element to it. The men whom Vespasian appointed, in every single case except one, had reached praetorian rank before the Civil War, and even in some cases, consular rank. They were therefore men of the old regime, the time of Nero mostly. Vespasian himself had risen during the reigns of Claudius and Nero through the various offices, consul in 51, and then to command of the Eastern army, having been governor of Africa, which was usually regarded as one of the last offices to be held before retirement (which, of course, was why he had been selected to command against the Jewish rebels – he seemed to Nero to be at the end of his political career). He and his colleagues were thus men who had already been selected by those emperors, in part on the basis of their presumed loyalty, in part as proven competent officials, though their willingness to serve under Vespasian suggests strongly that they had been less than satisfied with the policies pursued by those final

Augustan emperors. It might also suggest that Vespasian had known this full well under those emperors, and that they had formed a discreet group of (mostly silent) opponents. The men who served with Corbulo had perhaps been less than silent, at least amongst themselves, when in the East. Galba, from his own very high social prestige, was able to speak out to some extent, which was why he was sent to Spain, where he was able to conspire and plot the overthrow of Nero's regime. Vespasian had therefore to choose his consuls and governors very carefully, since several of these men outranked him in prestige and experience and family history – at least before he became emperor.

Where possible the governors of provinces, commanders of armies, and occupants of the magistral offices below the level of consul had to be considered as eligible for the position of consul. In all cases they held their offices at the emperor's gift, and clearly they represented a set of people who were chosen by the emperors because they were perceived to be his supporters. One major element in his choice was heredity. Respect for, and pride in, heredity was deeply woven into Roman society, and the emperors were affected by this as much as anyone. Vespasian's origin was always a source of enmity towards him: he was, in effect, a *novus homo*, a new man, with no senatorial ancestors – hence the multiple consulships. Yet an exaggerated respect for heredity might conflict directly with the imperial need for efficiency and competence if it excluded other, more capable, new men. A second element in choosing consuls was the general expectation among the senators. Any man who spent time as a praetor, and especially those who followed this with a spell as commander of a legion or a governor of a minor province – both praetorian posts – and had performed competently in those offices, could reasonably expect to become consul within a few years. To disappoint such expectations would be to build up a reservoir of resentment (as with Corbulo's officers) which would, at the least, make an imperial regime increasingly unpopular. So, although an emperor could choose who should be consul, his choice was circumscribed and he was limited to a particular set of men at any one time.

Vespasian's choice of men to be consuls was the beginning of a process by which these men and their descendants became the new ruling aristocracy of the empire, or in the case of iterating consuls, increasing their aristocratic status. The murderousness of the Emperors Claudius and Nero, and then the Civil War, had done much of the preliminary work by killing off large swathes of the earlier aristocracy, those whom Ronald Syme dubbed the 'Augustan Aristocracy'. How consciously Vespasian was attempting to construct the new ruling set is unclear, though it is quite certain that he was choosing consuls very deliberately, with the particular short-term aim of building personal support, and bolstering his own unsteady position. His own and his family's near-monopolization of the ordinary consulships was clearly intended to establish his family high in that aristocracy in place of the prestige of heredity. Later, his younger son Domitian seems to have been much more deliberate in aiming to shape the aristocracy. He not only chose to promote certain men as consuls, but also operated to eliminate – that is, kill off – others, which Vespasian had largely refused to do. It was Vespasian, however, who began the process.

Consuls – Vespasian's Choices

Frontinus' consulship was well placed in relation to his praetorship, since that was often succeeded by a legionary command and a year's break. It can seem therefore that it arrived in a normal sequence, at an expected time. Yet Vespasian's early years as emperor were not normal, and the consular list is composed of the unexpected. In order to see how unlikely Frontinus' consulship was, it is necessary to look at Vespasian' choices of consuls in detail.

Vespasian's first consuls were selected near the end of 69, when it became clear that he would soon be in control in Rome, though he had acted as emperor, and had taken imperial decisions since June. The selection was done at a distance from the city, for he did not arrive in Rome itself until the autumn of 70. Any consular list prepared during 69 by other emperors had been voided by the successive deaths of his four imperial predecessors, though the final occupants of the office saw out the final days of 69, even though they had been Vitellian appointees. One of these, C. Quinctius Atticus, was accused of committing arson and sacrilege in the fighting in the Capitoline Temple; he admitted the former crime, and is not heard of again.[12] Neither is his consular colleague, Cn. Caecilius Simplex, to whom no crime other than supporting Vitellius is implied, though his daughters did marry into consular families later on, so it would seem that he retained his senatorial status.¹³ Vespasian was not being overly, or unnecessarily, vindictive.

The pattern of the early years of the reign emerges even in Vespasian's first consular list, that of the year 70. Vespasian and his son each took one of the two ordinary consulships for that year, though they were held *in absentia* (which was the reason Frontinus as *praetor urbanus* presided at the opening of the Senate on 1 January).¹⁴ The constraints within which Vespasian worked in choosing his other consuls reduced the possible candidates very severely, and many of those he did choose had to be worked hard, not just as consuls, but in subsequent offices as well. C. Licinius Mucianus, as governor of Syria, had pushed Vespasian to take the final step and to proclaim his intention of opposing Otho and Vitellius by claiming the throne while still in Syria. He was therefore fastened hip and thigh to Vespasian's cause, and was awarded a second consulship. Besides Mucianus, four other men were appointed who had been crucial military supporters in the Civil War. M. Ulpius Traianus had been commander of Legio X Fretensis in Palestine (he had been governor of Baetica while Frontinus was in Spain, and they may have been acquainted earlier; they certainly were now).¹⁵ L. Annius Bassus had been legate of Legio XI Claudia, and had successfully persuaded the governor of the province of Dalmatia, M. Pompeius Silvanus Staberius Flavinus, after much dithering, to finally take the Flavian side; Pompeius eventually received a third consulship, from Domitian.¹⁶ Petillius Cerialis was another suffect of this first year, a family member, and went on to command in the German campaign, in Britannia, and receive a second consulship. Finally, there was a consulship for the son of one of Vitellius' commanders, L. Laecanius Bassus Caecina Paetus, whose name shows him to have been adopted by one of Nero's consuls.¹⁷ He was related in some way to Caecina Alienus, who had finally joined Vespasian after deserting first Galba and then Vitellius; after such behaviour Caecina was not himself rewarded; perhaps Paetus was honoured in his stead. It was therefore not just the earliest supporters who had to be rewarded, but also those who were initially reluctant; rewarding them was actually all the more necessary with the throne unsteady beneath the new rulers. Expanding the numbers of loyalists by rewarding them in advance might do it; perhaps it had been the price they demanded for joining the Flavian side.

Q. Iulius Cordinus Cn. Rutilius Gallicus, from Transpadana, had been part of the group around Cn. Domitius Corbulo in the Armenian War in the 60s, as commander of Legio XV Apollinaris, and had been a long-time governor in Galatia; he was an early adherent of Vespasian, possibly brought in by Mucianus, his neighbour as governor in Syria, or perhaps it was in reaction to the enforced suicide of Corbulo. Preferring Traianus and Gallicus was a firm gesture of appreciation to those Corbulo men who had supported Vespasian from the start. One element in the movement behind Vespasian's venture was that of revenge by former colleagues of Corbulo against Nero and the group in Rome who had plotted the general's downfall and brought him to suicide; these were now, therefore, likely to be members of the 'silent opposition'.[18] Rutilius after his early consulship was given important posts in Africa, in Germany, and in Asia, and eventually received a second consulship by Domitian, having been continuously employed in these several offices from 70 to 85. His career had evidently stalled before the Civil War: he had been military tribune thirty years before his consulship, which meant that he was in his 50s when he finally reached that status; he had clearly been suspected of disloyalty by Nero and perhaps by Claudius.[19]

On the other hand, little is known of another new consul, L. Cornelius Pusio. He was from Gades (Cadiz) in Spain, but it may be confidently assumed that he was, or had been, useful to Vespasian in some way, perhaps in his home province of Baetica during the Civil War, for this is clearly the main criterion for promotion to consul in this early part of the reign. Presumably he had been one of Galba's supporters in 68, though his province had been governed by Otho, and he probably went with him at first, no doubt, like Vespasian, abandoning him after Galba's murder.[20] His family became rich from the proprietorship of a fish sauce plant at Portus Gaditanus; his son was consul in 90; it is possible he was related to the Annius family, and, distantly, to the Traianus family, which also came from Baetica.[21]

The known consular record for 70 is thus two ordinary consuls and five suffects. With five suffects known it would appear that at least one name is missing, possibly more (unless one of the *ordinarii* served a longer term than usual, though since both were serving *in absentia*, this is perhaps unlikely; this incomplete record is a problem all through Vespasian's reign). The names of the *consules ordinarii* are known for every year of the reign, mainly Vespasian and Titus, of course, and only two men who were not Flavian family members held that office in the first half of the reign. Vespasian held the office four times, Titus four and Domitian once (and two suffect consulships). In addition, four of the other suffects were men who were holding second consulships. As a result of these repeats and the gaps in the record, and the imperial monopolization of most of the ordinary posts, there are only seven other men who reached the consulship, and one precisely dated, on record in the first four years of the reign. Vespasian was keeping a very tight grip on the consulate.

Two repeat consuls have already been noted. Second consulships also went to Mucianus (who also gained a third, in 72, at which point he had held as many as Vespasian himself), and to Petillius Cerialis in 74, when he had returned from Britannia; seconds also went to three other men who had held their first consulships under Nero. These were therefore prominent original supporters of the new emperor. T. Clodius Eprius Marcellus' second consulship in 74 was probably awarded because of his unprecedented four-year stint as governor of Asia (70–73), a post usually held for a single year, and at the end of a man's career, like the analogous post in Africa, though Marcellus was disliked among his fellow senators because of his earlier career as a prosecutor for Nero.[22] His partner as iterating consul was T. Plautius Silvanus Aelianus, who had been praetor as far back as 42, and consul for the first time in 45; he had been praetorian commander of a legion in Claudius' invasion of Britannia in 43, and was therefore an old colleague of Vespasian's, who had also commanded a legion in that war. Aelianus had also commanded under Corbulo in the Armenian expedition in 61/62, had governed at least three provinces, and was Galba's successor as governor of Hispania Citerior. He may have been Vespasian's friend and colleague, but he had also earned a second consulship in any case.[23]

A family member, T. Flavius Sabinus, Vespasian's nephew, received a second consulship in 72; his first consulship had been in May or June 69, in a list prepared by Otho, probably as a move to conciliate or deflect Vespasian himself, who by then was almost openly considering mounting his own usurpation, and anyway commanded a very large section of the army. Sabinus' father, with the same name, had been city prefect during the Civil War, and was later killed by a rioting mob in the fighting which ended in the burning of the Capitoline Temple in December 69. The son had fought for Otho at Cremona, unsuccessfully (when Otho deliberately took many such men, usually related to his competitors, to the war against Vitellius in a vain attempt at blackmail). How loyal he was to any of the emperors he served – Nero, Galba, Otho, Vitellius, Vespasian – is quite uncertain, but probably he was one of those men who accepted whoever was in power, perhaps arguing that the welfare of the empire as a whole demanded it, and at least Vespasian was a relative. He had been *curator rei publicorum* (curator of public works) in the city after his first consulship, so his second came immediately after that post, and may perhaps be regarded as a memorial for his father. He was not active after 72, so far as is known, and was probably dead by the time of Titus' reign.[24] His compliant neutrality during the crisis, or perhaps one may call it his overarching loyalty to Rome rather than to a particular emperor, was a political reaction which Frontinus was to take at the end of his life, when confronted with yet another succession crisis. These men thus straddled more than one category – family, old friends, selected as conciliatory gestures to dead enemies, capable men, political neutrals, pragmatists.

L. Iunius Q. Vibius Crispus received his second consulship after his governorship of Africa in 72/73; he had been *curator aquarum* (the official in charge of the maintenance of the water supply of Rome) all through the troubles, from 68 to 71, and he was, like Nerva and Eprius Marcellus, useful in political affairs in Rome and the Senate. He became, according to Juvenal, a member of Vespasian's inner circle; also like Marcellus, he was evidently an efficient administrator, and, like Sabinus, he was, it seems, one of those indifferent to whoever was emperor.[25]

Only two men who were not of the immediate imperial family became ordinary consuls in the first years of the new reign. M. Cocceius Nerva, the future emperor, was ordinary consul in 71. He had been awarded an honorary triumph by Nero for some unknown activity during the Piso plot near the end of the reign, which would imply extraordinary loyalty to that emperor at a time when Nero's throne was tottering;[26] he was fortunate not to be denounced after Nero's death as a *delator* (informer). His ordinary consulship from Vespasian came in the second year of the new reign, which implies his early support for Vespasian's candidacy, and perhaps some decisive activity, but no precise reason is known. He had clearly been selected as consul in Vespasian's first list, formed after his return to Rome in the autumn of 70, and so perhaps as a result of information he had acquired about events within the city. Nerva only ever left Rome to visit pleasant villas within a hundred miles of the city; he was the ultimate Roman political insider, never having 'seen a province or an army', but he was always at the centre of affairs in Rome.[27] He knew his way about the politics of Rome as well as anyone else, and he was descended from a line of at least four consuls, which made him one of the Augustan Aristocracy. There is no sign that he had bothered to take up earlier political posts to which he could have laid claim – though he was *praetor designatus* in 66; whatever his earlier activities or connections, he would obviously be of considerable use to the new emperor.

Vespasian, of course, had been away from Rome since being sent to fight in Palestine in 66, or even since Nero's Greek tour the year before, during which Vespasian, an old man even then, fell asleep at one of the emperor's performances – the appointment to warring Palestine may be seen as a punishment, or as an exile.[28] Nothing is known of Nerva's activities during the tumult of 69; he must have been in Rome under all the brief rulers of that year; his knowledge of who had done what in that difficult year was no doubt extremely detailed and valuable to the new ruler; he was later to be a member of Domitian's *consilium*, and it is likely he was also a member of Vespasian's.[29] His promotion to consul was thus in the nature of an adlection; he was a senator by rank and inheritance, and a patrician; his appointment as consul was Vespasian's recognition of his helpfulness.

The other non-Flavian ordinary consul in Vespasian's first half-decade of rule was L. Valerius Catullus Messalinus, consul in 73. He was probably of patrician rank and so was holding the consulship in his 30s, but he did nothing notably active during his political career. He was perhaps, like Nerva, also a Roman insider, though his familial descent was hardly as illustrious as Nerva's. He was from Verona in Transpadana; his father had died young without having entered any political offices, though he had been a *pontifex*; his grandfather had been consul in 31, but earlier forebears had reached no higher than quaestor or monetalis. It must therefore have been Messalinus' personal qualities – 'smooth and acceptable' in a modern characterization – which brought him to office under Vespasian, though such qualities do not seem to fit very well with Vespasian. Much later, after a second consulship awarded by Domitian, he was reviled by Tacitus and Juvenal as an 'informer'. It was only under Domitian that he emerged as an imperial *amicus*, but he clearly had a high status under Vespasian if he could become an ordinary consul in the most precarious period of the regime and so early in the reign.[30]

These ordinary consuls can be relatively easily explained. It is more difficult to account for the more numerous suffects, but it is necessary to review each of them to establish exactly what Vespasian was doing by his selection. (Frontinus has not been forgotten.) There are only two known suffects of 71, L. Pedius Casca and C. Calpetanus Rantius Quirinalis Valerius Festus, a highly contrasted pair. Pedius is little known, though he had presumably occupied preliminary posts up to praetor in Nero's last years if he was eligible for the consulship as early as 71; he has been claimed to be another of Vespasian's cronies, but the evidence for this could do with being expanded and clarified.[31] It is possible he was a provincial governor in the civil war year and had come out quickly for Vespasian.

Valerius Festus, probably of patrician rank, had been governor of Numidia and commander of Legio III Augusta from 68/69 to 70/71. He was therefore holding a crucial office in the years spanning most of the crisis. Calpurnius Piso Licinianus had been making moves aimed at claiming the throne himself. Valerius Festus had then taken his place, adding Africa to his province of Numidia. Festus' usurpation of the African governorship was thus illegal, but such details tend to be ignored during a civil war, especially if the usurper ends up on the winning side. (Note the difference in treatment between Festus and Roscius Coelius.) At first he had recruited troops for his relative Vitellius (Galba's method in Spain also), thereby doubling the size of the forces under his command, but soon he was communicating with Vespasian. At one point Vespasian had considered moving to Africa so as to exert more direct pressure on Italy from there.[32] This would have squashed any plan Festus may have had; he clearly decided to join him rather than go out on his own. With Valerius Festus aligned with him, however, there was no need for Vespasian's expedition. Festus could therefore reap the opprobrium of threatening to starve Italy by withholding the annual delivery of food supplies, and Vespasian could escape any blame; the contrast between their political skills is clear. Festus was no doubt rewarded with his consulship for taking Vespasian's side at the crucial moment; he went on to serve in other administrative tasks in the next years, governing Pannonia for three years after his consulship, then Hispania Citerior for two years, and probably finishing with a year in Asia; not a bad reward.³³ Given that, it seems probable that his co-consul, Pedius, had also rendered Vespasian some signal service during the Civil War; his absence from any governorship after his consulship rather suggests he may have been, like Nerva, a Roman political insider, and valued as such – or possibly he was now too old to take up any more offices.

The rest of the consuls in this first phase of the reign were all taking up the consular office for the first time. They included one Flavian relative, M. Arrecinus Clemens, who was consul in 73, the same year as Frontinus. Titus had been married to Clemens' sister Arrecina Tertulla, though they had divorced; Flavius Sabinus was married to another Arrecinus sister.³⁴ Clemens had been Praetorian Prefect until replaced by Titus himself.³⁵ It may also be that there is another imperial relative in the list, L. Flavius Fimbria, consul in 71. Little or nothing is known of him, but for him to become consul in that year, so early in the new reign, implies that he had already taken the earliest steps in climbing the *cursus* ladder under Claudius and Nero – as had Vespasian himself. He shared the same *nomen* as the new imperial family, though that does not guarantee a close relationship, nor even a relationship of any sort. On the other hand, it is difficult to account for him as consul as early as this part of the reign without either having performed a signal service to Vespasian, or being his relative. It has been suggested that he was the grandson of L. Flavius, who had been consul in 33 BC, but proof lacks; there are other Flavians active at the time, but these are not suggested to be imperial relatives.³⁶

Cn. Domitius Tullus, consul in 74, had served as a military tribune in Legio V Alaudae and as governor of Africa for two years. He commanded a major force of auxiliaries in the campaign along the Rhine in 70 under Petillius Cerealis' command; his consulship was clearly well earned, and came in the same batch as Cerealis' second, possibly not by coincidence. He was also very rich, having, along with his brother, inherited a great fortune from his adoptive father and he was one of the group of Narbonensians rising into the power set at the time (see Chapter 13). Pliny did not like him, which is not to say others felt the same; clearly the Flavians valued both him and his brother.³⁷

Five more suffects of this early period remain to be accounted for. Sex. Marcius Priscus was consul in 71 or 72. He had been governor of Lycia-and-Pamphylia during the war period in 69/70; his consulship as early as

72 rather implies that he had given his support to Vespasian in the early days of the usurpation, while he was governor, and possibly when Titus passed by his province on his way to Greece to offer Vespasian's allegiance to Galba, only to hear that Galba had been murdered. Priscus may perhaps therefore be counted as a supporter in the same way as Laecanius Bassus.

Concerning M. Gavius Atticus, consul in 73, and C. Pomponius and L. Manlius Patruinus, both in 74, no information survives to explain why Vespasian chose them, nor is it possible to enter into conjecture; on the other hand, it seems reasonable to suppose that they were his supporters, since they were promoted in this early period; what they had done to earn the accolade is simply not known.

Probably L. Sergius Paullus, whose consulship may have come as early as 70, though this is uncertain, was being rewarded for some assistance provided during Vespasian's time in the East. He was from Antioch-in-Pisidia, and had wide contacts in the local Italian colonial and Asian royal network which had been developing in the recent past.[38] The Italians in Asia were descendants of colonists settled in a series of *coloniae* planted in Asia Minor by Augustus; they had emerged quickly as the ruling groups in their cities, and some of them had become considerably wealthy. Paullus was the first of these to reach the consulship, and he was followed by increasing numbers in the next century – a provincial emergence comparable with the same development in Spain and Narbonensis, if a little later. Recruiting him into the governing group in Rome was an intelligent move since he could act as liaison between Rome and the network at home; he and Marcius Priscus in neighbouring Lycia–and–Pamphylia may well have co-ordinated support in Asia for Vespasian during 69, the one unofficially, the other officially. Rutilius Gallicus in Galatia had perhaps been another link.

A second consul who is not clearly dated was T. Vestricius Spurinna, probably serving in 72. He had been on campaign with Otho in the Civil War, though since that emperor insisted on forcing prominent Romans to accompany him (including Vespasian's nephew, Flavius Sabinus), presumably to foil any plotting in Rome while he was away, and incriminate the men in his cause, this did not necessarily mean that he supported Otho politically. His later career does, however, suggest a man well able to adapt easily to changed political conditions.

The consuls of the first part of Vespasian's reign whose contribution can be identified thus included a carefully selected group of Flavian family members – his two sons, his son-in-law Petillius Cerealis, his nephew Flavius Sabinus, Arrecinus Clemens, and possibly Flavius Fimbria. In addition, there was a set of prominent political supporters from the Civil War years, who were, or may be supposed to have been, involved in the earliest planning of his bid for the imperial throne, or had supported him in the East and Africa fairly early on. These included Licinius Mucianus, Plautius Aelianus, Vibius Crispus, Eprius Marcellus, Valerius Festus, and perhaps Cocceius Nerva from within Rome. Others were picked up during the early stages of the campaign, such as Laecanius Bassus, Rutilius Gallicus, and perhaps Marcius Priscus and Sergius Paullus. A third group were military commanders who had come out in his support from the start, many of them formerly part of the army of Domitius Corbulo in Armenia – Pompeius Collega, Ulpius Traianus, Annius Bassus, and Domitius Tullus. There were several other men in this first five-year set whose role is not now visible, but it may be confidently asserted that, given the political record of the rest of the consuls in this period, they had probably demonstrated early and useful support for the Flavian cause. One rather unexpected element is the presence in the list of two men who had been Vitellian supporters, and one who had campaigned at Otho's side. Vespasian had begun his bid to the throne only after the murder of Galba, and he had been explicitly fighting against both Otho and Vitellius, the first because he murdered Galba, the second because of his sheer usurping opportunism; the award of early consulships for Valerius Festus, Ti. Plautius Silvanus Aelianus, and Vestricius Spurinna, though their presence in the list can be accounted for by other considerations, might be seen in part also as a gesture of reconciliation towards the supporters of the emperors who were Vespasian's particular enemies in the Civil War (unless, of course, they had all earned their rewards in some clandestine way).

Frontinus Consul

There remains Sex. Iulius Frontinus to be discussed. He hardly fits with this collection of experienced and distinguished consuls, several of them serving for a second time, all of them, so far as can be seen, having risen through the cursus in Nero's reign. Contrast his rise from a two-day praetorship to consul in three years with another man who was adlected to the Senate by Vespasian, Plotius Grypus. He had been adlected before Frontinus reached his praetorship and commanded a legion in the Civil War, and yet he had to wait until 88 to become consul. All the signs are, therefore, that Frontinus was being exceptionally well treated by Vespasian, who will have detected in him an ability which was most unusual. He certainly earned Vespasian's gratitude for his success against the Lingones, and for befriending and assisting Domitian in that expedition. This rapid rise will also have created feelings of envy and jealousy towards him amongst his less-speedily promoted contemporaries. That he was sent off to Britannia in the aftermath of his consulship may well have been deliberate, to avoid the snide remarks which will have followed him – just within his hearing, of course, and behind his back – and as a test for him, to prove that his promotion was justified.

He had praetorian rank, but only as recently as 70. He may have reached the Senate, adlected, under Galba or Vespasian, in 69, but only under Vespasian did he achieve political office. He had probably fought in Armenia under Corbulo, as an *eques* in an auxiliary regiment; he had probably been a government official in Spain and Africa, but also as an *eques*. By abdicating his praetorship to allow Domitian to take the post, he put Domitian and his father under an obligation. Despite all this and other considerations, he cannot then have been by any means in anyone's reckoning in the running to be consul within two years of being praetor. But Frontinus may also fall into other categories of men favoured by Vespasian. He was a Corbulo man and a Galba man; he was an efficient soldier and administrator, well experienced and thoughtful in both roles; these were all qualities which would have presumably guaranteed him office in the course of time. It is likely that he would have succeeded under any emperor, though hardly as early as only two years after his abdicated praetorship. But he had commanded in the fighting in Gaul and had succeeded in gaining the surrender of the Lingones without costing any Roman or Gallic lives (after the heavy casualties to many the Roman forces in the war, and of Gallic lives in the German campaign) and so without leaving a lasting antagonism behind; he had made a good impression on both Domitian and Mucianus; if he had been given the task of founding the new legionary fortress at Mirabeau he had performed successfully. He had proved to be amenable to the new emperor's wishes by his praetorian abdication. His consulship in 73 was presumably Vespasian's reply to Frontinus' personal favour as well as a test for a coming man.

But to have been made consul only two years after his brief praetorship – he must have been selected for the post by mid 72 – it is likely that there were still other considerations involved. After all, his experience contrasts sharply with the double and triple consuls all around him, and the more one considers his promotion the most unusual and unexpected it seems. Several reasons can be suggested, though no account of their relative importance can be made. Apart from his politics in and before the Civil War, whatever they were, he had been associated with two members of the imperial family in 70 and had efficiently subdued the Lingones; presumably Domitian and Mucianus had reported on him to Vespasian in a favourable tone. It is possible that Vespasian already knew him, or of him, from his time as African governor, and from Corbulo's men in the East. He was therefore a safe political pair of hands; a suitable man to command the large army in Britain (which Vespasian had entrusted to his relative in 71–73).

There is perhaps more. Petillius Cerealis went from the suppression of the German revolt to govern Britannia, but he was always impulsive and erratic. He had led Legio IX Hispana to destruction in the Boudican revolt, and had made a mess when in command of 1,000 cavalry during the advance of the Flavian army into Italy. His conduct in the German campaign was bizarre, his womanizing constant and distracting both to him and his men. (It all seems like the sort of behaviour some people expected Domitian to indulge in if he ever got command of an army.) Cerealis' conduct of the fighting in Britannia was probably no better than his earlier exploits, and he had been involved in a campaign in the north which perhaps was seen as more demonstrative than successful. (See Chapters 4 and 5.) Therefore there was probably a call for his rapid replacement by a more careful and considering man. Cerealis was recalled after only two years, when the usual term of office was at least three. He was consoled with a second consulship in 74, and this would require his return from Britannia to Rome by late 73 (having taken up the office during 71). His successor had already been chosen. Frontinus was that successor and in order to be eligible for a major military governorship like Britannia he had to have the rank of consul; therefore he was given a suffect consulship early in 73 and dispatched to Britannia in time to take over from the departing Cerealis later in his consular year.

Why Frontinus was selected is now fairly obvious. He had a good military and political reputation, and he was a commander who had shown that he was a successful Flavian supporter. He would, unlike Cerealis, obey his instructions, whatever they were, carefully and without fuss. And appointing such an unlikely man would put him under a further obligation to the Flavian dynasty, though it might also annoy other prospective senators. If he failed it could be blamed on his inexperience and on Cerealis' legacy; if he succeeded it would redound to the emperor's reputation – no doubt he understood all this. He must have seemed a highly useful imperial supporter, worth binding to the dynasty. He was rewarded therefore with his consulship, a chance to shine in Britannia, and in the result with a governorship which lasted nearly five years.

Chapter 4

Governor of Britannia, I: The West

The province to which Frontinus had been sent as governor was only just recovering, thanks in part to Cerialis, from its troubles during the Civil War, and it presented a major opportunity for a vigorous and mature governor. It also proved to be a major educational opportunity as well, which led to further Roman – and Frontinian – advances elsewhere.

Britannia had been the scene of warfare for thirty years when Frontinus was appointed governor in 73. This was three times as long as it took Julius Caesar to conquer the much-larger Gaul, and the conquest of Britannia was still not completed. In fact, it never would be, leading to the need to continue the province's occupation by a large military force until the very end. It seems clear that the Romans in Claudius' reign had no real notion of their ultimate aim when the invasion force was landed in Kent, nor of the size and difficulty of the task; it was a conquest undertaken because, for the emperors of the Caesarean dynasty, it was unfinished business – Caesar had withdrawn, Augustus had thought about it and refused, Caligula had flinched – and it was a convenient source for Claudius to acquire some questionable military glory, so it had to be attempted.

It is probable that the initial Roman intention had been to secure control of a series of Celtic kingdoms which had developed in the south and southeast, which was the area into which Caesar had campaigned; the joint Catuvellauni-Trinovantes kingdom, the Regni, the Dobunni, the Durotriges, the Dumnonii, the Iceni. An early frontier, marked roughly by the line of the Fosse Way, lay diagonally across England from Exeter to the Humber. This seems to have been the first halting place, a line which was convenient rather than one which was intended to be definitive or permanent.[1]

There is, in fact, no convenient geographical line across England at which a conqueror could easily stop and form a permanent frontier. Probably the Fosse Way line was adopted by the first conqueror and governor, Aulus Plautius, having conquered the kingdoms of the south and southeast; but, if it was ever more than a temporary halt, the line was soon seen to be unsatisfactory from the Roman point of view. The second governor, P. Ostorius Scapula, was compelled, by the continuing enmity of, above all, the former Catuvellaunian King Caratacus, to advance into the northwest Midlands, the country of the Cornovii, and to the Marches of Wales. Caratacus was eventually captured, and at that point the advance stopped, but the Romans had been compelled take over more territory.[2] In the pause they raided the Welsh hills, and secured an alliance with the ruler of the Brigantes in the north. That ruler, Queen Cartimandua, had received Caratacus in his defeat and had then handed him over to Scapula.

This advance produced a new frontier line, between the estuary of the Humber and that of the Mersey, with the Peak District hills in the centre; it was considerably better than the Fosse line, especially when protected by the alliance with the Brigantes; but there was also a north-south line between the Severn and the Dee. The revolt led by Boudica in 60 interrupted an attempt to reach into North Wales, compelling the governor Suetonius Paullinus to withdraw his forces from an attempt to conquer Anglesey; the result was one of the longest frontier lines which could have been devised.[3]

The original invasion force of four legions plus auxiliary regiments was reduced by the withdrawal of Legio XIV Gemina and some *auxilia* in 66 for service elsewhere.[4] The governor Trebellius Maximus (63–68) appears to have been ordered to reduce costs and organize the conquest on a permanent basis, without further expansion.[5] But then 8,000 soldiers were withdrawn by Vitellius during the Civil War in 69, gravely weakening the Roman situation.[6] The original garrison had been a heavy military presence for a small and unproductive province, and its size is a good indication of the continuing Roman military problem of ensuring the control and defence of their conquest. Shifting the line back and forth might be seen as prudent, and showing the flexibility of the military dispositions, or it might be seen as a sign of Roman military over-extension, especially with the reductions in the Civil War. It was not long before successive emperors were enlarging the military manpower of the empire – Domitian, Trajan, and Marcus Aurelius all added several legions to the overall Roman strength, while Hadrian and Antoninus

Pius carefully avoided wars of conquest, and Septimius Severus added still more; all these are signs of the continuing pressure on the frontiers and on military manpower. The reduction in Britannia in the 60s, by contrast, rendered the province distinctly under-garrisoned and vulnerable.

The Military Coup

The army in Britannia was paralysed by internal quarrels during the Roman Civil War of 69. The governor Trebellius Maximus, who had been in office for six years and had carried through the reduction in the force, quarrelled with the legate of Legio XX Valeria Victrix, M. Roscius Coelius. The latter was supported by the other legionary commanders, and Maximus removed himself to the continent.[7] Britannia was then ruled by a legionary commanders' committee until the Emperor Vitellius, to whom Maximus reported, appointed a new governor.[8] The quarrel seems to have had nothing to do with imperial politics, since both Trebellius Maximus and the legionary commanders were Vitellians. Legio XIV Gemina, removed to the continent earlier, was returned to Britannia but then almost at once it was sent back to the continent as a reinforcement for Vitellius' forces, who were threatened by the Flavian advance from the east. The legion notoriously behaved badly wherever it was. A small part of it took part in Vitellius' victory over Otho in the first Battle of Bedriacum in April 69, but then the Flavian army of the Danube legions invaded Italy. The vexillations which had come from the British legions were in the front line of the second battle near Bedriacum, and suffered heavy casualties in the Vitellian defeat.[9]

In all this the most surprising element is that the population of Britannia, which had fought repeatedly against the conquest between 43 and 60, did nothing. By the end of the inter-Roman fighting the four legions of the garrison had been reduced to three, and these three had been seriously reduced in size by sending vexillations of perhaps 2,000 men each to support Vitellius; the number of *auxilia* in the province was also reduced. The Vitellian forces were then defeated with heavy casualties, particularly amongst the British legions. Numbers cannot be guessed, but it looks very much as though the original garrison in Britannia had been reduced by at least half, or even more. The original forces, four legions plus auxiliaries in 68, will have contained perhaps 40,000 men; half of that was not enough to hold Britannia, if the original Roman staff calculations back in 43 had been anywhere near accurate.

Vettius Bolanus and the Brigantes

When Trebellius Maximus reported to him, Vitellius sent a replacement governor, M. Vettius Bolanus, but no extra troops.[10] In the circumstances, any attempted expansion of the province was out of the question, not that there was any talk of it while the issue of the fighting on the continent remained undecided. The defence of the Roman position was the only real option for the new governor. The extent of the province in 70 therefore was bounded by a frontier line across northern England from the Humber to the Mersey, with the Brigantian kingdom as a client state to the north; to the west the frontier lay along a line from the Mersey to the Severn estuary. This line was actually a region, not a line on the ground, a frontier, not a boundary. The legionary fortresses at Lindum (Lincoln) and Viroconium (Wroxeter) anchored the northern line, and Viroconium and Glevum (Gloucester) controlled the western frontier, with Isca Dumnoniorum (Exeter) dominating the southwest; the farthest part of the southwestern peninsula, beyond Exeter, may not yet have been conquered or occupied. The area enclosed by these frontiers and by the seas to east and south (the modern Midlands and southern England) was, of course, the wealthiest and most productive part of Britain, but in the north and west there were highland regions from which raiders were liable to emerge, and some of them had been roused to oppose the Romans in the past by Caratacus, while the Silures of South Wales and the Ordovices in the North had successfully resisted earlier Roman attempts at conquest. In the north, the Brigantian kingdom had been fairly stable for at least two decades under Cartimandua, but her position partly depended on Roman support, as she showed by surrendering Caratacus to the governor. At first it was clear that the northern frontier was guarded by the Brigantes, but the recent war put that in danger, and this soon changed.

Soon after Bolanus arrived in June or July 69 (he was appointed by Vitellius in April), trouble began in Brigantia. The weakened Roman authority in turn weakened Cartimandua's position, for she and the Romans supported each other. Her consort, Venutius, who had parted from the queen and had attempted to overthrow her once already, now tried to do so again. Bolanus, who had been one of Corbulo's legionary commanders in the Eastern war, succeeded in rescuing her, and resisted Venutius' pretensions. This involved using a force composed wholly of *auxilia* to fight several battles, according to Tacitus. Venutius achieved control of the Brigantian kingdom; no doubt the removal of Cartimandua disheartened her supporters.[11] The kingdom therefore changed from a client state to a hostile neighbour. On the other hand, Venutius apparently did not attempt any invasion of the province.

It is unclear just how the Brigantian kingdom was organized, but it was too large and geographically diverse to be easily controlled by either Cartimandua or Venutius – it stretched from the Humber to beyond the line of the future Hadrian's Wall, more or less precursor of the later kingdom of Northumbria. Neither of the Brigantian rulers had anything like an efficient governmental apparatus at their disposal. It has been plausibly suggested, in fact, that it consisted of a group of small sub-tribes, more or less autonomous, with the Brigantes being the largest, richest and so the dominant one. Certainly Venutius appears to have lived at a separate location from his estranged wife (perhaps the marriage was political only), he perhaps at Stanwick fort, just south of the River Tees, she possibly in the Elmet region in the Wharfe and Aire region (but these are not certain), so that the basic Brigantian kingdom consisted of the Yorkshire Vale – certainly the richest area in the north – with a surrounding group of sub-kingdoms. When the Romans eventually did set out to conquer the state, they advanced in sections – Yorkshire first, then Lancashire, the Eden Valley, Cumbria, and so on – which all seem to have been dealt with separately, which suggests they were politically distinct.

Apart from the Parisi in East Yorkshire, which were probably fully independent of the Brigantes, four or five names seem to indicate sub-tribes. The Setantii can be located in the north of modern Lancashire, where Fleetwood was Setantiorum Portus, so the Ribble Valley was probably their territory, and the hillfort Ingleborough suggests itself as their political centre. The Carvetii were in the lower Eden Valley and along the south Solway coast, with, at least later, their centre at Luguvallium (Carlisle); the Corionototae were possibly located north of the later Hadrian's Wall in coastal Northumberland; the Tectoverdi were in the same general region, their lands possibly along the lower Tyne, to be bisected by the later Wall.[12]

In light of this casual information, which is partly speculative, and certainly incomplete, it is possible to suggest that other sub-tribes, whose names have not survived, might have been located in such areas as southern Lancashire, between the Mersey and the Ribble, in the upper valley of the Eden, and in (the modern County) Durham, all examples of discrete geographical regions at some distance from the central Brigantian lands. The geography of the north of England dictates that central Yorkshire was the location of the most powerful group, that is, the Brigantes proper, which, being surrounded by such smaller tribal units, could exercise its (somewhat distant) power over them. The location of Stanwick fort, just south of the River Tees, might be that of the chief place of the tribe of the Durham area.

Surveys of the 'native settlements' of the North of England show the densest population amongst the independent Parisi of eastern Yorkshire, and along the southern Solway coast, part of the Carvetii lands. The most curious anomaly, however, is Lancashire. The Setantii seem to have had a reasonable density of population, but the land to the south, from the Ribble to the Mersey, shows very few settlements in the Iron Age, and this is repeated during the Roman period. The Yorkshire Vale is relatively well populated, as would be expected, but it was clearly its size and therefore its relatively numerous population which gave the Brigantes their political power.[13]

When Cartimandua was expelled by Venutius (or, alternatively, rescued by Vettius Bolanus), Venutius gained control of her territory. Bolanus was strong enough to march into Brigantia and defeat Venutius in battle, but not strong enough to hold on to Brigantian territory; indeed, he had been instructed not to make the attempt, and his main aim had been to rescue Cartimandua and not to conquer. His shortage of troops was obviously the main reason for his restraint, besides his instructions. But then suddenly, as a result, the Romans were faced not by a northern ally, but by a much larger and now hostile enemy state.[14] Bolanus had had to fight several battles in rescuing Cartimandua, and perhaps to prevent raids in defence of the province. In the process of the campaign he built forts (possibly only temporary) and signal stations, according to the poet Statius later, in a poem. Statius was a friend of Bolanus' son, who was presumably the source of his information.[15]

Bolanus' fighting took place in the second half of 69, and so in the six months or so between his arrival in the island and the end of the year. He had clearly been a vigorous and relatively successful governor, particularly given his shortage of troops, but his fight had been defensive. (It may be noted that there had been fighting on many other sections of the Roman frontier in the same years.) Bolanus' reputation as a failure is founded on Tacitus' assessment, which, as with Bolanus' two successors to prevent raids, was designed to enhance the reputation of Agricola by denigrating or ignoring the achievements of the other governors.

Bolanus was reinforced in the next year by the return of the vexillation of Legio XX and the appointment of its new commander, Cn. Julius Agricola, but then XIV Gemina was taken away again, and Bolanus himself was replaced early in 71 – he was a Vitellian appointment, and Vespasian was now emperor. The two remaining legions were probably still under strength, after the casualties suffered at Bedriacum, even if the surviving troops had been returned to the province. On top of all this, yet another governor was sent out to replace Bolanus, Q. Petillius Cerialis, fresh from his erratic campaign in Germany.

Petillius Cerialis

Cerialis arrived early in 71, having had to continue his campaign in the Rhineland until September 70. It is possible that he had been promised the province of Britannia by Vespasian before being sent against the rebels in the Rhineland; this, if it had become known, and Cerialis is unlikely to have kept quiet about it, would certainly have further inhibited Bolanus, since he could not start a serious campaign of conquest if this had been reserved for the new emperor's son-in-law to accomplish.[16] But since Cerialis brought with him another legion, II Adiutrix, and a large number of auxiliary regiments, it was really only now that there was sufficient armed strength in the province to make any new progress. Bolanus' work in the north had certainly softened up the Brigantes for conquest, but no more than that. The defeats suffered by Venutius will have reduced both Brigantian strength and his authority.

Cerialis brought a very large reinforcement as well as the legion, mainly auxiliary regiments from Germany. Some of these were newly recruited Batavians, a tribe which had been involved in the rebellion but had submitted before having to put up a debilitating fight; nine of their cohorts were transferred to Britannia.[17] Others were former members of Vitellius' forces, including Ala Gallorum Seposiana and Ala Gallorum Petriana, a double-strength unit. This was a sensible use of formerly enemy forces, and in accordance with the normal Roman practice, these forces were being moved away from their homelands (the new recruits) and from the places where they had been stationed in the rebellion (the existing units). Others arrived with Cerialis, because the legions in Britain had been on Vitellius' side in the Civil War – though perhaps only their commanders, and unenthusiastically – and needed still to be watched. There were at least three Flavian auxiliary regiments, the I Hispanorum Equitata, mounted infantry, and two more cavalry units, Ala II Asturum and Ala Gallorum et Thracum Classiana. Besides the newly recruited Batavians, there was Ala I Tungrorum, and at least a dozen more cohorts, all mainly recruited in Gaul. (As ever, the Romans were using recently conquered peoples to conquer the next victims.) It has been calculated that, apart from the four legions, the force in Britannia in 71 had fourteen cavalry *alae*, and fifty-five infantry *cohorts*.[18] The garrison therefore consisted of about 20,000 legionaries, at least 7,000 auxiliary cavalry and more than 25,000 infantry auxiliaries, a force a quarter again larger than the original invasion force. This much-enlarged force was available for all the governors of Britannia from Cerialis' appointment in 71 until reduced for some to serve in Domitian's Chattan War in 83.

The first task Cerialis faced was to bring the legions back into proper discipline, which Bolanus had apparently not managed to do, so Tacitus reports.[19] Given his record of occasional disasters it is not likely that Cerialis was the man for that sort of job. Instead his instinct was to come out fighting as a means of controlling and encouraging the soldiers, and that is what he did in the north. Perhaps this had been Bolanus' attitude as well, but he did not have Cerialis' resources, and he did not use the legions in his Brigantian fighting, possibly because he distrusted them. Cerialis' ultimate task, however, and that of his successors, was to complete the conquest of Britannia, and so then to release the large forces bound up there for use elsewhere. He seems to have campaigned to seek out and defeat the local forces, but could not develop a serious network of permanent forts and signal stations beyond those of Bolanus' campaigns, which was the sort of system which was needed in order to hold the supposedly conquered territory. He was superseded late in 73, so he may not have had long enough to finish the task, which, of course, was more difficult on the spot in Britannia than it seemed in Rome. He must have had to spend some time settling in and distributing the new forces, some of whom will have had to build their own camps. He is, however, credited with founding Eboracum (York) in 71, so this would seem to have been one of the garrisons. The beginning of the city, however, was only a minimal fortified camp, presumably for an auxiliary force; it was only later that a major legionary fort was built there.[20]

From south of the Humber, conquest northwards was constrained by the Pennines to the west, and by the wetlands of the lower Ouse and the Humber estuary on the east. The Roman road towards York from the south emphasizes the latter constraint by swerving westwards to avoid the wetlands before turning east for York. But north of the Humber, and separated by the wetlands from the Brigantian lands, was the country of the Parisi. The relations of Parisi and Brigantes are not known, but the former would seem to have maintained their independence, so they were not one of the Brigantes' sub-tribes. The Roman approach to their territory was directly north from the legionary fortress at Lincoln, where there was a crossing of the Humber to Petriana (Brough-on-Humber); the route continued north to the area of Derventio (Malton), which seems to have been a major Parisi centre. Given the probable hostile relations of Brigantes and Parisi, an alliance of Romans and Parisi is likely, and will be assumed later in this chapter.

It is generally assumed that Cerialis campaigned through the whole territory of the Brigantes, as far as Luguvallium of the Carvetii, where a fort dated to '72/73' has been located, and so was built in Cerialis' time, though again this is only an estimate.[21] This would suggest that there were other forts of Cerialis' foundation elsewhere, between central Yorkshire and the Solway, along the route between Eboracum and Luguvallium, over the Stainmore Pass and along the Eden Valley. Luguvallium, however, seems to be the only one so far located, apart from a temporary marching camp at Bowes within the Stainmore Pass. The dating of Cerialis' governorship is also assumed for a line of forts along (the future) Dere Street, but only one, at Roecliffe, 28km north of York, has produced a firm date.[22] Nevertheless this would suggest that the whole Dere Street route was used by the Romans, and that it was fortified with a line of forts – York and Roecliffe being two of them. It may be no coincidence that the Carvetian lands included Luguvallium; Cerialis is credited with being a skilful diplomat, and it is quite possible that one of his methods was to contact the several Brigantian sub-tribes and offer each of them his protection; this would contribute to reducing Brigantia, perhaps by making treaties with the client kingdoms separately and so treating them as independent and under Roman suzerainty. This would fit with the general Roman method, and the interpretation made here that the Parisi were also Roman allies.

Frontinus Governor

Frontinus was the next governor of the province, appointed probably during 73, in association with, and in succession to, his consulship.[23] He replaced Cerialis as governor either later in that year or early in 74. Cerialis was suffect consul in 74, taking up the office in May, and it is likely that he returned to Rome well before that date – the journey itself would take a month or more, longer in the winter. Frontinus thus began his three-year term as governor most likely very late in 73.

This governorship merited one grudging sentence in Tacitus' hagiography of his father-in-law Agricola, who was Frontinus' successor. All too often this is followed or copied by modern historians. A recent account of Roman Yorkshire also gives Frontinus no more than a single sentence.[24] He is at best given the minimal credit (by Tacitus) for the conquest of the Silures of South Wales, but given that no actual fighting is recorded, it is obvious that this is a less than complete account. Frontinus was governor for over four years, late 73 to early 78, so it seems a small achievement for an active governor. In fact, I will argue here that Frontinus did much more, and that some of Agricola's so-called achievements were actually made by Frontinus.

In advance of leaving Rome, Frontinus could well have been provided with advice from a series of former governors and legionary commanders. These included the emperor himself, who had commanded Legio II Augusta in the original invasion in 43, and had conquered the southwest. Bolanus and Trebellius Maximus were still alive and probably in Rome, and Suetonius Paullinus had fought for Otho in the Civil War. Cerialis and Frontinus no doubt discussed the situation before Cerialis left the province, assuming that their presences there overlapped. He may also have met Agricola, whose term as commander of Legio XX did not end until early in 74, and who had been in Britannia as a military tribune in Boudica's time. There will thus have been plenty of advice available, no doubt some of it contradictory, but the most valuable, because of the source, would be from Vespasian. How prescriptive the emperor was in his advice and/or instructions is not known, but it is evident from Vespasian's earlier measures, sending Cerialis with large reinforcements, and from Frontinus' own actions, that the new governor arrived in Britannia with clear instructions and a plan of action already formulated.

Given the unusually large forces already concentrated in Britannia, and the apparent success of Bolanus and Cerialis in controlling the Brigantes, it is probable that the emperor added the instruction that a major attempt should be made to finish the conquest. This would then allow the removal of a large proportion of the soldiers for use elsewhere. Vespasian was thus continuing the Roman mission to expand the empire (as he was also doing elsewhere, in Syria and Germania). Two years later, partly in response to Frontinus' successes in Britannia, he carried through the ceremony of extending the *pomerium* of the city of Rome, a mark of the expansion of the empire last done by Claudius with reference then also to conquest in Britannia. (The advance in Germany, and the annexation of Syrian kingdoms, were also commemorated.) Vespasian may well have pointed out to Frontinus that, with the Brigantes quiet, the obvious next step would be to establish direct control over the tribes of Wales; doing so would permit a strong concentration of forces from a westward orientation to concentrate in the north. To have a soldier as emperor would permit a clearer view of the problem in Britannia, which included hostility from both the west and the north.

Legionary Bases

Certain changes to the disposition of the Roman forces in the province had already been implemented, mainly under Trebellius Maximus, whose reputation for indolence, manufactured once again by Tacitus, appears to be quite inaccurate.[25] The legionary bases until the early 60s were at Isca Dumnoniorum (Exeter, Legio II Augusta), Lindum (Lincoln, Legio IX Hispana), Burrium (Usk, Legio XX Valeria Victrix), and Viroconium

(Wroxeter, Legio XIV Gemina). Trebellius had carried out a serious reorganization of these bases: II Augusta moved from Isca Dumnoniorum to a new legionary base at Glevum (Gloucester), which was being built in the mid-60s; XIV Gemina was eventually relocated permanently to the Rhineland, and XX Valeria Victrix was moved from Burrium to Viroconium. This left the supervision of the Silures to II Augusta, from a distance, for the base at Burrium (Usk) was abandoned. Only IX Hispana stayed in its original base, at Lindum, for the moment. No doubt the basic reason for all this was to reduce the legionary garrison; XIV Gemina had already moved out to the Rhineland by 67, before the Civil War.[26] The shuffling of forces reduced the legionary garrison to three legions, implying that Nero's government had decided to abandon any intention of 'completing' the conquest of the island, though to be sure the Parthian War had demanded the movement of forces eastwards.

Most of these changes had happened before the Civil War, or at least they had begun, and were the work of Trebellius Maximus, whose governorship was thus preoccupied with these internal matters and involved little fighting – which is what gave Tacitus the opportunity to belittle him. Strategically each legion was now charged with guarding a particular section of the frontier. IX Hispana was obviously concerned with the frontier against the Brigantes to the north, in the Yorkshire plain, which was the heartland of the tribe's territory, and it was to be the unit used mainly by Cerialis in his campaigns there; he had commanded an earlier version of the legion in his earlier stint in Britannia as commander of the legion during the Boudican revolt; how pleased the legion was to be honoured in this way and to receive its former commander is not known, for he had led it then into a comprehensive disaster (though he himself had survived). It was backed up by auxiliary regiments in several forts west of the River Trent, and in southern Yorkshire.

Legio XX Valeria Victrix at Viroconium (Wroxeter) faced the North Welsh region, mainly the Ordovices tribe, but it might also have to pay heed to the western part of the Brigantes kingdom, in southern Lancashire, where there was probably a sub-kingdom of the Brigantes, though the area appears to have been very thinly populated. Against these areas there were auxiliary forts closer to the Ordovices and as far as the Mersey.

At Glevum, II Augusta was clearly on guard against the South Wales tribes, particularly the Silures, but also had a watching brief over the southwest, with which it had long been familiar after thirty years being stationed at Isca Dumnoniorum; part of the legion had remained at Isca when most of it moved to Glevum; more forts were spread through the southwest in support.

The old legionary base at Burrium (Usk) had been abandoned in favour of Glevum; in effect, a partial Roman withdrawal. The move put the barrier of the River Severn between the legion and the tribal territory of the Silures. The change was also in part the result of changing Roman priorities, as the Brigantes, after Venutius' takeover, developed into a serious problem.

On the other hand, apart from the legionary fortress at Burrium, the forts which had been occupied by *auxilia* facing the Silures were not abandoned. A sequence of three large forts and several smaller ones controlled the frontier region facing and inside the tribe's main territories. The large forts were at Cardiff, Monmouth, and Clifford, the first two large enough for a legionary vexillation or perhaps two auxiliary regiments, the third about half that size. The other, smaller forts, at Hindwell Farm, Canon Frome, and Castleford Farm, were placed north, east and south of Clifford; others were at Abergavenny, west of Monmouth, and possibly at Chepstow, between Monmouth and Cardiff. Burrium continued to be occupied by an auxiliary unit until the mid-70s, and would complete a neat network of forts. Their distribution, however, was clearly defensive, aimed at containing the Silures, even though several of the forts were established within the tribal territory.[27]

There were, therefore, two major problems facing Frontinus when he arrived. The most recently active problem was the Brigantes in the north, where Cerialis and before him Bolanus had been victorious against Venutius, but where the Brigantes still held the tribal territory, in effective independence, depending on whatever settlement had been organized by Cerialis. The other problem was the Silures in the west, inactive for a decade.

It is evident that the withdrawal of XIV Gemina had seriously increased the vulnerability of the province, and that conquest to north and west had been impossible during the Civil War, and under governor Bolanus. The British tribes had shown an ability to fight in coalition in the past: a coordinated attack, led by a man like Venutius, who was regarded by Tacitus as an outstanding commander, could well, at the least, penetrate deep into the province; at the worst it could drive the Romans out completely.[28] The real problem was that, for the past decade, the Roman conquest had stalled, and had halted at a point which left them with an unsustainably long frontier to guard – from Cardiff to the Mersey, and across to the Humber. The line the Romans eventually settled at, along Hadrian's Wall, was a frontier of about a hundred miles in length, the line they were defending in 71 was double that, over 230 miles, and with fewer troops. This was the problem Frontinus was tasked to solve, which had to be settled before any further attempt could be made to 'complete' the conquest.

The Conquest of the Silures

The Silures was the dominant tribe in South Wales, inhabiting the fertile lowlands and the adjacent hills from the River Wye in the east to the Gower in the west, that is, roughly modern Glamorgan, with extensions; their northern boundary lay along the Black Mountains and Brecon Beacons. From the new legionary fortress at Glevum beyond the Severn, some of the Silurian territory was under Roman occupation; to the west, the area of modern Carmarthen and the River Towy was their western boundary. Beyond them to the west were the Demetae and the Octopitae, between them occupying modern Dyfed.

Along the North Wales coast were three major tribes. The Venedoti were in Anglesey, the Gargani in the Lleyn Peninsula, and the Deceangli occupied the northeast as far as the Dee estuary. The Deceangli had submitted a decade or more before, agreeably and peacefully accepting Roman supremacy. South of these tribes were the Ordovices whose territory stretched from the North Wales hills south to the upper Severn valley. All these were Frontinus' concern as well as the Silures. It will be seen that some penetration of Roman authority has been made already, in the north with the Deceangli, and into the Silurian lands, but the Deceangli had not been occupied, and there was a large area in Mid Wales where no apparent tribal organization is known.

The Silures had fought hard and successfully against the Roman encroaching forces in the 50s. A legion had been defeated, a cohort had been destroyed, and the Silures thereby had retained their independence, and a formidable reputation. And yet the Roman forces maintained the line of forts within their territory; possibly their reputation had been exaggerated. Frontinus is credited, in the only written notice of his work, by Tacitus (in that single sentence), with conquering the Silures.[29] Such is Tacitus' method and prejudices, if it had been a hard fight he would probably have distorted the point into criticism, as he did with Bolanus. (Archaeological work has demonstrated that Frontinus also had an effect in North Wales and probably among the Brigantes as well, items not mentioned by Tacitus.) Frontinus was, in other words, very busy in his four years as governor, and arguably he achieved as much as his more celebrated successor Agricola, who was governor for much longer, and who has benefited from the survival of the brief biography by Tacitus, his son-in-law. Frontinus' work was the essential foundation for Agricola's activity, just as the work of Bolanus and Cerialis prepared the way for Frontinus himself in the north.

Despite their reputation, the conquest of the Silures seems to have taken only a short time, and Frontinus spent most of his term as governor being busy elsewhere. The celebration in Rome of extending the city's *pomerium*, if it was in part a result of the conquest of the Silures, happened in 75, suggesting that the work in South Wales had been completed by then. The aftermath, the laying out of the roads, building forts, including a new legionary fortress, no doubt took a considerable time, but the initial conquest can only have taken a single campaigning season.

It may be conjectured that a decade and a half's familiarity with Rome and Roman society had weakened any attachment the Silures felt to maintaining their independence. The tribe's neighbours, the Dobunni to the east and the Durotriges to the south, conquered thirty years before, were now contented subjects. No doubt there were advocates for continued Silurian independence, but only enough to force Frontinus into a single campaign.

Whatever the precise political condition of the tribe, Frontinus defeated any recalcitrants in a single season. This was, no doubt, achieved by a mixture of diplomacy, conciliation, generosity, and the mailed fist where necessary. He followed this with a programme of fort building to cover the whole of the tribal territory, aiming to maintain Roman control. Legio II Augusta was moved forward from the new base at Glevum, the fortress founded only seven or eight years before, to a new legionary base to be built at Isca Silurum (Caerleon), on the Usk like Burrium, but closer to the coast, and so with easier communications to receive reinforcements and supplies. A hill fort at Llanmelin was close to Usk, but it was apparently closed down when a new town was founded only a short distance away to the south, at Venta Silurum (Caerwent), close to the legionary fortress. This would indicate that the tribe was being organized as a regular Roman *civitas*, a pseudo-city-state.[30] In turn this was an indication that the local chieftains were to remain in charge of the tribe. Those Silurians who had lived at or near Llanmelin were not much disturbed by the move to Venta Silurum; they could continue to farm the same lands and control the same tenants as before. Other new inhabitants may have come from a coastal hill fort at Sudbrook a few miles away on the Severn estuary.

The dating of the founding of Venta Silurum is here assumed to be at or just after the conquest by Frontinus, which in turn is taken to have been swift and relatively bloodless. There are Flavian-period remains in association with the bathhouse planted squarely in the centre of the town, next to the forum-and-basilica, which is dated rather later. The outline, as shown by the (rather later) walls and ditches around the city, is approximately rectangular (about 18 hectares). Apart from one right-angled corner of the city wall, there is nothing in the plan which is specifically military, though in all probability soldier surveyors were needed to lay out the site. There may have been a fort on the site at first, though none has been located, but it looks very much as though the town, even if laid out by military engineers, as one might expect, was essentially civilian from the beginning.[31]

At first only the chiefs from the tribal area will have moved to the new town, with their families and servants/slaves. They would thereby change their political role from tribal chiefs to Roman councillors, and move from a windy hill fort (if that is where they lived) to a new city with the usual Roman amenities, such as hot baths, stone buildings, shops, plumbing, and underfloor heating. There is no doubt that they would benefit from the move in terms of creature comforts, and, of course, the Roman garrison at Isca Silurum would be able to watch them more easily. And the chiefs would remain rich.

This sequence implies that the mailed fist was perhaps less in evidence in the campaign than the diplomatic glove and the persuasive voice. One of Frontinus' possible advantages was that he probably had some command of the Celtic language, or he may well have equipped himself with a competent translator; another advantage was that he had available a large number of auxiliary regiments under his command, brought over originally by Cerialis, and many of these were manned by men recruited in Celtic-speaking Gaul; the communication problem was thus evaded. The new legionary base at Glevum was better positioned than the old at Burrium, and he could base the legion there until it could be moved forward to Isca, an even better place than Glevum or Burrium from which to dominate the tribal territory. Out of the large number of his auxiliary regiments he could afford to bring in an overwhelming force, and to leave plenty of other forces to watch the Brigantes and the Ordovices, who were also watched by three of his legions. Some legionary detachments from the local legion could then be found to occupy the series of forts and fortlets by which the Silures' territory would be occupied and the tribe subdued.

This conquest took one campaigning season only, that of 74. It had been carefully planned, probably during the winter of 73/74 (which is a good reason for assuming that Frontinus might have arrived late in 73 or early in 74). To accomplish such a conquest in such a brief time called for not just good and careful advanced planning, but overwhelming force and perhaps surprise. The large force Frontinus could deploy included the legion at Glevum (theoretically 4,800 men) and perhaps 30 auxiliary cohorts of infantry and several *alae* of cavalry – a total of 20,000 men, more or less – a quarter of the legionary and half the auxiliary strength of the province. This force arriving suddenly would clearly overwhelm the tribe and would decisively discourage any resistance. It would be all the more effective if preceded by careful diplomatic preparation, designed to persuade the tribal leaders that resistance would be futile, and that acquiescence would have its advantages. The existence for a number of years of the fortress at Burrium had surely had its persuasive effect, as will the experience of the Silures' neighbours, the Dobunni and the Durotriges, who had been Roman subjects for a generation. The massive force Frontinus could deploy was perhaps in the end largely redundant, though deploying it would salve Silurian pride.

The Control Network

If the chiefs of the tribe had been conciliated first by a combination of diplomacy, gifts, and an overwhelming military threat, the military imposition of a network of roads and forts could proceed rapidly, probably at the same time as the building of the Caerleon legionary base. The river valleys of the Silurian territory (the Towy, the Tawe, the Usk, the Wye) provided a series of convenient north-south routes from the Bristol Channel coast into the Brecon Hills. These routes, which, of course, already existed as roads and tracks, having long been formed by the inhabitants, only needed to be improved by the military engineers to their necessary standards. That is, the outline of the network which Frontinus imposed on the Silures already existed.

The roads were now planted with forts at convenient distances, so that, along with the improved roads following the lines of the old tracks, the whole formed a net which enfolded, commanded and controlled the tribal territory (or, if greater force is envisaged, as a 'straitjacket').[32] Some of the roads were eventually paved, but it is unlikely that this was done at once. All Frontinus needed was to designate the necessary routes and choose the fort sites.[33] The priority would be to construct the forts, which could be built to a practiced standard – rampart and palisade – with the troops living in leather tents at first. This could all be done within a short time, perhaps no more than a few days. It would then be improved with wooden barracks and eventually stone, depending on how long the fort remained in use. This sequence has been detected archaeologically at most of the forts which have been excavated.

The legions, of course, routinely formed entrenched camps each night when on the march, doing so within an afternoon (a surveyor having gone ahead to locate a suitable site), and the auxiliary regiments would do the same. (Frontinus probably undertook this task when in the East as a junior officer.) The legionary base could be set up almost as quickly, the troops using the pick, as Corbulo had noted, and shovel, though converting the primitive preliminary work into more durable and comfortable stone buildings would take some years; the fortress at Chester took five years to build, and as a legionary base it would obviously have some priority.[34] The essential point was to have the regiments in place and in camp, and spread throughout the tribal territory, quickly; elaborations and permanent structures could follow gradually.

The road network in the Silurians' land has two east-west lateral roads, RR ('Roman Road') 60 along the coast from Glevum to Maridunum (Carmarthen), and a road north of the mountains, from Caerleon through

Abergavenny and Brecon Gaer to Carmarthen (RR 62 and 623). These enclosed the tribe's territory and were dotted with forts, five or six along the coast, six or seven along the northern route. These two roads were linked by other roads through the mountains, RR 621 from Cardiff towards Brecon Gaer, with three forts along the way at Caerphilly, Gelligaer, and Penydarren (though the northern part of the road has not been located)[35] and RR 622 from Neath to Brecon Gaer, with a fort at Coelbren and some fortlets on the way.[36] Three of the forts functioned as major route centres, Caerleon, Brecon Gaer and Carmarthen, each with three or four roads joining them to other forts. The whole system was in place within a little more than a year of Frontinus' arrival, since the crucial road system fort at Brecon Gear was in existence by 75.

In contrast to the variety of fort sizes facing the frontier before 75 the forts guarding these roads are generally of a small size. The legionary fort at Caerleon was 20.5 hectares, but none of the others was larger than 3.5 hectares, which five of them (Cardiff, Neath, Brecon Gaer, Llandovery, and Llandeilo) approximate to. Four of these were sites towards the west, presumably to enclose the Silures the more effectively, to deter infiltration from or to the rest of Wales, and to separate the tribe from the peaceful tribes in the west, the Demetae and the Octapitae. The others were mainly a little over 2.0 hectares down to 1.5, a suitable size for an auxiliary infantry regiment. These minor variations in size within a fairly narrow range can be accounted for by the precise sites they occupied – the basic purpose for each fort, at least on its foundation, was defence, and so the best plan was chosen, even if it was not quite regulation. This series of forts was fairly expensive in manpower, of course, but given that there were over fifty regiments in Britain, not extraordinarily so.[37]

Between these permanent camps there were marching camps; at Y Pigwn there was one of 15 hectares, large enough for a full legion, and another, smaller station at Pen y Gaer. Several of these have been noted to the southeast, probably from the original campaigns against the Silures in the 50s.[38] They may have been used during the campaign of conquest, when a whole legion would be suitably intimidatory.[39]

Within the system of roads and forts, Brecon Gaer emerges as a major road junction, the linchpin of the road system across the north, with roads leading off to the west, east and southeast (RR 62), southwest (RR 623), and northwestwards (RR 63) to Caerleon, Carmarthen, and Caersws respectively. The forts on these roads were situated between 20 and 45km apart, the shorter distances being in the lowlands where much of the population was located. This was both comprehensive in that nowhere was more than 15km from a fort, and economic in manpower in that the total garrison, excluding the legion, was probably no more than 2,000 or 3,000 soldiers.

The forts almost universally attracted a civilian population, which provided manufacturing and services for the troops. They lived close by in a *vicus*, a movement which appears to have begun almost from the moment the fort built. Not only that, but when the forts were abandoned by the military, a large proportion of these *vici* continued in existence as civilian villages. For a part of the population the Roman arrival was an economic advantage.

The Roman army thus became a major economic factor in the life of the Silurians. It was also an active agent in seeking out resources. Taxation of the population (which would expand their local acquaintance with coinage) was one aspect, as was recruitment, forced or otherwise, into the Roman army, but probably more attention went on the search for minerals. This had already happened in the territory of the Deceangli, who produced lead (and presumably silver). The gold mine at Dolaucothi, west of Llandovery, was rapidly occupied and exploited, with a supervisory fort at Pumsaint.[40] Further west, the only fort at this early period in the territory of the Demetae was at Wiston, where mining took place; this was less successful, and the fort and the mine were abandoned by about 100.[41]

Extension Northwards

This network of roads and forts between Caerleon and Carmarthen sufficed for the Silures, and the fact that the area remained quiet thereafter is a testimony to the system's effectiveness. The garrison could begin to be reduced in a fairly short time. One fort (Caergwanaf) was abandoned for a time, then reoccupied, and finally abandoned completely c.85; it was a centre for iron mining and manufacture, and continued to be so until the third century. The fort at Llandovery was reduced in size in two stages, from 3 hectares to 2 then to a fortlet of 0.49 hectares. The proximity of the fort at Pumsaint was probably sufficient.

But this network amongst the Silures was not the whole of Frontinus' work in Wales. It is very probable that he extended Roman power and control into North Wales as well. This usually is credited to Agricola in his first campaigning season, but all that is said (in Tacitus) about it is that part of the Ordovices attacked and defeated a Roman force, and Agricola marched to defeat them in turn. This is not the conquest of the Ordovices, however, but merely the suppression of a small rebellion by a fairly small group of the tribal warriors – the sort of resistance which might well have happened during the Silurian conquest. That is, the conquest of the Ordovices had been achieved before Agricola's governorship, and the only Roman governor who could have done it was Frontinus; furthermore, the occupation pattern in the north bears his hallmark as well.

The fort system of the Silures was Frontinus' work, a network of sixteen forts linked by a network of roads. The rest of Wales, three quarters of the country, was dotted with only a few more forts than that, and they are in two major groups, linked with each other and with the Silurian network. The similarities of the three systems indicate quite clearly that they were the work of the same man.

The first line of forts was laid across central Wales from the legionary base at Viroconium (Wroxeter) to the mouth of the Dyfi River, four forts and three fortlets, forming a line of demarcation. The second group is in the north, enclosing Snowdonia, a set of eight forts. The roads linking the central Wales forts to the southern network were guarded by seven more forts.

The only written record of events in the north is Agricola's brief expedition among the Ordovices. The evidence for the establishment of these forts in Mid Wales is therefore entirely archaeological. Agricola, in fact, after his brief Ordovician campaign and a subsequent visit to Anglesey, concentrated in the north of Britain – after all, the Ordovices had been conquered already. He was therefore in North Wales only briefly, probably less than a campaigning season. Tacitus claims he 'cut to pieces the whole fighting force of' the Ordovices, and that resistance on Anglesey was abandoned as soon as an auxiliary force, without equipment, swam across the Menai Strait. This is all notably vague, and cannot be accepted at face value, but he certainly defeated the Ordovician rebels, and the inhabitants of Anglesey clearly submitted. From then on, he had no more to do with Wales; he hardly had time to organize a road-and-fort network.

It follows that in all Wales, there were no forts founded before Frontinus took up the governorship in 73, except those along the borders, and none after Agricola departed for the north, in 78. Any fort which is dated by the archaeologists as 'early Flavian' was therefore Frontinus' work, and it is worth pointing out that what Frontinus had done in the Silurian country was very similar to what took place along the central Wales road, and in the Snowdonia area. Given that the Ordovices were hostile (their breakout in 78 destroyed a Roman cavalry unit which entered their territory), it would make sense for Frontinus to establish a defence line along the upper Severn to prevent them from raiding into Silurian territory, and to establish control of the land between the two great tribes – hence the forts between the Severn and the Silures. Some of the Silures were presumably ready for any disturbance which might encourage them to rise against their conquerors. The heavy military presence in their territories implies suppressed hostility. Preventing the nearest hostiles from interfering would make sense, in the same way that establishing the network of roads and forts all over the Silurian territory was aimed at the same solution.

The Demetae and the Octapitae in the far west did not receive this sort of treatment, and there are no signs of any Roman forts west of Carmarthen (except at the mine at Wiston). Only a single Roman road has been noted in their territory (RRN 20), heading straight west from Maridunum (Carmarthen) for Wiston. The conclusion must be that these two tribes submitted to Rome very readily, probably even before Frontinus dealt with the Silures; enmity between the Silures and their weaker western neighbours is to be presumed. This would open the way for an easy Roman diplomatic intervention, and clearly assist in subduing the Silures.

The line of forts along the upper Severn Valley – the legionary base at Viroconium (Wroxeter), occupied from 47 until about 90,[42] Forden Gaer, Pentrehyling, Caersws, and Pennal on the estuary of the River Ystwyth,[43] with three fortlets (at Llanfair Caereinion, Hafan, and Pen y Crocbren),[44] was clearly designed to control that route, and to cut the Ordovices off from easy contact with the Silures. These forts and fortlets are all about 25km apart, and form a zone of division between the south and the north, controlling the route along the Severn and blocking in the Ordovices. Caersws is the route centre, with connections to east, west and south (with

Brecon Gaer) and probably with the north, though the road has not been precisely traced. These forts have mainly been dated to the Flavian or 'early Flavian' period, which would mean during Frontinus' governorship. Along the roads connecting this line of forts with the Silures, the RR 69 from Llandovery to Pennal, paralleling the coast, and the RR 623 from Llandovery to Caersws, driven through the centre, the forts and some fortlets along the roads are similarly dated. There are three forts on the road between Pumsaint and Pennal – at Llanio, Trawscoed, and Penlleyn, with a fortlet at Erglodd,[45] and two on the centre road, at Caerau and Castell Collen, with two fortlets.[46]

The network in the north controlled the route north from the port and river crossing at Pennal to Caerhun on the Conwy estuary, with four or five forts, at Tomen y Mur and Brithdir fortlet, while Bryn y Gefelliau was possibly founded later;[47] the road northeastward connecting Pennal with Chester, had only two forts, at Caer Gai and Llanfor.[48] This was Ordovices territory, a thin skin of control, suggesting the tribe mainly subsided to obedience. In addition there are two more forts in the northwest, at Caernarfon, controlling the crossing to Anglesey – a considerable town developed on the island in response, at Tai Cothinau – and at Pen Llystyn in the Lleyn Peninsula.[49] All these forts have been dated to Flavian or early Flavian times. Some have been dated to Agricola's visit to the area ('77/78'), but that dating is clearly derived from Tacitus, on the assumption that Agricola's short visit will have resulted in the founding of forts. The only one which he could have founded was Caernarfon.

The political situation in the north of Wales was similar to that in the south (and in the north of England) in that the most powerful tribes (Silures, Ordovices) were surrounded by weaker neighbours. In the south, the almost complete lack of a Roman military presence in Dyfed implies that the Demetae and Octopitae took the Roman side, so they did not need to be governed and controlled. In the north the Deceangli and the Venedoti (in Anglesey) received no military garrisons, though some watchtowers were established on the Anglesey coast, but the Ordovices were surrounded by forts and roads in much the same way as the Silures. In the Lleyn peninsula the Gargani were watched by a single fort, at Pen Llystyn, on the eastern border of their territory, just as the Demetae were watched by the garrison at Carmarthen, on their border.

This combined diplomatic and military arrangement was further combined with two new substantial forts to the east in the Cheshire plain, at Mediolanum (Whitchurch) and the new legionary fortress at Deva (Chester), the latter founded by Frontinus and completed in Agricola's time, and the other new legionary fortress at Isca Silurum, also founded by Frontinus. It all meant that the resistant Welsh tribes – the Silures and the Ordovices – were surrounded and interpenetrated by Roman allies, Roman roads, and Roman forts. The North Welsh network enveloping the Ordovices would seem, by the forts' dating, to be as much Frontinus' work as that netting the Silures. But apart from the (uncertain) dates it bears all the hallmarks of his method as applied to the Silures. The minor Ordovician rising when he handed over to Agricola, and Agricola's single campaign there and into Anglesey, the latter no more than a demonstration, bear witness to the effectiveness of Frontinus' work before Agricola arrived. By enclosing the militant tribes by these networks of forts, Frontinus was protecting the weaker tribes, thus vindicating the implied agreements with them.

It is worth noticing, however, that the approach to controlling the Ordovices was very different from that applied to the Silures. The Silures were directly controlled by the network of roads and forts throughout their lands, so that their land was sliced up by the network; the Ordovices were controlled by being surrounded by a line of roads and forts, and part of their territory; centred on the north-Welsh mountains, was certainly garrisoned. There were very few forts within their own territory, but the surrounding roads were controlled in detail.

So we have three different means of extending the Roman imperial control over Wales: first, alliances with the Demetae and the Octapitai, the Venedoti and the Gargani, and the Deceangli and other tribes; second, the relatively dense network of roads and forts throughout Silurian territory; and third, the surrounding of the Ordovician mountain territory by a line of fortified roads, rather than a detailed occupation as with the Silures. The implication is, of course, that the Silures were still regarded as the most dangerous of the Welsh tribes, a conclusion which is fortified by the stationing of a legion in their territory; the reason, no doubt, was that in numbers they will have been the largest of the tribes, occupying as they did the wealthiest part of the country.

There is one further point to make. It is sensible to consider the Roman approach to each of the tribes, since it is clear that each was treated as an individual political unit. It seems that Frontinus was able to take an overall view of the entirety of Wales. His schemes of fortification fall into an overall system which clearly was the result of an understanding of the geography as well as the population distribution and political boundaries of the country. The key to the eventual country-wide system is a sequence of four major forts. The legionary fortresses obviously were planted to control the major routes into Wales – the south coast, the upper Severn, and the north coast. But within Wales there was a second line along the centre, along which a group of forts, each over 3 hectares in area, were established – Neath on the south coast road (3.3 hectares), Brecon Gaer and Caersws (3.14 and 3.9 hectares respectively) where the route to the north links with the cross routes, and Llanfor (3.6 hectares), on the route from Pannel to Chester; on the north coast Caerhun (1.97 hectares) was a little smaller but was in a very advantageous strategic position.

These four larger forts held larger-than-usual garrisons, probably an infantry and cavalry regiment. Their positioning gave them access to large areas around them, and they were relatively close to each other and to the surrounding forts. This was a carefully worked out method of control, and it is worth noting that, as the Roman military presence was reduced from about 120 and earlier, these particular forts were maintained far longer than most of the rest.

The whole scheme of control of all Wales coheres into a well-thought-out system. This is the work of a man with a clear vision of achieving a swift and painless conquest, and a method of holding that conquest for long enough to persuade the Welsh population that it was in their interest to accept it. This was Frontinus' achievement.

Roman Celebration

In Rome in 75, the year after Frontinus' conquest of the Silures, and possibly of the Ordovices also, Vespasian carried through the ceremony of the extension of the *pomerium*, the alteration of the sacred boundary of the city, as a mark of the extension of the bounds of the empire.[50] This was a major event, which could not take place after a mere paper victory and conquest; only a clear and decisive conquest of new territory would count, and the Silures, the Ordovices, and their neighbours were a decisive advance of the Roman frontier, extending the size of the empire by 20,000km^2. Other advances had taken place in Vespasian's reign already: the annexation of two Syrian kingdoms, the final conquest of the Jewish rebels (but both of these were within the bounds of the empire already), and a minor advance in the angle between the upper Rhine and the upper Danube in Germany (see Chapter 7). This seems quite sufficient to account for Vespasian's celebration – apart from the useful publicity value of the ceremony – but it may be noted that only the German and Silurian territories were real conquests against opposition and additions of territory to the empire (the Syrian acquisitions were of kingdoms already part of the empire, and the defeat of the Jewish rebels did not really count); only the Silures and perhaps the Ordovices could be said to have been physically conquered. The ceremony is thus a good, if somewhat indirect, confirmation of Frontinus' success. Vespasian must have been well pleased with his choice of governor, a man who, like himself, had risen from the ranks of the *equites* by sheer ability, and having the further capability to be in the right place at the right time to seize his opportunities.

Chapter 5

Governor of Britannia, II: The North

It is hardly usual to credit Frontinus, said to have conquered the Silures but no more, with campaigning in the north of England, which is supposed to have been Agricola's achievement. But it is evident that Agricola's conquest of North Wales only exploited, or perhaps finished off, Frontinus' work by defeating a forlorn rebellion, and his visit – it was no more – to Anglesey was perhaps a tribute to his former commander Suetonius Paullinus, who had invaded the island before being recalled by Boudica's rising.

Bolanus and Cerialis had earlier both operated in the north of England. Bolanus did not establish a firm control of any part of the area, though he defeated Venutius; Cerialis' campaign may have been somewhat superficial, though he is certainly credited with marching through Yorkshire and over the Pennines, as far as Luguvallium, and establishing forts along the way. Agricola's campaigns in the North are not always very specific as to location, but he was operating north of Yorkshire and well into the Scottish Highlands. Yorkshire, the main Brigantian region, seems to have been under Roman control as a result of the wars of Bolanus and Cerialis; that is, Agricola began in Cumbria and moved on into Scotland. There was therefore a gap between the frontier as established by Bolanus – the Humber-Mersey line – and the lands in which Agricola campaigned. Yorkshire, Lancashire, and County Durham were in that space, and it is in this area where Frontinus operated in the period before Agricola's arrival. It may be well to recall that Frontinus was the governor of Britannia, so he was responsible for the government of the whole province. Even if he did not campaign in the North, it is all but certain he went there.

The Fortress at Deva

One of the major developments Frontinus was responsible for was the foundation of the new legionary fortress at Chester, to which the Legio II

Adiutrix was eventually moved, though it became the base of XX Valeria Victrix in the end.[1] This had been the site of a temporary fort earlier during Suetonius Paullinus' campaign into North Wales, but the site had apparently been abandoned until Frontinus returned and founded the new, much larger, permanent legionary fort. Paullinus' fort was mainly to act as a temporary base from which the campaign into North Wales could be launched, but Frontinus' fortress was designed as a major strategic base where the resident legion could dominate North Wales and the routes north across the Mersey, into Lancashire, and on to Luguvallium and the Solway area. Its founding can be dated to 74, from some securely dated lead pipes found there (formed from lead mined from the territory of the Deceangli).[2]

The essential point is that posting a legion to Chester was a major strategic move in the process of controlling Wales and, further, it marked the intention to extend control into the lands to the north. The legion stationed there was in command of routes leading both west into North Wales, specifically along the coast, and north into Lancashire, which is relatively flat as far as the River Ribble. It was part of the fort system hemming in the Ordovices, along with the legion at Viroconium, commanding the route along the upper Severn valley, and the forts established by Frontinus around Snowdonia, so that for a short time three legions faced Wales, stationed at Isca Silurum, Viroconium, and Deva.[3] The legion at Viroconium was moved away in about 90. Deva was also a base from which to campaign northwards, and a suitable place for a naval base on the Dee estuary.

The Brigantes

The Brigantes had been damaged by the campaigns of Bolanus and Cerialis, though we do not know the details. The tribe, however, had not been fully conquered in the way that the lands to the south had been, or as the Silures' land was now. Some forts had been established from South Yorkshire to Carlisle, apparently by Cerialis, but so far as can be seen only along the line of Dere Street. There was much territory still uncontrolled, and it seems probable that beyond the Stainmore Gap the forts were not maintained; the continued use of the fort at Luguvallium is uncertain. It took a series of Roman garrisons in their forts for a generation to ensure that attempts at resistance ceased in a newly conquered country, and some regions remained liable to uprisings. (The Silures, for instance, were not relieved of some of their garrisons until the 120s, and the legion stayed at Isca Silurum forever.)

Cerialis has been assigned the credit for occupying Yorkshire, but the land was in fact divided between two tribes, the Parisi in the east, from the Humber to the Cleveland Hills and the North Sea coast at Scarborough, and the Brigantes in the rich well-watered plain between the Parisi and the Pennines; similarly Lancashire, the Pennines, and the Durham region were occupied by non-Brigantian tribes, but which were part of the Brigantian political system.[4] The Pennines themselves, the passes through the hills, and the Lancashire lowlands, were regarded as Brigantian territory by the Romans, though it seems likely that Lancashire at least was nominally the land of other tribes which had been brought into the Brigantian system – the Setantii in and around the Ribble Valley and estuary was one such,[5] and another, whose name has not survived, probably occupied southern Lancashire. Similarly, the tribes north of the Tees as far as modern Northumberland, and in the Eden Valley and Cumbria as far as the Tyne-Solway Gap across the country, and perhaps even beyond, had become part of the Brigantian overlordship system; the Southern Uplands of Scotland, however, were occupied by other and independent tribes, the Selgovae, the Votadini, the Novantae, not part of the Brigantes' system. Like much of Wales, especially in the hills, the population was often thin on the ground, and quite probably pastoral in occupation.

Bolanus had battled Venutius' forces and had founded some forts and signal stations, but it is not clear how firm a grip he had achieved on the territory in his short time, and with the much-reduced forces he had had.[6] Probably the Yorkshire region was a badly damaged land, invaded and fought over, but still essentially independent, and maybe still under Venutius' rule when Cerialis arrived. The forts and signal stations Bolanus is said to have built during the campaigning were probably abandoned once he had fought Venutius to a standstill; for he then, it seems, withdrew all his forces, probably leaving Venutius still in control, but reduced in prestige and strength. Therefore, when Cerialis took over in 71, the frontier was at the Humber-Mersey line, with a legionary base at Lindum (Legio IX Hispana), and several forts in the Trent Valley, and along the northern limits of the Cornovii tribe to the west. Some of these forts – Newton-on-Trent, Rossington Bridge, Osmanthorpe, Broxtowe – were of legionary size, but were perhaps only temporary, or were occupied by groups of auxiliary forces. Others, at Templeborough, Chesterfield, Trent Vale, Whitchurch, were certainly for *auxilia*.[7]

Cerialis had clearly done better than Bolanus, but then he did have a full three seasons as governor (71–73) compared with Bolanus' six months, and he had a much larger and more obedient army. It appears probable that he had moved IX Hispana forward from Lindum to Derventio (Malton), where a vexillation seems to have been placed, and then to Eboracum (York), where a fort had been established, beginning this move in 71. The first Eboracum fort was of the size for an auxiliary regiment, and this is also the accepted date for the foundation of York. The legion only arrived later, therefore. Some of the forts in the territory of the Parisi may also have been founded by Cerialis. These last might well be forts for the protection of the tribe, with the Parisi acting as Roman allies as against the more overbearing and belligerent Brigantes. The territory of the Parisi shows no further indication of being occupied by Roman forces, other than the line of forts which seem to mark the tribe's western boundary, and the larger base at Derventio (Malton), possibly occupied by part of the legion in the first phase.[8] It will be seen that there is a good deal of vagueness here. The Parisi were thus probably Roman allies, and the line of border forts was Rome's contribution to their safety – and they also threatened the eastern flank of the Brigantes. Their main defence, however, was the marshes of the lower Ouse, the difficult Humber estuary, and the line of the Yorkshire Wolds on which the forts were placed.

This was likely the situation when Cerialis began his main campaign against the Brigantes, this time with the aim of deliberate conquest. He could gather a formidable force in Lincolnshire, Nottinghamshire, and Derbyshire, while leaving a powerful guard on the Welsh Marches to prevent any interference from the Silures or the Ordovices. The legionary fortresses facing Wales were then at Glevum and Viroconium, and he left himself without the use of these legions in his northern campaign. The foundation of forts at Eboracum, Roecliffe, Bowes and Luguvallium indicates his campaign route, first directly north towards and against the fortified Brigantian base at Stanwick, then northeast into the Eden Valley. There are three large marching camps along the Eden Valley, a day's march apart, which would suggest the route of a marching army in hostile territory, though they have not yet been dated.[9]

Cerialis, by following the invasion route, was ignoring his flanks. This would suggest that the attack on the Brigantes had shattered its political system, and that the subordinate tribes had been contacted by Cerialis' agents to persuade them to remain neutral, or to submit to Roman authority. Had these flanking tribes – the Parisi in east Yorkshire, the Setantii in north Lancashire, and the several tribes in Durham and Northumberland – been hostile, his march as far as Carlisle (where he founded the fort) would have been highly dangerous. In addition, it is probable that the Carvetii of the Solway region were similarly contacted, and that his aim was to reach and reinforce them, and secure their territory for any further advance northwards. One senses that Cerialis was overconfident, expecting the conquest to be easy.

Tacitus explicitly says that Cerialis had to fight many battles.[10] He was facing Venutius and his tribal army. Venutius is said to have been a competent commander, but he disappears from any record at this point. Presumably he died, either of old age or in battle. One place which Cerialis probably seized is the great fortified camp at Stanwick in the Tees valley but, despite Sir Mortimer Wheeler's advocacy, there are no signs that the place was the site of a battle – it was in fact indefensible from a well-organized army.[11]

This was Cerealis' full achievement. He'd had rather less than a full three years to govern. He arrived sometime in 71, probably after the winter when the sea routes reopened, and he left Britannia late in 73. His consulship was scheduled for May 74, and he would need to get to Rome before that – again the difficult sea crossing to Gaul in the winter was to be avoided. He was replaced, therefore, late in 73 by Frontinus, who arrived with a different set of plans.

In the north, Frontinus found that, in two years, Cerialis had established only a precarious control over Yorkshire, but that he had buttressed his conquests with submissions and/or alliances with several Brigantian sub-tribes. It was a system Frontinus was able to accept while he dealt with Wales, which took no more time than Cerialis' activity in the north, but was achieved more competently. It may well not have been until 76, therefore, that Frontinus was able to attend to the north in detail. Then he was able to take over Cerialis' achievement and improve on it. Again though, he could not make much progress in advancing the Roman frontier; that was to be Agricola's problem in this long contest.

The Parisi

It is worth considering the way the Parisi were dealt with in more detail, in part as a contrast to the system Frontinus put in place, and as a means of interpreting the tribe's situation. From Lincoln northwards, a Roman road led to a crossing of the Humber at Petriana (Brough-on-Humber). Beyond the Humber this road was lined with forts. The line looks very much like a defensive frontier laid out to protect the Parisi, rather as Frontinus' line of forts along the upper Severn Valley separated the newly conquered Silures from the Ordovices. From Petriana the Roman road drives directly north along the Wolds, leaving Derventio (Malton) to one side, and on to two forts at Cawthorne and Leas Rigg in the Cleveland Hills, from where a patrol could easily cover the last section to the coast only a few kilometres further on.

The line of forts-and-roads parallels the eastern edge of the floodplain of the Ouse, and continues the line of the Yorkshire Wolds. This line probably marked the western and northern boundaries of the Parisi territory. Forts at Brough, Hayton, Stamford Bridge and Cawthorne lie along the clear line of this fortified road, which is the defensive boundary of the tribe.

These are the only forts, apart from Derventio, within the territory of the Parisi, standing a little behind the tribal boundary. This suggests that the Parisi did not need to be dominated and controlled by Roman forces as did the Brigantes, though no doubt these forts could do that as well. None, apart from Derventio, can be said to be planted to control the tribe, and large areas of its territory had no Roman presence. Derventio itself was a cavalry fort, one holding two infantry cohorts, of 3.24 hectares (note the similarity in size to the four forts along the centre line in Wales). Others, like those in Wales, were 1.2 to 2.0 hectares. Most of the tribal territory was never under Roman military occupation. The fort at Hayton also marks another road connecting Petriana with Eboracum and Stamford Bridge. The distances between the forts from Petriana to Leas Rigg and Petriana to Eboracum are regularly between 15 and 30km, the usual day's march in every case.[12] This was a system laid out at one go, defending the Parisi rather than occupying the tribe's territory, and as such it was Cerialis' work.

Eboracum

A second route of advance to the northward for Cerialis was probably in fact the main one, since control of the Parisi did not provide a helpful base to campaign into other parts of Yorkshire. The route lay to the west of the Humber estuary, and is marked by the forts at Chesterfield, Templeborough, and the fort at the crossing of the Don at Doncaster; a second route came in from the east, a branch of the road from Lindum. The road then went on to Castleford and York. It swung to the west by way of Castleford, keeping clear of the floodplain. Cerialis' foundation of York was little more than a fort of the usual relatively small size, fit for an auxiliary regiment at most, and designed to control the crossing of the River Ouse.[13] It was some time before it would be realized that this was a particularly important strategic point.

All these forts may be dated to the early 70s, or the 'early Flavian period', that is, either to the governorship of Petilius Cerialis or, less likely, that of Frontinus; the traditional date for the foundation of York is AD 71, though that seems to be derived from the fact that Cerialis took up his governorship in that year; it seems unlikely that he managed to subdue the Brigantes sufficiently by that date, though one of the prime methods would be to found forts in their territory in his first year, as a statement of intent – just as did Bolanus. The line of forts along the road north from York includes at least two which can be assigned to these early dates, and imply an advance beyond York into North Yorkshire at least.

Occupation of Southern Brigantia

If Stanwick was a major political centre for the tribe it will have been one of Cerialis' targets, and he certainly campaigned as far as Carlisle where the fort is dated to '72/73'. How firm his grasp was in the Yorkshire area is not clear, but the southern part of Brigantia was certainly occupied in Cerialis' time. Bolanus may have begun the process, by his many battles, but most of the work of permanent conquest was clearly done by Cerialis. The series of forts in southern Yorkshire, southern Lancashire, and northern Derbyshire and Nottinghamshire can be dated to the early 70s, that is, in the governorships of Bolanus, Cerialis and Frontinus, but the evidence for the individual forts varies. Of the forts south of York only one is well dated, that at Castleford, its occupation dated to 71–86, which in the circumstances of the conquest is disappointingly vague.[14] It was then replaced and rebuilt. Other forts along or near the route northwards are too often interpreted as 'temporary', or 'campaign' forts, and based on discovery but not excavation. The important crossing of the River Don at Doncaster was surely held,[15] however, and the fort at Newton Kyme, near Tadcaster, was placed on two successive sites and was then succeeded by a small fort.[16] However these more permanent forts, excavated or not, or presumed, can be assigned to Frontinus. Thus, if York was Cerialis' foundation as a site for an *auxilia*, as seems likely, it is best to see those to the south as planted during his campaign. Frontinus' work therefore was to select those forts which were to be made permanent, to begin building an earth-and-timber fort, and to construct more suitable barracks than leather tents.

On the western side of the Pennines, the main military sites in southern Lancashire were forts at Mamucium (Manchester) and at the crossing of the River Ribble at Bremetenacum (Ribchester). Mamucium was an important route-centre linking the new legionary fortress at Deva with the equally new legionary fortress at Eboracum, but also by road to Bremetenacum and to a possible fort at Wigan. On the Eboracum road there were forts of this early date at Condate (Northwich) in northern Cheshire; a fort at Slack (probably Camulodunum) guarding a point through the hills was founded a little later. From Deva to Camulodunum/Slack the forts were consistently about 30km apart, the standard distance for Roman roads. The southern Lancashire forts, however, were few and well apart. The conclusion must be that the land was occupied rather than conquered.[17]

In the lowlands on either side of the Pennines new roads were laid out from Mamucium north to Walton-le-Dale (a supply base rather than a fort) and Bremetenacum, both on the Ribble, though no other early forts have been found along that line. North of Bremetenacum was the territory of the Setantii (Fleetwood was 'Setantium Portus'), but again there are no early forts known north of the Ribble. Even in the Roman period the territory from the Mersey to the Lune was thinly occupied.[18] The conclusion must be that the Setantii quietly submitted, as did whoever lived in southern Lancashire, no doubt having been contacted diplomatically in advance. Their territory did not need to be occupied.

They could also form a buffer between the province and any hostile groups in the Lake District.

North from Eboracum and Bremetenacum, which are on the same latitude, there were only the forts at Roecliffe, Bowes, and Luguvallium at this early date; Bowes was only a marching camp, and the fort at Luguvallium does not appear to have been permanent, perhaps built by Cerialis while he conducted negotiations with the tribes in the region. Roecliffe, however, suggests that there were other forts along the route north, perhaps as far as the Tees, and so aimed at controlling Stanwick's people.

It is unlikely that the land north of the rivers Tees and Ribble was under direct Roman control – the land from York to the Tees would certainly be under Roman domination from York, especially once Stanwick was taken. It seems therefore probable that Cerialis could claim to have eliminated Venutius, and to have campaigned as far as Luguvallium, but he only established some sort of control over the land as far as the Tees and the Ribble. Stanwick, from its sheer size, was an obvious target for his campaign, and a place whose control was clearly required, but there is no real sign that he moved beyond the Tees other than for his brief campaign to Luguvallium.

The two ends of the Tyne-Solway gap were populated by several tribes whose names are known, and who had been part of the Brigantian political system – the Carvetii around Carlisle, and the names of three others are known at the eastern end of the gap, facing the North Sea. Like the Parisi and the Setantii they will all no doubt have been contacted diplomatically with a view to detaching them from the Brigantian political system, though the advance of an early campaign into the territory of the Carvetii around the Solway estuary suggests that a dusty answer may have come from that tribe. If Cerialis had to fight several battles, as Tacitus says, as well as advance and build forts at several places on either side of the Pennines, it may be that he had little time to consolidate his conquests. That was a process Frontinus excelled at.

The Roads and the Forts

The conquered area, from the Deva-Lindum line held by Bolanus, to the line of the Ribble and the Tees was seamed by roads on which forts were placed – a version of the same system Frontinus used in the land of the Silures.¹⁹ The road north from Brough-on-Humber guarding the Parisi has affinities with that along the upper Severn, separating the Ordovices from the lands to the south. Given that Cerialis seems to have spent much of his time as governor in campaigning and founding only some forts, it is probable that the overall system of forts was eventually organized by Frontinus, on the basis of Cerialis' work.

There were four roads laid out from south to north. On the east was the road from Lindum, crossing the Humber to Petriana and on to Stamford Bridge and Cawthorne and Leas Rigg, which marked the boundary of the Parisi. Second, through inland Yorkshire, was the main route which became Dere Street from Doncaster to Eboracum and on to Cataractonium. In the west, where there were roads aligned the same, one went from Northwich over the Mersey to cross the Ribble near its estuary close to Walton-le-Dale (and later on it would reach Lancaster). The fourth road was through Mamucium to Ribchester, along the Pennine foothills; this eventually dipped into the Eden Valley and reached to Luguvallium, but at first it went no further than Bremetenacum.

These north-south routes were connected by east-west roads through the several Pennine passes – Mamucium to Eboracum through the southern Pennines (with the main pass guarded by the later fort at Castleshaw and the earlier at Slack), and Bremetenacum to Eboracum by the Craven Gap. Later roads connecting Wensleydale and Ribbledale, and Cataractonium and Luguvallium through the Stainmore Gap and the Eden Valley, were organized and fortified – the line of at least three matching camps in the Eden Valley suggests the passage of Cerialis' army. All these roads were sown with forts, though those in the hills may have been developed later. Frontinus, having spent at least two years in Wales, may have had two more years for the north, but some of the work will have been done already; the network is notably sketchier than that in Wales, partly because the forts are not yet certainly founded, and partly because of the flatter geography; but, also, too many are simply unexcavated and undated, and some are no doubt still undiscovered.

The dating of many of these forts is therefore vague, for 'Early Flavian' might cover fifteen years and the governorships of four men, from Bolanus to Agricola. Any or all of them could well be the work of any or all of these men, though Agricola is usually credited with them since he is the best known – but Agricola worked primarily north of these forts, from the Tyne-Solway line northwards. Some of the southern forts in Lincolnshire and Nottinghamshire were likely to be earlier than Frontinus' time, indeed before Bolanus' time.

If Cerialis really did move the IX Hispana forward from Lindum northwards as soon as he arrived it was mainly to fight, not to build. Bolanus had used an *auxilia* force in his rescue of Cartimandua, but heavier metal would be needed to secure Brigantian territory, specifically the Yorkshire region, by conquest. The presence of a full legion in the region would be properly intimidatory. Cerialis seems to have put part of the legion at Derventio (Malton), with a legionary vexillation or an auxiliary regiment in the fort at Eboracum at first. So no doubt there was plenty of work still to be done when Frontinus arrived in the province and it is likely that the legionary fortress was his work. He was the founder of the other new legionary fortresses, at Deva and Isca Silurum (and even possibly at Mirabeau), so Eboracum would complete the set. He is the obvious man to have perceived that the position of Eboracum was the best for the third of his legionary fortresses, with his forces equally spread and strategically placed for control, not for conquest; his work here was consolidation. Lindum was now in a backwater, and Viroconium was becoming unnecessary with a heavy auxiliary garrison controlling Wales. The legions were equally spaced: Isca-Deva-Eboracum.

The Roman military was a well-oiled machine when it was under firm and clear direction. Cerialis' erratic nature may not have been as systematic in his attention to details as the fortification system in the Brigantian southland seems to be, but Frontinus was just the sort of a man to bring order out of a series of provisional expedients; a surveyor needs to be careful and to attend to detail. Perhaps we may assume that the initial fort at Eboracum and the Parisi defence line were Cerialis' work, since both of these seem likely to have been initial moves in the conquest of the north, and so will have taken place during his conquering process, while the early date for the forts at Roecliffe and Bowes require that there was already a force stationed at York. Exactly when the auxiliary camp at York was replaced by a legionary fortress is not clear. The camp dates from 71, when Cerealis' forces invaded Brigantia, though this is claimed for the date of Cerialis' arrival, and the invasion could well have been a year or two later; whether he had the time and the manpower to build a legionary fortress seems unlikely. He possibly began the process, but building would take at least as long as the fortress at Deva – five years – so much of the building was left to Frontinus to do, even if Cerialis had laid the foundations.

The details of Cerialis' unfinished work, there and elsewhere, as well as the fortresses at Deva and Eboracum, were therefore left to Frontinus to sort out and complete. Probably he concentrated on the southern Brigantian region as far north as the Tees. It appears from excavations, however, that Luguvallium, isolated and distant from any prospect of support, was retained. It shows signs of having been established by Legio II Adiutrix, brought across from Nijmegen in the Netherlands by Cerialis. The fort was occupied by a cavalry unit, possibly Ala Sebosiacum, until Agricola ordered its refurbishment in 82/83.[20] The *ala* was possibly therefore sent to replace the legionaries by Frontinus, and to act as support for the local tribal authorities, but it was somewhat isolated, and there is little indication of Roman presence between Carlisle and the Ribble before Agricola's time. This would allow Roman control south of the Tees to be consolidated, and as far as the Ribble in the west, both of which river lines would make an efficient defence line if no further advances were immediately contemplated. (But he must have known that the next governor would receive the same instructions as Cerialis and himself – to complete the conquest of the island, which, as Agricola was to discover, was not possible in a single governor's term, even when doubled, as it proved.) The two newly established legionary fortresses, Deva and Eboracum, the firm control established in Wales and southern Brigantia, were the bases from which Agricola could operate to secure the next advance; Luguvallium fort was a sign of Roman intent.

Frontinus' Britannia, a Summary

When Frontinus arrived in the province, in late 73 or early 74, the north had probably been secured as far as the line of the Tees, if perhaps a little precariously, and he could devote his attention to the west. This was necessary, since any further advance northwards would be endangered by an attack, even the threat of one, out of Wales. The Silures were rapidly conquered, perhaps as a result of preliminary diplomatic work, perhaps because of an overwhelming Roman force being displayed – or most likely by a combination of the two. A new town as a tribal capital, Venta

Silurum, was founded, and a Silurian population was encouraged to live there. The new legionary fortress at Isca Silurum was a more convenient site than Burrium (and more likely to exert influence and detailed control over the tribal state than the fortress at Glevum). It also provided a potentially substantial market for the Silurian farmers and craftsmen. Persuasive diplomatic work among the Silurian leaders, perhaps assisted by the experience of their neighbours to the east and south, and who had become accustomed to the Roman influence with the fortress at Burrium in their territory, had perhaps been successful. By 74 the Silures had been at peace with Rome for a decade and a half. A resumption of fighting might have seemed pointless in the face of the sudden increase in Roman military power. The advance of II Augusta from Glevum into the midst of their territory once more was similarly persuasive. Whatever the precise reasons, the tribe was taken into the empire in a single campaigning season.

Frontinus is credited with conquering the Silures and must therefore be credited also with the successful diplomacy involved and with the founding of the new town and the new legionary base, for the whole set of developments stand together. It was also he who was responsible for laying out the net of roads and forts which enveloped the Silurian territory, and that along the line of the upper Severn. This network was clearly a military occupation, and was equally clearly conceived as a whole from the start. The submission of the Silures may have been quick, but 'conquest' implies some fighting, and the detailed garrison imposed on it implies continued uncertainty as to tribal intentions. The upper Severn line may also be the means of defence for the newly subdued tribe against the Ordovices, the other tribe which made some resistance, but it is best to see the road-and-fort network which covered all Wales, including the net which surrounded the Snowdonia region, as a single system, conceived as a whole, and executed by Frontinus. This will mean that the other tribes were reduced to subordination as well, some by diplomacy alone, and in Frontinus' time.

He continued the same work in the land of the Brigantes. No doubt diplomacy was at work in amongst those peoples who retained tribal links with the Brigantian system, as with the Parisi and others. It was, however, less easy to lay a network over the north than in Wales. Within that overall system, however, a different approach had been adopted for each tribe, some conquered, some conciliated, which was another subtle means of separating them, but it was also a tribute to Frontinus' application, and to his understanding of the capabilities and susceptibilities of each of the tribes. One may recall his careful, non-violent, approach to dealing with the Lingones, whose great numbers were discounted in a sense by his conciliatory diplomacy. (Tacitus, of course, did not find such an approach appealing.)

Among the Brigantes, again, we can see that the conquest had been bounded by a network of roads and forts laid over the conquered land, with due regard to the physical landscape – two major north-south roads on each side of the Pennines, linked by connecting roads through the mountain passes. Some of this had been done by Cerialis, especially in Yorkshire, a relatively easy region to deal with, but it is possible to detect developments by Frontinus, such as the concentration of IX Hispana in the new legionary fortress at Eboracum, analogous to the placing of II Augusta in the midst of the Silures, and the completion of the new legionary fortresses at Deva and Eboracum. The forts for the *auxilia* were concentrated in the Yorkshire lowlands, between the Pennines and the line of forts protecting the Parisi, and they could therefore be planted rather farther apart, and rather fewer need be built, than in hilly South Wales. The southern half of Lancashire in particular received only two certain forts, at Mamucium and Bremetenacum, which is a possible case of advance diplomacy once more, together with the open country. (A fort has been suggested, on rather flimsy grounds, for Wigan; another, at Kirkham in the Fylde, north of the Ribble, is better attested; Walton-le-Dale was a supply base, not a fort.) All these places are connected by two roads, lying north-south, one through the centre, the other close to the Pennines.

How far Frontinus had the responsibility for this layout is not known, but he was certainly the architect of the Silurian system, and that in Mid- and North Wales; that amongst the Brigantes is very similar in concept. The allied tribes were left largely unoccupied, but were bolstered by smaller forts – Derventio, Bremetenacum, maybe Wigan, Luguvallium – while the conquered were held by a dense network, and the whole system was anchored by the new legionary fortresses, which were either in the midst of the conquered territory or were frowning at it from nearby.

The legion at Deva was the strategic centrepiece for the whole system in both the North and North Wales, and it is a little surprising that it had taken so long for the Roman military to appreciate the usefulness of the position. With II Adiutrix there, three legions faced the Welsh tribes, one planted amidst the Silures, two watching the Ordovices from Deva and Viroconium; but II Adiutrix was also paired with IX Hispana at Eboracum and faced towards the north as well (as at Luguvallium). And the conquered lands were heavily garrisoned with dozens of forts. This was not intended to be a permanent distribution and occupation, since the overall intention was to conquer the rest of the island. But the two northern legions were well placed to advance further northwards, and IX Hispana had done so in stages to Eboracum; the Deva legion was presumably patrolling into southern Lancashire as well as watching North Wales. The conquered lands were also guarded by the allied tribes – the Setantii, the Carvetii, the Parisi – while the legions at Isca Silurum and Viroconium could watch Wales, again surrounded by allied tribes which still occupied perhaps half of Wales – the Venedoti, Deceangli, Demetae, and the others. Frontinus had laid out the board in preparation for Agricola's campaigns.

Other Work for the Governor

There was other work than campaigning and fort building for a governor to do, of course. It must be assumed that the legionary commanders and the engineers could do the detailed work of planting and constructing the forts; these were, of course, of a basic pattern all through the empire, but each one would need adaptation to the ground they were to be built on – at Cawthorne the early forts were square, but the final one was oblong, with apsidal ends, on a plan quite unlike any other Roman fort. Their precise locations would need to be decided, and these may have been the governor's decision, particularly a governor with Frontinus' skills and experience. The general layout of the network will have been Frontinus' decision, as may be the locations of the forts, and the size of the garrisons; his would be the allocation of the units to the several forts. The officers had the necessary skills, as did their junior officers, to build the forts and lay out the roads, and could be left to get on with that work themselves; suitably inspired, if only at the prospect of greater comfort for themselves, they would be pleased to be able to work with only distant and occasional supervision. No doubt Frontinus would periodically turn up to inspect the work. In Brigantia much of the initial work had been done, and only decisions on the permanent abandonment of the 'temporary' forts needed to be made. There are a number of these temporary forts, scattered throughout the region, many of which were not taken up as permanent bases – this, it would seem, was Frontinus' work, after Cerialis' less organized methods.

The foundations of the legionary fortresses would require greater gubernatorial attention. None of the fortresses begun during Frontinus' period in office was finished in his time, with the result that an inscription on a lead pipe, dated 79 and naming Agricola, means he has been credited with the whole work.[21] Isca Silurum is dated only to the 70s, which clearly meant that most of the construction was done under Frontinus, who also chose the site – and therefore probably in 73 or 74, one of his first acts. Eboracum's first (small) fort is dated, conventionally, to 71, and the legionary fortress may have been founded in the next two or three years, and so by Cerialis, but it had to be built, again, mainly within Frontinus' governorship. He was thus responsible for all of these fortresses, which were founded by him on sites chosen by him (in at least two cases) and mainly built during his time. They may have been completed under Agricola, but that was all.

Beyond that work, the governor had also to attend to the general government of the province, and this included legal and criminal affairs, as well as the defence of the province and military matters. There is some indication that Frontinus gave a boost to the development of urban centres in other parts of the province. It was in his time that the new forum-and-basilica at Verulamium (St Albans) was begun – it was opened in a ceremony in 79, and so again Agricola was taking credit for Frontinus' work; it had taken over a decade for the town to recover from the Boudican devastation, and then to build its new administrative centre.[22] Similar work at Isca Dumnoniorum (Exeter) and Corinium (Cirencester) has been detected and seems to be related to Frontinus' urgings.[23] He founded Venta Silurum, probably at the same time as the legionary fortress at Isca. The removal of the legionary base from Isca Dumnoniorum to Glevum and then from Glevum to Isca Silurum left the associated civilian settlements at the abandoned bases somewhat bereft, no doubt, but they all survived. At Glevum it seems that the fortress was not wholly abandoned, and was then handed over to civilian occupation. The city retained the outline plan of the legionary fortress all through its life.[24] These towns were in wealthy regions and could be expected to, and did, survive; there is no reason to believe that the Roman government left them to rot; part of II Augusta did stay at Isca Dumnoniorum after the main part of the legion moved to Glevum, no doubt to continue to supervise the western peninsula, which was rich in mineral deposits which Rome always eagerly exploited. Camulodunum (Colchester) and Londinium (London), like Verulamium, had been destroyed in the Boudican revolt, and, if only for prestige reasons, were well on the way by this time to full recovery, assisted by government funds and expertise.

This was all no doubt very expensive. Moving troops was a costly process. Building forts and fortresses could be done in part by the labour of the soldiers, at least the initial foundation and the temporary rampart and timber forts and the tented accommodation, but the heavy work of construction in permanent timber, and later stone, was surely done by local labour, at least in part – one does not train soldiers expensively to be cheap labourers. The acquisition of the building materials could be made in part by requisition, and some labour could come from conscription, paying minimum wages, but the cost was substantial nonetheless. We do not know the cost of such work, but, if the soldiers were conducting campaigns most of the time, or were on vigilant garrison and patrol duty, which was their expertise, and would be necessary in the early years after the conquest, they could not at the same time be building forts; hired labour would be necessary.

In the years 71 to 77 perhaps three dozen or more forts and three legionary fortresses were built in Britannia, and roads were laid out throughout Wales, and over a similar area in the north. These roads will have followed existing tracks, and these will have had to be improved in parts, no doubt, any paving could be laid down gradually, and by conscript labour, but some initial cost was certainly involved, if only to provide the conscripts with food, and the food needed by the workers had to be supplied in considerable quantities – note the use of ports at Isca Silurum, Pannel, Caerhun, Caernarfon, and other places, while York and Chester were both river ports with access to the sea.

In addition, the big municipal buildings in the cities in the older parts of the province were no doubt subsidized by the central government. The cost of all this had to be borne by the imperial treasury, since the population of Britannia itself, which remained a fairly poor province, could not possibly have afforded all this work, particularly as it seems that several cities – perhaps all cities – were busy building their own facilities at the same time – forum, basilica, baths, temples, and so on. It is noticeable that most cities had no walls to surround them for many decades, despite frequent wars in the north of the island, and when they were built they appear to be constructed of local resources and at local expense – in other words, the towns could not afford such expensive buildings by themselves for many decades, again leading to the supposition that imperial funds had to be available for the early buildings.

Not only that, but the network of roads and forts absorbed military manpower at a great rate. Ignoring the legions, which were on permanent stations, there were, in Frontinus' Welsh system, forts which are classed as for *auxilia* at almost thirty locations. If each held one auxiliary regiment, half of the regiments brought to Britannia by Cerialis were absorbed in these Welsh garrisons. Probably some of the forts were only partly occupied, or occupied only part of the time; some of them were certainly reduced in size, and hence in the number of troops located there, within only a few years; some will have been occupied by vexillations from the legions, but other forts have not been discovered yet. In military manpower Frontinus' system was extremely expensive. Then the same system was applied to Brigantia, if on a somewhat lesser scale – ten or a dozen auxiliary forts. There would be few left for a field army for Agricola's assault on the north.

The imperial treasury had to provide the cash. This was an imperial decision, one which was the responsibility of the emperor himself. Bolanus will not have received any extra cash, since he was a Vitellian appointee in the midst of a civil war, and then Vitellius was defeated; by early 70 it would be known that he would not be serving much longer. Cerialis, Frontinus, and Agricola, on the other hand, were all Flavian loyalists, and had to be supported, particularly as they were intended, as seems probable, to aim at the conquest of the whole island. Hence the extra legion and the huge garrison of *auxilia* brought by Cerialis. If they were able to provide good news – news of victories particularly – for the glory to be assumed by the new emperor, they would need adequate financial resources. All three accordingly did provide victories.

The extension of Frontinus' scheme into the north was probably less expensive in manpower than that in Wales; the area was partly allied territory, and had partly been conquered and occupied before his arrival. But the new forts in Lancashire and Yorkshire had to be built and occupied. There is some sign that some forts, in peaceful areas, could be quickly abandoned – Derventio (Malton) was one, but they had to be built first.[25] When Agricola arrived, one wonders how much military manpower was still available for his campaigns. He was almost compelled to adopt Frontinus' method of advancing by forts, rather than campaigning to fight battles. The army of auxiliaries used to defeat Calgacus in the Highlands was partly found by abandoning existing forts and reducing the garrisons in others, of which there is some evidence in Wales, and in the North of England. He would need to return these garrisons after the victory to reaffirm Roman determination to remain, particularly since he withdrew from supposedly conquered northern Scotland. He did not have the manpower to occupy northern Scotland in the way Frontinus conquered Wales, and without such occupation there could be no conquest.

Frontinus' British conquests were exactly what Vespasian required, enabling him to carry through the extension of the *pomerium* in 75. It has been suggested here that Frontinus had an interview with Vespasian before he set out for Britannia, Vespasian being familiar with the province from his time as a legionary commander. If so, instructions as well as advice will have been imparted. Much the same instructions were surely provided for all these governors, even without an interview – though Tacitus implies that Agricola was the only one[26] – but it is more likely that a face-to-face talk would be especially impressive, and all the more so since Cerialis' achievement had been so limited, and Vespasian had an old familiarity with the province. It would not be surprising if the emperor had been considering how Britannia might properly be included in the empire ever since his legionary command at the time of the initial invasion and conquest. It would also not be surprising if he pointed out that the conquest of the Silures and Wales was a necessary preliminary to the conquest of the north.

The three governors appointed by Vespasian contrasted in style and abilities; of them, Frontinus was probably the most capable at organizing the conquests and delivering the network of forts and roads; Cerialis' style was more impatient and improvisatory than that of the more organized Frontinus;[27] Agricola was perhaps well-organized, but his attention lay northwards, over which it was considerably more difficult to establish control. Of the three, only Frontinus could have organized the Silurian and Ordovician conquests, hemmed in the Ordovices, laid out numerous roads, and organized the fort system, both in Wales and the north, and founded three legionary fortresses and three dozen forts, all in four years or so, while also encouraging existing cities to build up their municipal centres.

Frontinus' method of conquest – and control – was new. No other part of the Roman Empire had been conquered and held in such a detailed way.[28] Normally the land acquired was superficially occupied, and the main force was then sent to guard the new frontier. This permitted rebellions to occur behind the frontier. There is no sign of such a rebellion in Wales, even after much of the garrison network had been dismantled. So Frontinus was successful, in Wales and in part of the north, but his method was so absorbing of soldiers that it was difficult to advance any further.

It was the increase in the force in the province which had arrived with Cerialis in 71 that made it possible for Frontinus to begin his campaign at once on his arrival in Britannia and to implement his new system. Cerialis had revived the discipline of the army in Britannia, and he had brought in all those extra regiments. If Frontinus arrived in the winter of 73/74 the troops could have been alerted to start the campaign as early in the new regime as possible; also, such an unusually early arrival by a governor would demonstrate the imperial urgency involved, quite apart from the advantages of attacking the victim at a time, the beginning of spring, when supplies after the winter were short.

The conclusion I reach after all this is that the work done by Frontinus was crucial to the future of the province, and enabled Agricola to mount his military expedition into the north, while at the same time it also prevented him from 'completing' the conquest. (The alternative would be for unrest in Wales which would also prevent further conquests in the rest of the island.) Nero had wondered aloud if holding Britannia was worthwhile, and Vespasian must have wondered about the future of the province when its garrison had been so severely reduced by the exigencies of the Civil War.[29] He could have left it with its small garrison, and been content with only a small expansion beyond what his original commander, Aulus Plautius, had settled for thirty years before at the Fosse Way line. The only part of the conquests of Cerialis, Frontinus, and Agricola which were profitable would be Yorkshire and Lancashire, and perhaps some of the mineral resources, such as the gold at Dolaucothi and many lead mines; the empire could get along well enough without the Welsh mountains or the Pennines and Cumbria, and certainly without Scotland. But Frontinus' successful capture of the Silures and the Ordovices made it strategically possible for Agricola to move north, though his campaign ultimately failed to extend the empire much beyond what Cerialis had briefly achieved in his disorganized way, and which Frontinus had organized as a permanent possession. The line between the Tees estuary and Morecambe Bay would have been as satisfactory (or unsatisfactory) a boundary as the Tyne-Solway line or the Forth-Clyde line. In effect, Frontinus had completed the inclusion of the profitable part of Britannia into the empire, and there was no real need, and no profit, in going further.

Chapter 6

Frontinus on War

By the time he returned to Rome in late 77 or early 78, having handed over the province of Britannia to Agricola, Frontinus had accumulated considerable experience of warfare: probable military tribune in the East under the inspiring command of Domitius Corbulo, a fellow Narbonensian; command of military surveyors in Africa and Spain; possible officer in Galba's legion in the Civil War; praetorian commander of a legion in Gaul; and proconsular governor of Britannia with four legions and over sixty auxiliary regiments under his command, and a considerable conquering achievement to his credit. This was probably as extensive and varied a military experience as any man in the Roman Empire could have gained without being emperor, and it was in effect his whole life from adolescence to adult maturity. In the process he had also gained wide experience of the empire, and, to a thinking man, of its problems.

At some point in this experience of war he resolved to write a treatise on the *Art of War (de re militari)*. This book has disappeared, but he also made a collection of military anecdotes and examples, possibly as a preparation for his *Art of War*, possibly to be an illustrative supplement; it is this which has survived.[1] This collection was published under the title of *Stratagemata*. This is, interestingly, a Greek term, usually translated as '*Stratagems*', as here, though that is scarcely an adequate rendering of what he attempted. It is curious that Rome, a pre-eminently military empire, should have to resort to a Greek term in this matter. It was the most successful military state of the ancient world; perhaps only Assyria was able to rival it in the sheer concentration on warfare as the essence of the life of the state. And yet there appears to have been no Latin term which Frontinus could use for his collection of military examples. That is, it appears that the Romans had not approached war in any exercise of intellectual capacity until Frontinus, unlike a number of Greek writers. It was perhaps an example of Roman practicality, or perhaps of Roman anti-intellectualism. As with his pamphlet on surveying, he had noted the absence of earlier accounts and was aiming to fill the gap.

Both in *Art of War* and in *Stratagems*, Frontinus' purpose was to provide instruction for commanders. He selected events from the past to illustrate how to accomplish military results. This included the importance of discipline, intelligence in and for commanders, care for the soldiers, and all the many qualities required of a serving commanding officer. *Stratagems*, at least, and no doubt *Art of War*, was directed squarely at officers, not at the soldiers. This is, of course, much the same managerial audience which he had addressed in the surveying book.

The connection between the two military books is not clear, but since he had to research both, and another on 'Homeric tactics', which he is noted as producing, as a coherent group of studies, it is very probable that *Stratagems* was collected first, since he would need to accumulate such information before beginning *Art of War*. It is also probable that in assembling his book, *Stratagems* could have acted as an appendage to *Art of War,* and at the same time was the raw material from which he crafted the latter. That *Stratagems* survived in three decent copies (derived from a single one) and numerous bad or part copies, where *Art of War* (and the account of Homeric tactics) have disappeared may be because the *Stratagems* is more approachable and perhaps more useful than the full accounts. Later attempts to prescribe a military system for commanders have always failed: *Art of War* was less useful than he must have wished and intended; the *Stratagems* were entertaining, if no more useful. Command in war is certainly, however, as much an art as a learned process; the successful commanders succeed by inspiration as well as knowledge of warfare. *Stratagems* continued to be copied throughout the medieval period and into the early modern, which supposes that military men professed to find the collection helpful, though it was likely that amateurs and students favoured it most.

Stratagems was organized in four books, originally three, in each of which Frontinus' examples were marshalled in groups, each group dealing with a military issue. For example, the first set is 'On Concealing One's Plans', and includes Greek, Roman, Carthaginian, and Pontic examples, which, with the addition of some Persian and Parthian examples in other parts of the book, more or less covers the range of his selections. (For present-day historians, who use *Stratagems* as a quarry from which to find otherwise unknown material, quite a number of his stories are useful in that they come from sources which have been lost; almost as useful are the examples which vary a little in wording from other sources.) Frontinus' reading was wide and not confined to Roman and Greek examples, though these certainly predominate.

There has been a rumbling on-and-off controversy about the fourth book, which had been judged to be an addition by a different author to the earlier books I to III, but now is thought to be originally by Frontinus after all. Frontinus stated in his preface to Book I that three books was the intended length of the book as a whole.[2] It seems that he later added another selection, Book IV, dealing with some of the topics he felt he had ignored, or adding further illustrations. (One wonders if this addition came after some others had been consulted and offered advice.) This change of plan has confused modern critics into believing that the fourth book came from elsewhere. But it has all the same style and limits of method as the first three. The present belief is that the four books are all by Frontinus, and that he added the fourth book later.[3] The controversy, however, has not gone away, though opinion now has edged towards accepting the authenticity of the fourth book. Some of the items in the text are duplicated elsewhere, which is regarded by some as interference by another outside author, but these may be quite deliberate repetitions by Frontinus, using a single example for more than one purpose; he also notes cases where more than one commander has used the same stratagem – the case of Corbulo's firing the head of the decapitated traitor into the enemy's conference chamber is such an example. It is obvious that some items can provide illustrations for more than one category. These are not important matters. Excessive criticism is rarely productive. And it is hardly unknown for authors to change their minds and their plans during the middle of the writing of a book.

The date of composition, as with all of Frontinus' writings, is not known. Four items in which the campaign of the Emperor Domitian in Germany features have been assumed to mark the earliest date for composition, since they could only be included once they had happened. This is hardly convincing. There is no reason to believe it was written all in one go. The quantity of work, the gathering of examples, extracting quotations, organizing the material, means that he will have spent a long time – years, probably – in composing the work, and probably it occasioned a good deal of travel to find his sources, though no doubt most will have been available in libraries and houses in Rome. He was probably writing both books, *Art of War* and *Stratagems,* and perhaps that on Homeric tactics, at the same time. There is no reason to suppose that he did not work through his examples over and over again, inserting new ones, discarding unsuitable ones, moving them around (and perhaps ending up with so many that he eventually realized that he must include them as Book IV), seeking out missing ones, reorganizing the order of presentation. The text as it now stands was undoubtedly the work of many years and many revisions – that is the only way such a work could be composed. No single date can possibly be suggested for its composition, unless a period of years.

If we knew when the book was published, if that is the correct term, we could suggest a date for the starting of the work, but we do not know that either, except that it was probably finished before the reign of Nerva, since from 96 he was very busy supporting two new emperors, Nerva and Trajan, and as *curator aquarum,* and served as consul twice in that time, in 98 and 100. One clue is in a book called *Tactics* by Aelian, who, feeling diffident about composing yet another book on military art, visited Frontinus in his villa at Formiae and was reassured by the latter's enthusiasm. The date was in the reign of Nerva (October 96 to January 98). Aelian explains that by that time Frontinus had 'a glowing reputation in military matters'.[4] He does not say that he was an author of military books, but that was clearly why Aelian was visiting and consulting him. Nor does he say that Frontinus was a distinguished general, though he was, but that his reputation was high in 'military matters'. This would suggest, rather pressing the wording, that Frontinus' book or books were in the public domain by Nerva's reign. And since Frontinus was in his late 60s by then, it is highly unlikely he was still writing it. He had been without any obvious public employment since 86 when he returned from the governorship of Asia, and the dozen years which followed may be seen as the most obvious period during which the book was finished.

When he began to compose the book (or books) is even less easy to discover. The collection of the four books of *Stratagems* could well have been originally a hobby, a collection built up in a commonplace notebook, for example, possibly in the hope of eventually becoming a commanding general himself. The idea of using the material for *Art of War,* and then of publishing the *Stratagems,* would thus have come to him later, possibly after that ambition was clearly disappointed, or after more experience of command in Britannia and Germania. We can probably assume the book was not started before his praetorship in 70, since he was then busy in countries with fewer libraries than Rome, and moving about in several successive employments. One curiosity is that there are no references to his work in Britannia, even though there are several to his work with Domitian in Germania several years later.

Examining his career, one can suggest some periods when he is unlikely to have been working on the text. His early life, until his praetorship, was spent in the lower ranks of the army, or in work as a surveyor, during which time he could have collected several of those personal anecdotes which he eventually included, but hardly the full set of historical examples he used. His experience of high command only came from 70, first in the reconquest of the rebellious parts of Gaul, and then between 73/74 and 77/78 in Britannia. This will have provided him with the experience of command and campaigning which would be a necessary background for tracking through what needed to be said in his *Art of War*.[5] In Britannia he was clearly busy, but less so in the winter than when on active campaign in the summers, though it is unlikely he would find the source material which he would need in the province. So it is most likely that he was working on the books after 77, perhaps inspired by his immediate British experiences. He was well enough known as a skilful commander to be summoned to accompany the Emperor Domitian for his German campaign in 83–85, and he was in Germany and then in Asia until 86, so if he had not finished the book by 82 (and he included cases from the German campaign in *Stratagems*) it will have been finished at some time after his return to Rome in 86.

Then there will have come the re-reading, the corrections, the checkings, the re-organizing, and the rewritings which any worthwhile author always has to do, especially in a book such as *Stratagems*, for which there were few or no precedents – though for *Art of War* he would have several Greek works on which to model his book – and with which he could also, author-like, carefully disagree. Because of all this, we should not expect the books to have been finished much before 90. One would think that a book on Homeric tactics, based on *The Iliad* and *The Odyssey*, might have been the most straightforward to write, given the limited sources available; *Stratagems* was a compilation, which became longer with his inclusion of the fourth book, and will have been a long time in the making; if the *Art of War* was partly based on *Stratagems* it was probably completed at the same time.

It is impossible to discover where Frontinus located all his examples for *Stratagems*, though Thucydides, Xenophon, Herodotus, Polybios, and Livy are likely to have been the most used, also, of course, Homer, as well as other historical texts which have disappeared since his day. His approach is systematic, dealing first with preparations for the fighting, then on specific situations a commander might find himself in, such as a march through enemy-controlled territory; he has a section on ambushes, both on laying them and on beating them. He has some anecdotes on the difficulties of supply and of distracting the enemy. A fourth part or section discusses how to control and inspire the soldiers. These are the topics illustrated in his Book I. The other three books essentially elaborate on the subjects he has introduced in that first book. Book IV, apparently added later, is a discussion on discipline and morale in the commander's army. (The experience of the Civil War was surely inspirational here, as was that of the British legions.)

He claims in his introduction to Book I that he is reducing the practice of war to an art, with rules and a system. (This is the best clue to the idea that *Stratagems* is an appendix to his *Art of War*, or at least that he was composing both at the same time.) He does not cite any other writer as having done the same, though he does comment that his title is from the term used by the Greeks, *strategos*, meaning commander or general – a clear indication of the audience he was addressing. Considering other military writers, however, it is clear that he was in fact the first to take all military affairs as his subject rather than sections of it or particular items, or particular wars, and historical accounts which might include discussions of wars, as Polybius did. Other writers on the subject tended to be historians, or to specialize in a single aspect of military affairs – tactics, or siege machines, for example. Frontinus, therefore, is thus both unique and very ambitious. Without precursors to suggest an approach, it would clearly be necessary to gather the material, as he presents it in *Stratagems*, before he could even begin to write *Art of War*.

The surviving discussions of military matters began with Aeneas Tacticus, who served as *strategos* of the Arcadian League in its early days, in the fourth century BC. His book discussed 'siegecraft', which was evidently a major concern for Greek and Hellenistic commanders – neither they nor the Romans were ever very good at sieges. Every other discussion of military technique before Frontinus was concerned with sieges in one way or another, a clear indication that sieges were seen as one of the major military problem areas. Philon of Byzantion in the late third century BC wrote on constructing siege machines, as did Biton in the second century BC. Asklepiodotos, Aeneas Mechanicus, and Heron of Alexandria similarly wrote their accounts of these machines, or at least how to build them, rather than on their use in war.[6]

Such machines were evidently a major interest for this group of technically-minded men, though not their only one. It is, of course, very significant that none of them wrote on other military techniques, nor is it clear that their machines were ever put to practical use. No doubt it was understood that tactics and strategy were none of their business. Their interest was essentially in the mechanical aspects of the machines, just as modern atomic scientists are less concerned about the consequences of their inventions than on how to build their bombs. There seem to be few examples of their machines being put to actual use.

Frontinus' work, in *Art of War* and *Stratagems*, is therefore original. There had been, of course, discussions by historians of tactics in battle and of strategic concerns in war, but no earlier attempt seems to have been made to bring together so much information on these topics into a coherent discussion, covering all aspects of warfare.

What is missing in earlier compilations is any discussion of actual warfare. Such discussions may appear incidentally in historians' accounts, though it is often seen as a purely historical matter, suggesting that they did not see the need, and that one battle was very like another; until Frontinus an overall view of warfare was ignored by military specialists. The ability of generals was clearly limited by the nature of the forces they had available to command. These consisted essentially of spearmen in a Greek phalanx, and swordsmen in a Roman legion, marshalled into disciplined groups, together with cavalry which, in the absence of a stirrup, was unable to mount a really powerful charge, and which were notorious for poor discipline. Innovations to the basic hoplite phalanx or legionary arrangement were slow to arrive. For example, Epameinondas of Thebes acquired a great military reputation by simply increasing the number and depth of spearmen, and so the weight of the charge, in one wing of his array.⁷ Hellenistic sea warfare was similarly a variation on the massed charge of oar-powered ships, the variation consisting, like Epameinondas' phalanx, in massing ships on one wing, or in producing bigger ships.

The number of creative generals – inventive in the actual conduct of war, that is – in the ancient world was few; one would include Philip II, Alexander, Hannibal, Scipio Africanus, and Julius Caesar, but few others; others gained victories by driving a large army up against a smaller, or using disciplined forces against undisciplined, as in warfare in Britannia. The professionalization of warfare was something which only came late to the Greco-Roman world. Commanders were usually appointed for single campaigns, and it was only with the Punic Wars – Hamilcar Barca, Hannibal, Scipio Africanus – that some commanders were kept in place and in command over several years on end, though a few Roman commanders in the conquest of Italy served several times. And even then it was unusual to find a long period of time when a general held lengthy commands – the Roman revolution tended to produce them, but it is worth recalling that Julius Caesar was essentially an amateur, with little military experience when he took command of the conquest of Gaul; Pompey the Great, for example, also learned his military skills on the job. In the Empire, however, professionalization to a degree did occur - many Roman Emperors commanded in campaigns (rarely very well), and some non-emperors did so as well – such as Domitius Corbulo. Even so, it was not a recognized profession, for which one would train – hence Frontinus' perception that a book or books like his was needed.⁸

Frontinus was therefore writing, not for the military geniuses, but for the normal Roman commanders, who by this time might fight a battle once in a lifetime, or (like Frontinus himself) never, even though many of them had command of an army when acting as a governor of a province. By his time governors and generals were more likely to face irregular fighters than formed armies. Therefore much of their military experience was in a more mundane area, such as ensuring the discipline of their soldiers, conducting marches, organizing and acquiring supplies, or surviving an ambush on the march – low-level warfare and administration – or perhaps not at all if they simply left these tasks to the centurions and military tribunes. It is thus in these areas that his collection of anecdotes concentrated, giving hints on how to avoid or solve problems in such areas.

Whether his books ever had an effect on later commanders we do not know, but Frontinus himself was the sort of general who was very comfortable with administration; he acted slowly and carefully with the obvious intention of winning a war without fighting, if possible. He convinced the Lingones to surrender by exercising strict control over his own forces, so not giving the enemy any further cause for anger. The conquest of the Silures was evidently achieved by diplomacy and the use of overwhelming force, which made resistance unprofitable. His roads-and-forts network was essentially an occupation system enforced by regular patrolling. In the Roman Empire, where skilled military manpower was always in short supply, the resultant lack of Roman casualties could be particularly helpful.

So the question arises, why Frontinus felt moved to compose this new account, covering all aspects of warfare, an account which was succeeded in the next century by five or six further wide-ranging discussions by other experts on the subject (just as his book on surveying stimulated others to produce similar books). Onasander, a generation before Frontinus, had produced a treatise on generalship for a former governor of Britannia, Q. Veranius, but while this topic is different from earlier military discussions, it is still very restricted in scope.[9]

Maybe it was Onasander's rather restricted, amateur, and inadequate treatment which drove Frontinus to be more comprehensive. The other military books which followed Frontinus also dealt with specific military topics – Aelian on tactics,[10] and Apollodorus of Damascus on that old favourite, siegecraft (he was an engineer, of course, the builder of the Danube bridge for Trajan, like Philon and Biton and Heron and the other earlier writers).[11] Arrian, writing historical accounts of the events of Alexander's great expedition and of his successors, and of his own military career in his own work in Anatolia, also produced an account of the Greek phalanx, a military system which had in fact fallen out of use with the successes of Roman legions, as long before as the Romano-Macedonian wars in the second century BC. (Frontinus' book on Homeric tactics was equally on an outdated military system, unless it had relevance to barbarian methods of his own day.) This is closer to Frontinus' aim, but it is descriptive and autobiographical rather than analytical and educational.[12]

Polyainos used Frontinus' anecdotal method in a book of stratagems which he dedicated to Marcus Aurelius, an emperor of the classic sort, who was pulled into a war with entirely no military experience – if anyone needed advice, he did. Polyainos' collection consists of a set of military exploits organized not by military topic, as is Frontinus', but under the names of the practitioners, a rather less than useful method, unless one is a modern historian.[13] And finally in this group there is 'Pseudo-Hyginus', who wrote of the layout and construction of a military camp – another limited topic.[14] All these aspects – generalship, camps, discipline, and so on – had been dealt with in Frontinus' *Stratagems*, and also possibly in his *Art of War*.

The widening of interest from the Hellenistic preoccupation with the technical accounts of siege machines to other technical military and historical subjects – camps, the phalanx, tactics, and so on – may be ascribed in part to the influence of Frontinus' books, but also to wider military developments. Between the generation of Pompey and Caesar and that of Vespasian, Titus, and Frontinus, the methods of warfare used by the Romans had changed. They had attacked, and been defeated by, the Parthians, who used adaptations of nomad and Hellenistic tactics; they had faced warfare in dense German forests, in which Augustus lost three legions in an ambush – the only means by which the German warriors could hope to fight successfully. Even as Frontinus was compiling his books, the Emperor Domitian was fighting a series of difficult wars along the northern frontier in Germany, in Pannonia, and in Dacia, in one of which Frontinus had actively participated (see Chapter 7), while Agricola was also failing to complete the conquest of Britannia, which Cerialis and Frontinus had set under way. And so it went for the next century, with only occasional advances, and much work in defence. It was perhaps clear to Frontinus, if not to others, that the expansion of the Roman Empire had effectively ceased, except for the capture of relatively marginal and unimportant places. (Domitian for one was not convinced, but his plan to expand north was foiled by his own murder – see Chapter 9 - and his effective successor, Trajan, also not convinced that expansion was no longer feasible, diverted into conquering Dacia and then ventured into another hopeless war with Parthia.)

The first- and second-century Roman commanders, including the emperors, were captivated by the past achievements of the legions, and failed to adapt. It behoved the ruling group to become much more militarily astute if the empire, having reached its apparent maximum size, and unable to expand further, was not to go down to defeat and ruin. It was in this area that Frontinus' work would be most useful, in detailing some of the alternative methods of war. But the essential point is that the empire's expansion was now too painful to be sustained or continued. This was shown in the wars of Domitian and Trajan. The plague brought back to the west by the army of Lucius Verus in 163 made expansion not merely difficult but essentially impossible because of the new shortage of manpower. Scotland was the test: Agricola failed to conquer it, and so did Septimius Severus a century later with the whole military might of the empire at his disposal; those failures forced the empire to maintain an army of an uneconomic, even extravagant, size in Britannia, a clear case of imperial over-reach; half a century after Severus, the empire abandoned exposed and untenable regions – Dacia, Mauretania, the Nile beyond Aswan, the Agri Decumates.

War, therefore, had to be understood more widely by those who would conduct it, and they must also understand that the old methods were changing, while the intricacies of command and campaigning were never part of a Roman gentleman's education, or indeed, in most cases, of his experience. This was the burden of those proclaiming treatises on the subject from Onasander onwards, but they were too often looking backwards. When Agricola fought the great battle of Mons Graupius in the Scottish Highlands, he used the auxiliary regiments alone; the legions stood aside as the reserve, the very reverse of the original intention of the two forces; Bolanus had done that also in his campaign in Brigantia, as perhaps did Frontinus in Wales, who spread auxiliaries out in his garrisoned forts. Agricola used this method, which was thus becoming usual in Roman warfare, to preserve the legions, composed of citizens, whereas the *auxilia* were not yet citizens – but also because the *auxilia* were a much more flexible set of units, and so far more useful to a thoughtful commander than the legions. (One may recall the evolution of British arms in 1914–1918 from the use of full regiments in attack to employing battalions and brigades as the basic units; again flexibility was the aim.) The use of non-citizen auxiliaries to do the work of citizen legionaries is of course a fairly typical example of an empire using newly conquered subjects as cannon fodder in its urge to expand. But so conservative was Rome in all its aspects, it was not until the great and calamitous crisis of the third century that legions were reduced to the size of *auxilia*.

The *auxilia* brought into Roman imperial warfare the successful elements of barbarian war, with the result that it was necessary for generals to think much more deeply about their methods and how to use their new Roman forces. The phalanx and the legion had been successful when they only fought each other: phalanx against phalanx was a brutal shoving match, no military skill needed, nor any generalship other than that involved in the preliminary manoeuvres; legions against legions similarly. Both methods involved heavy casualties for both sides. Phalanx against legion tended to favour the legions, which used a more open array and so were marginally more flexible – but recall the comment of Aemilius Paulus when he saw the Macedonian phalanx charging him at the Battle of Pydna, that he was frightened almost out of his wits.[15]

This was Mediterranean warfare, innovation not required – though when an innovation actually came, it was often successful, simply by surprise – as with Epameinondas' thickened phalanx, or Philip II's use of a longer spear, the sarissa. But the minor, even trivial, nature of these innovations mainly emphasizes their lack elsewhere and elsewhen – and there were costs elsewhere, as in even lesser flexibility. The inclusion of armoured cavalry, the cataphracts, in Hellenistic armies could be devastating to infantry, but such forces were very expensive to raise, train, and maintain, and so were few – and the tactics to defeat them were relatively straightforward. The employment of elephants was of the same order, and even easier to counter – a bowman taking out the mahouts would render an elephant out of control. Innovation tended therefore to stimulate successful counter tactics of an equal simplicity. But the barbarians and the Parthians, with their successes in the first century BC, were forcing the Romans to adapt again, and it was a slow process in the face of enemy innovations and the ignorance of commanders. The variety of warfare was one of the themes of *Stratagems*.

For it was a fact that the legions failed against both Parthian cavalry and against German ambushes. Any successful war fought against Parthia only ended in withdrawal from conquests; Severus' eventual successful conquests in Mesopotamia were against an empire in manifest decline; the German frontier scarcely moved for four centuries. Innovation in tactics was clearly needed if Roman armies were to prevail; the recruitment of German *auxilia* and Parthian horsemen was one method, but this evaded the issue of innovation within the Roman forces. Frontinus' account of the variety of fighting methods he had found, and of the ingenuity of several notable generals, was aimed at improving Roman military methods. For, except for civil wars, it would be the horse-borne archers and armoured cataphracts of the Parthians that the Romans would face in the East, and guerilla raids and forest ambushes in Germania, and mountain warfare in the north, in neither of which methods of warfare was the legion a suitable weapon to use. Frontinus was producing a book, based on his own experience in the East and in Germany and Britain, and on his research into the wars of the Mediterranean empires during the past millennium, which had the object of guiding later commanders into using more flexible systems of command; it was not prescription, only an indication of alternatives. And this is in fact what happened, so that the Roman way to victory in the third century and later was organized to use heavy cavalry and light infantry, with legions in the end only the name for small garrison units. But it took a long time, and Domitian, Trajan, Marcus Aurelius and Septimius Severus all persisted with the legions, and recruited more of them. Whether Frontinus' book – which did survive, and so was possibly read – had any direct effect we cannot tell, though the emperors seem to have paid little attention; it was, however, a symptom of the need for change.

Chapter 7

Comes in Germania

Rome

Frontinus' time as governor of Britannia ended late in 77 or early in 78. As with many events in his life chronological precision is unobtainable, but his successor in Britannia, Agricola, took up the office in 78, and Frontinus returned to Rome. He was by this time a prominent senator, active, and the victor in a war which had been unfinished for the previous decade. He is suggested to have been an *amicus* of the emperor, who was always in search of reliable friends or at least agents, and he certainly had earned the status.[1] He was also a slightly older contemporary of Titus, Vespasian's son and heir. For the next three or four years he was presumably at the centre of affairs in the imperial capital, and it was an eventful time.

Vespasian died in June 79. Earlier in that year there had been a conspiracy of some sort which resulted in the executions of T. Clodius Eprius Marcellus (consul in 62 and 74) and A. Caecina Alienus (consul in 69), two previous supporters of the emperor, the latter one of the victorious commanders of the Civil War. Exactly what was involved and who or what was the target of the plot is unclear, though only Vespasian and Titus can be considered to have been obvious or worthwhile targets. It may not even have been clear to Vespasian, but he was probably already ill and did not wish to leave the plot festering when he died. He had always struck hard when a threat to his dynasty was apprehended.[2]

Titus therefore was able to succeed his father without difficulty. He had been a successful soldier and commander and he might have been expected to go on campaign now that he was emperor. But events intervened. Only two months after his accession, the volcano Vesuvius erupted. It was not a disaster which affected Pompeii and Herculanium and their region alone, but one in which volcanic ash spread over much of the eastern Mediterranean, affecting agricultural production in many areas, for at least one growing season. The episode in the Bay of Naples, however, badly affected the villas and estates of the Roman elite (including Frontinus), so imperial attention was certainly required. Imperial assistance was well-publicized. It was followed, not coincidentally, by an epidemic of some disease.[3] A fire in Rome next year destroyed much of the city, including the temple of Jupiter on the Capitol; the temple was thus burnt for the second time in a dozen years, and the city was badly damaged by a great fire for the third time since 64.[4] Titus responded with governmental generosity, with both cash and tax remissions.

So, whatever Titus might have hoped to do in foreign affairs, the domestic disasters took priority, and soaked up large reserves of imperial resources. There was no interruption to Agricola's aggressions in north Britannia, and the advances made under Vespasian in Germany were held. The construction of a new legionary base for Legio III Augusta at Lambaesis in Numidia, which operated to extend the African frontier south and west at the expense of occasionally hostile local tribes, continued and was completed.[5] The establishment of new *coloniae* at Aventicum in Switzerland and Doclea in Dalmatia continued and were completed.[6] But all these were projects which had been underway under Vespasian. Titus hardly had a chance to develop any policies of his own.

The new legionary base at Lambaesis was another stage in the progressive enclosure of all North Africa within the empire, beginning with Caligula's execution of the last Mauretanian king in 40. Claudius formed two Mauretanian provinces. The civil and military functions held by the governor of Africa were separated, and now Legio III Augusta had finally moved to what proved to be its permanent headquarters, its third move. There had been occasional episodes of violence and conquest in this development, and in all, the process was not dissimilar from the still-continuing expansion of the empire in Britannia, but it was much more successful, at least for a time.[7]

Frontinus in Rome was a senior senator, no doubt involved in the projects of recovery from the various disasters, especially since he owned a villa at Terracina, and probably one at Formiae. His achievements in Britannia were the basis for Agricola's campaigns from 78 onwards, and he would be able to explain to others, including Titus and the Senate, what Agricola was doing, when, and where. It is assumed that he attended the emperor's *consilium*, the group of senior men who advised the emperor

VASIO

Vasio was probably Frontinus' home town. There are major remains of Roman buildings in the town, and this would suggest that Frontinus grew up in a well-run civilized place. It was well inland, and besides being a Roman civitas, it had Celtic inhabitants too.

A street beside the remains of the basilica. (*Adobe Stock*)

The Civic Theatre much restored.

Domitian was the emperor for whom Frontinus did most of his political work, from resigning his praetorship after one day in his favour and mentoring him in Gaul in 70, to his command in Germany and Asia Minor; it is probable he disapproved of the coup in 96 in which Domitian was murdered. (*Ted via Flickr (CC BY-SA 2.0)*)

Arausio (Orange), was at a major road junction, a place travellers passed through on the way from Gaul to Rome: the triumphal arch was a constant reminder of the fact of the Roman conquest. (*Carole Raddato via Wikimedia (CC BY-SA 2.0)*)

SURVEYING

This was the profession Frontinus took up, or was assigned to, after his first military post in the east. He worked, so it seems, mainly in the western provinces, as a surveyor, but it stood him in good stead in his later work in Gaul, Britain, and Germany – and it was the subject of his first extant book.

It is unlikely that Frontinus included illustrations in his books, but, especially in the surveying manual the text cried out for them. They were added at some point between his publishing the book and the creation of the surviving manuscript copy in the fourth century. These are in a section discussing civic layout.

Another manuscript illustration of the surveyor's work, in this case centuriation, the delimitation of plots of land for retiring soldiers, whose pension this was. Land survey of this type was a practice inherited from the Etruscan past. There are visible relics of these layouts in North Africa and Spain, where it is believed Frontinus worked. He will also have seen examples in Narbonensis and Italy.

FOUR LEGIONARY FORTRESSES

Frontinus can be credited with founding the fortress at Mirabeau-sur-Beze, after the suppression of the Lingones uprising in 70. Little remained of the building until it was found in a survey; here are the remains of barrack blocks. (*Carole Raddato via Wikimedia (CC BY-SA 2.0)*)

One of Frontinus' early actions was to found a new legionary fortress at Caerleon in place of the earlier one at Usk. This became Isca Silurum or 'the City of the Legion'; what survives, as at Mirabeau, is the foundations of the barrack blocks. (*Public domain*)

Chester – Deva – was the third fortress founded by Frontinus in the 70s. Strategically placed close to the River Dee estuary, and commanding the road into North Wales, it survives, in its civil version, to this day; above is a model of the military site. (*Łukasz Nurczyński via Wikimedia*)

York – Eboracum – began as a fort for a unit of infantry; Frontinus, having appreciated its situation, refounded it as a legionary fortress, his fourth in the space of perhaps five or six years. This was presumably done on the orders of Vespasian, but it is impressive nevertheless. No other Roman commander can boast of such a record. And York, like Chester, was a permanent foundation. Above is the Multangular Tower, a later addition to the walls. (*Mkooiman via Wikimedia*)

GOVERNOR OF GERMANY

Frontinus' main work in Germany, as governor and assistant to Domitian was to plan a new line of frontier forts, extending the Roman territory to include the area called the Agri Decumates. The most elaborately restored is Saalburg, whose entrance is shown here. (*Adobe Stock*)

Another fort, less elaborately restored, is at Stockstadt, a good example of what remains for many of the Roman forts in Germany, founded on the new boundary decreed by Domitian. (*Carole Raddato via Wikimedia (CC BY-SA 2.0)*)

GOVERNOR OF ASIA

Ephesos was the main governing centre for the province of Asia under the Romans. For Frontinus' governorship there is only the occasional item of evidence, but one may be certain that he spent some time in the library founded some time earlier by Celsus, and recently restored by the Austrian excavators. (*Benh LIEU SONG via Wikimedia*)

An 'administrative quarter' in the southeastern part of the city has been suggested by the Austrian excavators. There is no sign of the governor's palace, but it was probably in this area. Considerable building work was done here in Domitian's reign, including the fountain whose remains are shown here; no doubt Frontinus was involved in the planning. (*Adobe Stock*)

One of the few indications of Frontinus' presence in Asia is the 'Frontinus Arch' at Hierapolis. It gains its name from an inscription by his granddaughter placed on the arch, indicating that he had encouraged the construction. (*Carole Raddato via Wikimedia* (*CC BY-SA 2.0*))

AQUEDUCT MAN

Frontinus' last job in the empire, apart from acting as deputy to Trajan and holding two more consulships, was to take charge of the aqueduct system of Rome. Quite probably one of his recommendations was that a new aqueduct was needed; this became the Aqua Traiana a decade after his death. (*ShockWave2 via Wikimedia*)

on policy and projects.[8] He was probably also in Vespasian's *consilium* in the last year of the emperor's life – the emperor would no doubt wish to hear of his work in person, given his earlier experience of the province, and Titus made no great changes when he inherited, and he scarcely had time to reshape the group to his own wishes.

The New Emperor

Titus died after a short illness on 13 September 81.[9] Rumours that he had been poisoned, or otherwise murdered, usually naming Domitian, surfaced in many guises once Domitian succeeded and became unpopular. They can all be dismissed as fantasies.[10] Titus was only 41 when he died, though that was a reasonable age for a Roman male to reach, even if emperors could expect to last longer, unless assassinated. Any unexplained death of a prominent ruler in the ancient world produced such rumours of poison, partly because medical knowledge was not competent to discern many fatal illnesses. Titus was sincerely mourned by many who appreciated his charm and generosity, and who could then ignore the much fiercer reputation he gained as his father's praetorian prefect.

As Titus was dying, Domitian acted decisively to secure his own accession, visiting the camp of the praetorian guard with the promise of a donative, which was confirmed next day by the Senate, where honours were voted for the dead emperor before Domitian, who by then had the backing of the guard (which he no doubt made clear to the senators), was voted the imperial powers and the title of Augustus. He now had *imperium* (imperial rule) and *tribunician potestatis* (legal authority of a tribune) and the office of *pontifex maximus* (chief priest), and, a little ludicrously for a man of only 30, *pater patriae* (father of his country).[11] The speed of his actions, and their sequence, provides an object lesson in a Roman imperial *coup d'état*, and had clearly been thought through in advance; no doubt Titus will have helped by advising his brother.

In the period between 78 and 81, Frontinus presumably mainly lived in Rome, and was kept busy by the emperors, but this is only assumption, as is the theory which puts him in the successive imperial *consilia* because of his achieved eminence. This is the same uncertainty which envelops so much of his career.

Comes in exercitus Germaniae

Until recently, Frontinus' life between his governorship of Britannia, which ended in 77 or 78, and his taking up of the post of *curator aquarum* (supervisor of the water supply) in 97 has been largely a blank, but there are a couple of notices which have seemed to be quite isolated from anything he was doing. He held the governorship of Asia in 85/86, which is usually taken to be the last post a senator would normally hold. The assumption, if it was considered at all, has been that he was busy writing during much of this intermediary period, or that he was out of favour with Domitian. But there was always a suggestion that he was involved in Domitian's German campaign against the Chatti in 83–85, and two epigraphic notices seemed to support that. But now it is reasonably certain that he was made *comes* (commander) of the emperor with the *Germanicus exercitus* (the army in Germany) in 82 or 83, and held that position until 84. The posts he held between 81 and 86 make it clear that Domitian held him in favour at least in these years. By 86 he was in his late 50s, and was perhaps regarded by the emperor (still in his 30s at the time) as too old.

Frontinus' actual office in Germany is a matter of some speculation (as is so much in his life). The term *comes* is frequently used, but there seems no actual attestation of this in the ancient sources. His name has been inserted – with a question mark attached – as governor of Germania Inferior between 81 and 84, though this is only conjecture.[12] And if this initial date is correct, he was appointed to the post by Titus, who lived on until September of that year. That he accompanied Domitian on his campaign in Germania in 83–85 is, however, attested by the notices he included on the subject in *Stratagems*, and by the existence of two inscriptions locating him in the Rhineland in 84. If he was officially *comes*, he was thus taken on by Domitian while still in office in Germania Inferior; Domitian's German operations were in Germania Superior, which Frontinus was not permitted to enter as governor of Inferior, hence the need to assume his appointment to a superior office.

In fact, the epigraphic notices suggest rather more than that. One is from the legionary base at Vetera in Germania Inferior, the second is from Oppenheim on the upper Rhine south of Mogontiacum, which is in Germania Superior. There is a contradiction here best resolved by assuming his appointment as *comes* to assist Domitian in Superior.

These two notices would certainly imply that he was active over the whole frontier. The association was partly personal, since they had earlier experience of working together in Gaul in 70, and was presumably based also on Frontinus' experience in constructing a frontier out of fortifications designed to hold conquered territory.

The term *comes de exercitus Germaniae* may fit well enough his position with Domitian. There is, in fact, no record of a governor of either of the two German provinces, Inferior or Superior, in office in the years of Domitian's campaign, other than Frontinus in Inferior. In fact the Rhine frontier region had an anomalous position in the empire. The province of Gallia Belgica extended from the North Sea and English Channel to the Rhine, and bordered on Raetia to the southeast, so that the governor of Belgica, located at Durocortum (Reims) was responsible for a very large territory and, in theory, a very large army. At the same time there were other men in authority in the two Germanies, which in effect were the military frontier commands, and their responsibilities were less governmental and more purely military, though they were also to some extent subject to the Belgican governor in certain aspects. Domitian could therefore assume military authority without being governor, and a *comes* under him could operate without disturbing the provincial system too much.[13]

Domitian had evidently come to the conclusion during the reign of his father and his brother that a good deal of work was needed on the imperial frontiers. Vespasian had been active in promoting frontier rectifications in the East and the expansion of the empire in Britannia and elsewhere, and a war was still going on in Britannia when Domitian became emperor, and another in a small way in Germany. Domitian had little direct experience of warfare – his expedition against the Lingones in 70 had ended without fighting, and his father and his brother, not trusting his stability, had kept him out of military commands, but he had evidently come to the realization that he could rely on the experience of such men as Frontinus. As a result, the wars of Domitian as emperor do not seem at all amateurish. Competent commanders were available, and the evidence is that Domitian retained the loyalty of the military men, even if the men in Rome were backbiting and inimical.

Frontinus was one of these men, whether he was loyal to Domitian personally or loyal to the office of emperor, whoever held the post. Domitian had obviously taken note of Frontinus' work with the Lingones in 70, and of his achievements in Britannia, and of his father's approval. The Lingones' and the British conquests were very similar in the way that they were achieved, and compared favourably to those of his successor as governor, Cn. Julius Agricola. In the end, when all these men were dead, Frontinus' work would be seen to be the more permanent.

Essentially, the Roman frontier in mainland Europe, from the North Sea to the Black Sea, was originally a temporary line arrived at as a result of military victories, conquests, defeats, and subsequent neglect, and it had landed on the Rhine and the Danube more because they were clear lines to work with, rather than being sensible frontiers. That part of the frontier in Germany was the result above all of the failure of Augustus and Tiberius to conquer 'free' Germany beyond the Rhine and the Danube fifty and more years before. The frontier line along those rivers had been the line at which the Romans in their acknowledgement of defeat had stopped in their retreat, not the line they had reached in their advance, and had never been intended as their limit. But rivers, superficially easy to recognize as frontier lines, become increasingly inefficient and awkward in that role as time passes. They were as helpful to the enemy as they were to the Romans, being as awkward for the Germans to cross in raids as they were for the Romans in invading Germany. This was hardly the main purpose of the frontier from a Roman point of view. Furthermore, a river dominated and united a geographical region rather than dividing it, and so adopting it as a divider was to lay down a line which separated into two parts an economic territory which long had been united; this is especially the case in the upper Rhine, from Mogontiacum (Mainz) to Basel, where the river flowed through a flat, wide plain. Not only that, but a river is in fact relatively easy to cross, in both directions, by the people who live beside it, and who usually partly live on it and from it, while the people on either side have more in common than people further away. And so it needs as much manpower to guard it as any other line, and perhaps more than most.

Vespasian's Advance

In the case of the frontier in Europe, the line across the continent which the Romans had ended up guarding was particularly inconvenient. For a start, it would be difficult to draw an even longer line across the continent if one tried, and it was configured in such a way that military communications between Gaul – with its eight legions – and the Danube lands of Pannonia and Moesia – ten legions – by using these rivers was much longer than necessary. It must have been obvious from the start, say by AD 20, that to secure control of the great triangle of land between the upper reaches of the two Rivers Rhine, south from Mogontiacum (Mainz), and Danube west of Castra Regina (Regensburg), would be highly useful. On the other hand, frontier adjustments such as were achieved by Vespasian and Domitian could be seen as a confession of failure, in that it presupposed that the line at which Roman expansion had stopped was now permanent and only needed short adjustments. There is evidence that Domitian came to understand this, and made a start on changing it, late in his reign (though he did not know it was late in his reign at the time). The experience of his war in Germany in 83, with the frontier expert Frontinus advising, was part of this educational process.

Vespasian had pushed the line forward at the southern apex of the triangle by establishing a group of forts around Arae Flaviae (Altars of the Flavians) – a significant name – at the headwaters of the Neckar River, but this was only a minor improvement to the frontier line.[14] The advance was commanded by Cn. Pinarius Cornelius Clemens, who gathered a force of five legions, plus auxiliaries, to take control of the apex of the 'triangle'. Clearly this was a commander who wished, like Frontinus, to avoid fighting where possible – hence the overwhelming force he used for the task. A road was organized from Argentorate (Strasbourg) to cut off the long route which ran south of Lake Constance. It was then seen that this was only a minimal improvement, and more would have to be done. Vespasian had many other issues to address, above all holding on to his throne, and it is to his credit that even this advance was made possible. By the time Domitian took the throne, resources were greater and the imperial will could be more concentrated on the particular issue of the Rhine frontier, and the imperial imagination was now more active and more focused.

Vespasian's advance at the southern apex of the 'triangle' had reduced the journey from Mogontiacum to Carnuntum (Vienna) by a relatively small amount, but it had not economized on military manpower. Arae Flaviae (Rottweil) was the site of two forts on either side of the Neckar River, and there were four further forts arranged in a semi-circle to its north; two more forts, perhaps three, existed to the south, evidently along the road from the legionary base at Vindonissa (Windisch), which itself was south of the Danube by a day's march. It would seem that these forts were planted to hold Arae Flaviae, whose name, and the existence there of the dynastic cult, would encourage a strong defence. Their garrisons represented an increase of perhaps three or four auxiliary regiments in the force located in this part of the frontier area, and their presence implies that attacks were feared. (It was a very much reduced version of Frontinus' system in controlling the Silures by his net of roads and forts, but was closer to a more traditional linear frontier system.) It was a high cost for a fairly minor shortening of the journey time and the acquisition of the Arae Flaviae area.

The advance in the apex area between Rhine and Danube was accompanied by a move across the Rhine along the river between Mogontiacum and Argentorate. Several forts have been dated to Vespasian's reign – Gross Gerau, Ladenberg, and Heideberg – along with a new road built along the east bank.[15] A milestone from Offenberg, also on the east bank, in front of Strasbourg, bears the name of Cn. Pinarius Cornelius Clemens, the governor in the early 70s and dated to 74, and the commander of the advance in the south.[16] This was in fact from a district south of the forts, for it provides a context for this activity as well as the advance to Arae Flaviae. In the northern part the advance evidently consisted in the construction of the military road along the east bank, dotted with forts, but not very far in advance of the river. The cluster of forts around Arae Flaviae are linked with this new road as part of the easier passage between Mogontiacum and the Danube forts, though the saving in distance for travellers was not very much.

The Wetterau

To the north of Mogontiacum the line of the frontier turned through two right angles to draw a line around the lowland called the Wetterau, a rich agricultural area east of the Rhine, and there a line of forts was rebuilt in Vespasian's time. The forts had been damaged or destroyed in the Civil War by an invasion of the Chatti, the tribe of the lands to the north. These forts were also linked to a road, which drove through the centre of the Wetterau lowland northeastwards, the forts being on the Taunus Hills to the north. In this case the road was also recovered and repaired. There were four or five forts along this road – Hofheim, Heddenberg, Okaben, Freidburg – and this operation was aimed to recover the lands along the Main and Kidda Rivers. The road and its forts actually consisted of a long, 50km salient thrust into the German lands between the Main River to the south and the Taunus Hills to the north.[17] One cannot believe that the Roman commanders were at all happy about this salient, on low ground overlooked by forested hills, and the operation to control the road can only have been conducted with the intention of deliberately recovering and restoring the lost forts, both on the road and on the hills, and of expanding Roman control on either side of the line of the road.

The Roman high command had therefore located the Wetterau as the essential point at which control was required. This was, besides being strategically vital, also a rich agricultural area. Control of this area would allow the wide Rhine valley to the south to fall under Roman control relatively easily – it was partly already occupied by Pinarius' operations. The Taunus Hills and the Wetterau Valley were thus the hinge of a door. Control of that area would allow the whole line of the frontier to the south to swing forward eastwards. This had evidently only been understood as a result of the earlier advance and recovery, and thus in Domitian's early years. The Rhine Valley, another agriculturally productive area, the Black Forest, which, apart from wood, was also productive of various forest products such as wax, furs, leather, animals, and so on, and the territory east of the forest would thus come under control much more easily. The line of the frontier would be shorter with the domination of the whole triangle and not just its apex, and the whole region, the line being shorter, would require a smaller garrison, while the journey from Mogontiacum to Carnuntum would be shortened by more than 200 kilometres – a week's march, if not more.[18] But the essential element in the whole scheme was to control the Wetterau with a substantial garrison, and along with that it would be necessary to control and garrison the line of the Taunus Hills to the north. The Chatti faced the lower Rhine frontier and the Wetterau; south of both, the Hermanduri occupied the quadrilateral area formed by the upper Rhine, the Danube, and the hills of western Bohemia. The Chatti had long been Roman enemies, but the Hermanduri were among the most favoured of the German tribes; according to Tacitus they had the right to trade inside the empire still bearing their arms.[19]

Domitian's War

Domitian attended to matters in Rome for his first months as emperor, including the re-dedication of the temple of Jupiter Optimus Maximus on the Capitol, burnt in the fire in Titus' reign two years before. Then he travelled to Gaul, giving out that he intended to supervise the provincial census.[20] His aim in fact was to wage war in Germany, and it is worth considering his need to exercise this subterfuge; it suggests that the Germans across the Rhine were well informed about events in Gaul – the Hermunduri were not the only Germans who could enter the empire to trade – and perhaps in Italy. The movements of the emperor were apparently swiftly transmitted to the tribes outside the empire, and also that the emperor and his military men knew this; presumably the Germans were alert to the possibility that the new emperor would exercise his new power at their expense. They must have realized the propensity of newly installed emperors to validate their new power by a successful war. It also implies that the German enemy about to be attacked was seen to be formidable, and that subterfuge would confer a Roman advantage. The campaign by Pinarius, using five legions against only a relatively small section of the land to be acquired, was a lesson.

Why Domitian chose to work first on the German frontier is unclear. Several other frontiers also called for his attention, but certain details might provide a possible explanation. One is the earlier activity of Vespasian's small advances in the 'triangle', where the advance may now have been seen as inadequate. Vespasian had also sent a campaign to retake the Wetterau, lost during the Civil War. To most soldiers with experience of the German frontier these advances were useful but minimal, and represented still unfinished business, a factor which both Titus and Domitian no doubt understood. It was therefore a dynastic priority, an incomplete imperial task. A third element in Domitian's choice of this first task was that Frontinus was available to provide advice. Colleagues in Gaul a dozen years before, they had lived in or near each other in the city of Rome much of the time since, though Frontinus had, so it seems, been on better terms with Titus than Domitian was, but being emollient was perhaps one of Frontinus' qualities, just as he was clearly diplomatically capable.[21] It is clear the two men were friends, and it would not be a surprise if Frontinus, understanding that after Vespasian's death

Domitian was the heir apparent, should be assiduous in maintaining good relations with him.

That Domitian had chosen to attend to this part of the frontier first may be because it was clearly an unfinished task which had left several Roman forts exposed to sudden attack. The activity was clearly misunderstood, perhaps deliberately, in Rome, and Tacitus set the tone by ridiculing and belittling what was done, while Suetonius claimed that it was unnecessary.[22] Tacitus in particular should have understood, and probably did, what was being done, but allowed his personal anti-Domitian feelings to override his historical judgment, not for the first or last time.

Domitian used the four legions stationed in the upper Rhine region. Their new distribution had been another of Vespasian's measures. He broke up the system by which the eight legions on the Rhine were grouped in pairs, judging that this was dangerous from an internal security consideration – as had certainly been demonstrated in the Civil War – and that spreading them along the frontier line singly was more efficient in terms of defence, since the legions were now to be located to defend the frontier without having to march long distances to meet the invader; the assumption clearly was that attacks would come in smaller numbers than originally expected; in addition, spacing the legions out allowed two to cooperate to attack an invader from different directions. The new deployment was for more than internal security reasons.

Domitian brought I Adiutrix and XIV Gemina from Mogontiacum (the only double camp left), XI Claudia from Vindonissa and VIII Augusta from Agentorate, and added vexillations from the four British legions, a requisition in effect of another full legion. It was this which stopped Agricola's campaign; in any case it had clearly reached its limit after six years; in addition, an unknown number of *auxilia* were used, some brought in from Britannia. The emperor is said to have had a total of 30,000 to 35,000 troops on the campaign and in total he probably used a comparable force to that employed by Pinarius in the south ten years before.[23] The aim, as in any sensible campaign, was to succeed without having to do too much fighting by using overwhelming numbers, just as Frontinus had done with the Silures; but if it did come to fighting, the fight could be won easily because of those same numbers.

It must have taken some time to assemble these forces, especially bringing the troops from Britannia to the region, which may have been the object of Domitian's Gallic census subterfuge. The date of the start of the war has been placed at both 82 and 83; if the story in Frontinus of Domitian moving suddenly from his faux-census directly to a sudden attack is correct, he either spent a long time dawdling in Gaul, or the surprise was unsuccessful. It is surely unbelievable that he could gather 30,000 troops to invade the Wetterau and not expect them to be noticed and the victims alerted. This is especially so given that the Romans understood clearly enough that the Germans had good information of events in the empire – else, why the subterfuge? We may conclude that the surprise did not occur, though there was probably a deliberate misdirection as to the target.

However the preparations were disguised, the main fighting took place in 83, presumably in the Wetterau region and the Taunus Hills. An anecdote in Frontinus' *Strategems* describes how Domitian at one point ordered the cavalry to dismount and then pursue the fleeing enemy through the forest in which they had taken refuge.[24] So the assumption must be that the fighting which took place was relatively small-scale, guerrilla and ambush warfare, which is not surprising given the large legionary strength, which was almost guaranteed to defeat a barbarian army if it stood to fight.

The New Frontier

It was one thing to defeat the enemy – and this was certainly accomplished – but another to secure the contested territory in such a way that it was safe for the inhabitants. (Domitian was careful to ensure that those inhabitants, probably people of the Mattiaci tribe, did not suffer loss when his men built forts on their land – can one detect the advice of Frontinus here?)[25] A line had to be selected which would mark the boundary. (This was not to be a frontier, which was a wide space, with a fortification having a no-man's-land before it, of variable width, the whole space separating Roman from barbarian territory; instead it was to be a boundary, a line on the ground, which separated Roman territory from non-Roman along the line of forts. This would be where Frontinus' expertise and experience in Britannia would be especially valuable.

The watershed of the Taunus Hills was the base line, and along that line was placed a series of well-situated forts, depending on the terrain.

They were placed at irregular distances apart, but were sited to give the garrison forces command and visibility forward. The new line extended southeast from close to Antunnacum (Andernach) on the Rhine to the main Taurus line overlooking the Wetterau, in a line gradually trending away from the river. This brought a narrow section of the east bank into the empire. This was a narrow area only 30 kilometres long and 10 or fewer kilometres wide and in that short distance four forts were built.

From there the line continued southeast from the crossing of the Ems River which flowed down from the Taunus, but for a distance of about 40 kilometres there were just two forts. At Kemel the line turned through 90 degrees to follow the summit line northeastwards for about 80 kilometres; on that line there were five forts, and between them were watchtowers and signal posts, with extensive views to the north and east. This was the Wetterau line, and within the lowland area thus defended there were six more forts, to add to the seven already in place. These had been recovered (and presumably repaired and reoccupied) by the forces in Vespasian's time.

This was the main line which had to be defended against attacks by the Chatti, whose land was to the north, and its density of forts was greater than elsewhere along the frontier for that reason. It will be seen, even in this summary account, that the forts had been positioned with care and individually, taking into account distances, views, and the local topography. At the northernmost part of the Taunus line, a fort at Inheiden, the line turned from northeast to run almost due south, and continued in that direction until the fort at Grinario (Kongen), on the Neckar river where a Roman military fort in stone, replacing one of earth and timber, survives. For part of the way this line followed the Main River, then there was a dense line of forts – nine in only 50 kilometres – which took it to the Neckar River, and for 100 kilometres that river was lined with forts at regular distances apart, with just seven along the river line.

The variety of distances and fort densities along this line argues that a detailed survey had been taken before the work began, and that competent commanders and surveyors with an eye to the landscape and some knowledge of the capabilities of the German enemy had prepared the way, selecting the sites for the forts well in advance. Some of these qualities clearly attached to Frontinus. He may not have had serious earlier experience of German warfare, but he had an eye for ground and experience in surveying, while his experience among the Silures and the Brigantes was clearly directly relevant in the siting of forts. He would hardly have done the detailed surveying, but someone with exactly that experience determined the distances and situations of the forts, and took account of the variation in the needs of the defences; it seems very likely that Frontinus, using local Roman knowledge and experience, was deeply involved. It is hardly likely he actually did the work himself, but he was clearly capable of supervising the surveyors, something Domitian could not do.

One may contrast this careful siting with regard to distances and situations, with the mechanical layout of other Roman defence systems, notably the almost mathematical spacing of the forts and milecastles along Hadrian's Wall. In some cases the forts on the Wall pay no attention whatsoever to the landscape, and the Wall is driven along with only occasional reference to the best line. This would seem to have been according to decisions made at headquarters, perhaps on paper, and then built by the hapless infantry, with orders not to improvise, though changes during the building, clearly did take place, presumably after problems held up the work. Given the layout of the new German frontier line and its attention to local needs, it seems not unreasonable to conclude that, if Frontinus did not decide the layout in detail himself, he at least was active in giving advice.

Frontinus was *comes* of the *Germanus exercitus* in 83 and 84. The epigraphic notice left by him at Vetera was to give thanks to the gods for his recovery from illness; the other, at Oppenheim, was dedicated by his daughter Julia Frontina, so he presumably had his family with him on this tour of duty. (We have no information on his wife, and he had, it seems, two daughters.) He completed that tour in 84, the year before the Chattan War officially ended, in 85, though the fighting was mainly over by the time he left. (Possibly his illness ended his usefulness to Domitian.) He had clearly had wider responsibilities than simply advising the emperor, who was not concerned with Germania Inferior at the time (the *limes* which were being moved and reconstructed were entirely in Superior). The building of the forts and watchtowers and the signal stations would probably be completed by 85 or soon after. The forts began as a rampart and ditch, with temporary wooden buildings, the men probably living in leather tents within the ramparted area. The buildings would be constructed of wood in the first instance and gradually replaced in stone as they became clearly permanent. (This, for example, was clearly the process at Grinario, as it had been in Wales.) The watchtowers and the signal posts were also originally of wood all along the line, and if the wood was carefully selected the initial building would last for at least a generation – it was usual to replace the first wooden forts in stone, or to abandon them. The whole series of forts and so on were being built in an ancient forest, of course, with the materials for building acquired by felling trees. This in turn would both clear a field of fire around the new fort and provide a cleared view of the territory in front of the line, and supply the means for building the forts. The soldiers knew how to do this.

Domitian moved on in 85 to attend to a new crisis on the Danube. (He returned to fight another Chattan war in 88/89.) The frontier in Germany had been advanced from the Rhine to the Neckar, and on the Danube from that river forward and northwards for perhaps 20 or 30 kilometres. On the Rhine front the newly enclosed area was rather larger, 60 kilometres wide in the advance from the Rhine to the Main, and 100 from the Rhine to the headwaters of the Neckar. This was a large enough advance to call for a provincial reorganization, since if this extra territory was added to the old province (Gallia Belgica) it would produce a province of an even more unwieldy size. The Second Chattan War persuaded Domitian to make the necessary changes, and elements of the provincial reorganization were already present in the military commands. The whole of the German frontier area was now separated off from the Belgica province, and divided into two new provinces, Germania Inferior, from Bonna to the North Sea, and Germania Superior from Bonna to the Raetian border, names which, of course, already existed – the change was not profound. (This delayed revision of the provincial organization might explain why Frontinus' inscriptional evidence suggests he was operating in both Inferior and Superior.)

Each of these new provinces, therefore, had a stretch of the frontier to guard, and at the same time acquired some territory stretching well into the interior of Gaul. For some reason the boundary of Germania Superior was drawn to include a bulge of territory in Gaul which included, curiously enough, the land of the Lingones; one wonders if Domitian and Frontinus conspired to do this in memory of their original meeting. Certainly the new boundaries did not make much geographical sense, though by attaching the land of the Lingones to Germania the new province gained control of a strategic area, which in turn suggests that one of the reasons for the new provincial organization was to ensure internal control as well as that of the new frontier line. This was all arranged after the Second Chattan War in about 90. One result was that the garrisons of both provinces could be reduced, though since this was to meet a crisis on the Danube, it was not necessarily intended to be a permanent reduction; it does suggest, however, that Domitian's second war was regarded as decisive, and in fact the settlement which he reached with the Chatti ended the forward imperial movement for the next century and a half.

From the central government's point of view these new provinces also partly solved the problem of the heavy concentration of forces along the Rhine by the reduction which followed. Each of the new provinces included the legionary bases for four legions, reduced to three in 90, whereas earlier the *Germania exercitus* had included eight legions, plus of course the auxiliary regiments. The lesson of the uprising on the German frontier in the Civil War was that, first, double legionary camps were dangerous, a problem largely addressed by Vespasian, and enhanced to Domitian by the attempted coup by Saturninus in 89, which took place in the last of the double camps – this was broken up immediately afterwards. Second, it was seen that large and possibly idle provincial garrisons were equally dangerous, and this was addressed by Domitian's division of the military forces between his new provinces; the concentration among *auxilia* recruited from the same tribe could easily be dealt with by moving them about; it was normal, of course, for these units to serve away from their homelands.

The land taken in across the Rhine was included in Germania Superior and acquired its own label, the Agri Decumates, supposedly meaning 'ten counties' or something similar. The frontier line established along the Neckar was pushed further forward by a few kilometres about fifty years later, to form the so-called Antonine Limes, aligned in a mathematically straight line for 100 kilometres; as such it was inevitably a weak defence, ignoring as it did the land along which it was lain; the empire was relying, it seems, on the goodwill of the allied tribe occupying Bavaria, the Hermunduri. It was, of course, a mistake in the long term.

The net result of Domitian's German campaign was not just the acquisition of more territory for the empire (and a solution to the problem of the over-concentration of Roman military power in the area). The real gain was to establish a much better frontier defence line, since that in itself had helpful consequences (a solution destroyed by the Antonine Limes line). Control of the Wetterau allowed the Roman forces to dominate a much larger frontier area beyond the actual frontier line, to north and east, and permitted the advance of the line eastwards from the upper Rhine to the Neckar and beyond, and allowed the reduction of the frontier garrison. The fact that the frontier in Germany continued to exist for two centuries in a condition of general peace is another result of the success of Domitian's campaign. The heavy concentration of forces in the forts of the Wetterau was offset by the saving of troops along the Rhine and the Danube sections of the frontier, and allowed the move of troops from the Rhine line forward. It also allowed the temporary removal of legions and *auxilia* from Germany to deal with crises on the Danube and in the East, just as the ending of Agricola's campaign in Scotland permitted the removal of the vexillations of the British legions which Domitian used in the Wetterau campaign, and of a full legion later. A generation later, the eight legions of Vespasian's reign had been reduced to four, and the *auxilia* by half also, a saving of perhaps 20,000 men or more, to be deployed elsewhere.[26]

How much Frontinus had to do with all this is, of course, uncertain, since he is never mentioned in the very brief and inadequate written sources for Domitian's campaign. 'No record exists in ancient literature of this truly gigantic work of Roman engineering', as one informative book on the *limes* puts it.[27] However, the fact that he is known to have accompanied the emperor must imply that he was, in effect, Domitian's second-in-command, or perhaps his chief of staff, a position which would be the more effective in the light of his own tact and the evident good relationship between the two men. His experiences in Wales, in surveying, and in command of a four-legion force in Britannia was enough to allow the emperor to trust him; he was clearly loyal to the dynasty and this was also reassuring. And he had acquired further material for his books.

Chapter 8

Asia

Frontinus became governor of the province of Asia in 85, a term of office which would last a year.¹ This was a post to which many senators of consular rank acceded simply by surviving, and winning a ballot among the senators. It was held to be the pinnacle of a senator's career and it was limited to a single year, rather than the usual three years, so as to permit as many senators to share the honour as possible. An equivalent governorship was that of Africa, again held for one year and held at the end of a political career. Or, to put it another way, these governorships normally came to men who were thoroughly experienced in governing a province (though this was not a requirement, having been a consul was). Both Africa (which Vespasian had governed in the 50s), and Asia were unarmed provinces: they were, in other words, honorary positions, even sinecures.

The number of men who wished to hold such posts was increasing as the number of consuls who were eligible increased. In Domitian's reign the term of office for a consul was generally three or four months, except for emperors, who usually held the ordinary consulship for just two weeks, and were then succeeded by a suffect. In any one year, therefore, there could be six or eight consuls, sometimes even more (plus the emperor at times). And all these men could aspire to Africa or Asia. But it was often the case that Domitian would pack the list of consuls with extra men, whom he wished to reward, so that terms were reduced even more. Some men clearly died before they could reach the Asian or African governorships, while some would not wish to take up the post – it was a task, as in every Roman governmental post, which could be refused. So, as the number of qualified men increased, the length of time which passed between consulship and governorship steadily increased also. Under Augustus the gap had been five or six years; under Nero it was eight rising to ten; under Vespasian it varied but was generally ten; with Domitian it rose to fifteen years. Frontinus achieved the post only twelve years after his consulship, a clear indication of imperial and senatorial favour.

This expansion was, of course, the reason the governorship was only for one year. No doubt the emperor's preferences carried weight, but the Asian governorship was for a senatorial province, to which governors were allocated by lot; this would suggest that Frontinus was able to enter the lot as soon as he came back from his service in Germany. We have no idea who his competitors were, but he does seem to have received the post a few years earlier than he might have expected. No doubt the emperor's wishes were made known. He also took up the post in Asia only a year after returning from Germany, an unusually short period, which again argues imperial favour, though a certain degree of appreciation from the senators must be assumed also. This was all fairly conspicuous. So an early posting to Asia would seem to have been in the nature of a reward for his assistance in the First Chattan War.

The area he was to govern was a substantial part of Asia Minor, stretching from the Aegean coast inland for 500 kilometres, and from the Propontis in the north to the border of Lykia in the south, more or less the old kingdom of the Attalid dynasty, which had been willed to the Roman Republic in the 130s BC. It was a very large province, and one which was, like Africa, effectively ungarrisoned; this is not to say there were no troops there, though they operated as a police force rather than a defence force, and he had his own governor's guard. It was also one of the wealthiest regions of the ancient world, one of the richest parts of the Roman Empire, and therefore a source of much tax revenue – peace and calm here would be requisite. In this large area there was a large number of ancient and proud cities, each of which had their particular priorities. Some issued their own coins still – Smyrna issued some commemorating Frontinus' time in office.[2]

Certainly it was a region by now pre-eminent, economically and culturally, in the Greek world, and for a governor who spoke Greek and had intellectual credentials it will have been a rare treat to spend a year there; Ephesos, for example, was a major intellectual centre by this time. Some eminent Romans retired there. At the same time, the governor had a great deal of work to do in Asia, keeping the peace and dispensing justice over a large area above all; inter-city disputes were not rare; some governors, however, did nothing but enjoy themselves, leaving the burden of active governing to their subordinates and magistrates in the cities. From what we know of Frontinus this is unlikely to have been his reaction.

For a vigorous and active governor a year in Asia could require a great deal of strenuous activity. If he insisted on assuming the burden of the work, as Frontinus surely would, there would be much travelling. He was supposed (though not all governors did this) to attend the assizes in each *conventus* centre in the province, acting as a court of appeal for disputed local issues. In Asia there were thirteen *conventus* cities, several times the usual number. This would take him to Kyzikos on the shores of the Propontis, south to Halikarnassos on the south coast, and inland to Apameia Kelainai close to the border with Phrygia in the interior – not to mention the many cities along the Aegean coast. This would be a heavy burden, and might take him the whole year. It seems unlikely that he would have time to visit them all.

It is known, however, that Frontinus went to Laodikeia-ad-Lykon and to Hierapolis, deep in the interior. At Hierapolis his name is recorded in a bilingual inscription on an arch in the city.[3] A little further east from these two cities is Apameia Kelainai, where his grand-daughter Sosia Polla (whose husband was Q. Pompeius Falco, also a notable governor of Britannia and Asia – see Chapter 14) in another inscription produced some decades later, mentioned that he had benefited the city while he was governor, an unusually long local memory for a governor who was present for only one year and whose visit to the city must have been brief.[4] There are traces of him elsewhere, in the coins from Smyrna and in an inscription from Laodikeia-ad-Lykos,[5] and in an honorary inscription at Kos.[6] He clearly made his mark while there.

The Asian governor lived, when not travelling, at Ephesos, where there was a *praetorium*, or governor's palace, large enough to house the governor, his family, his staff, and his guards. He had as his staff a quaestor, who handled financial and other matters, and three legates, who could be dispatched to those *conventus* cities which the governor could not get to. These legates would be the governor's own choice; Frontinus had no sons, so there would probably be some competition for the posts. He probably had his daughter with him – she was in Germany with him, so she would no doubt go to Asia as well. One legate remained at Ephesos when the governor went on his travels, while the other two (or three if the governor stayed in Ephesos) could be dispatched to other parts of the province.

They might be able to deal with some local cases, and perhaps collect the tax receipts at the several cities, or maybe accept them from the local city governments and forward them to the quaestor. The governor's guard lived in barracks at the *praetorium*. This would be a prized assignment for all the governor's staff. They would be well fed, in comfortable quarters, have access to the baths in the *praetorium*, but spend some of their time in one of the great cities of the empire, and would only go out into the province when the governor travelled – and even then they would be in comfortable quarters when he halted. Small detachments of guards travelled with the legates also.

The governor might delegate some tasks to his legates, but the responsibility for everything lay with him, and at the end of his tour of duty he would have to present a report to the Senate and probably to the emperor. (In an analogous case, Pliny the Younger in the senatorial province of Bithynia-and-Pontus, referred his difficulties directly to the emperor.[7]) The quaestor may have worked at the finances, but the governor had to check his work; the legates might visit other places, but if they made decisions, the governor needed to be told and to ratify them; any which were too difficult or too controversial for the legate, who might be only a young man in his twenties, would end up with the governor. Maintaining public order was the governor's task, and that would include ensuring that the soldiers in the province did not oppress the population. A number of cases of this are known in Asia, particularly in the villages not far from the location of garrisons.[8] There were no doubt more.

Above all, the governor had responsibility for administering justice. Capital cases were automatically his, for the empire reserved to itself the right of execution. Relations between cities in the province had also to be supervised. By Frontinus' time relations between neighbouring cities were becoming steadily more unpleasant and acrimonious, and while to the Roman government this was not unwelcome, since it diverted local energies, it might in a crisis break out into violence. In the absence of any other conflicts in the province, and the likely ferocious reaction to cities fighting each other, cities had developed their own new sets of disputes, which might be about their boundaries, competitions for honours, competitive building of temples or theatres or baths. This was an activity very likely to exhaust any monetary resources the city had, especially if no provision for post-build maintenance had been made. (Pliny the

Younger's experience in the neighbouring province of Bithynia-and-Pontus thirty years later may be excessive, but he faced just these sorts of problems.)[9] The cities were in effect autonomous members of the empire, but being in the empire, and so subject to no external threat, some had a tendency to irresponsibility. The age-old institution of annual elections almost guaranteed this. As a result, the governors found they had to take more decisions which really should have been left to the cities – but the governors were also annual officials; disputes, like that in Africa between Ammaedara and Thysdrus, which Frontinus knew of from his surveying experience in Africa, might in such circumstances easily last half a century.

Constraint on the governor's practices and decisions was exercised in several ways. There was, first of all, a *lex provincia*, which was imposed by the Senate originally, and which would need to be consulted in awkward cases; this provincial constitution was individual to the province, and was often subtly different from other provinces; an experienced governor would need to show he was not applying his memories of other provinces to any new one. There was also the governor's own edict, published when he took up the office, stating the methods and principles he would apply.[10] And, more nebulously, perhaps the greatest constraint of all, there were the local provincial customs and practices, for it was normal for a governor to attend carefully to local traditions; ignoring such traditions might well spark a riot.[11]

Then there was the governor's own integrity. Administering justice was always a tricky business, and the governor only took on the important or especially awkward cases; such cases were very likely to involve prominent citizens, or whole cities, and the temptation to extend bribes to a governor to secure a favourable verdict was always present, and inevitably some governors would accept. The governor's edict might not be enough to stop either offer or acceptance.

Frontinus in his writings habitually emphasizes the need for men in authority in the empire – as surveyor, general, governor, administrator – to maintain the public good and reject or punish all sorts of wrongdoing, a matter which would include soliciting or accepting bribes. Unless he can be accused of hypocrisy throughout his life, his time as governor was likely free of corruption, at least on his part. (But this did not necessarily mean that his legates, quaestor, servants, or guards were as scrupulous; opportunities in a rich province were no doubt numerous and welcome.)

Frontinus went to Asia when the province had largely recovered from the extensive and impoverishing damage inflicted on it by the combatants in the civil wars which had brought an end to the Roman Republic a century before. It had taken a long time for that recovery to arrive, at least half a century, and longer in the most badly damaged places. The Civil War of 69 had barely affected Asia.

Abuses of the tax regime which had caused so much misery had largely been reined in. The *publicani*, whose demands and practices had provoked so many complaints, had been removed from the direct operation of the tax collection system by Julius Caesar, and gradually responsibilities for the collection had landed with the cities, whose administration became the imperial tax collectors. This did not necessarily mean that there was no oppression or corruption, but it was obviously on a smaller scale. The temptation clearly was for the local ruling oligarchy to shift the main tax burden onto the poor, away from themselves, a factor likely to operate when the city found itself in debt, or facing large expenditures. This, however, will have been well understood locally. The collectors were subject to local pressures, and to a certain degree of governmental supervision. The money collected went to the quaestor, and if he was honest and impartial (and supervised closely enough by the governor) accuracy was likely, and so oppression could be prevented, or at least reduced.

The *publicani* still operated in collecting customs duties at ports and borders, but merchants were a vociferous group, and had relatively easy access to the governor, since they were important and often rich, so any excessive demands would be complained about; the customs rates were published and could be consulted. It was hardly a just system, but unless the Roman Empire was to become an ever-vaster bureaucracy, it was probably the best that could be devised. But a great deal lay on the governor.

On the other hand, these administrative improvements had only a slow effect, and they depended heavily on the determination of governors to be honest, and in Asia the very limited time the governors were in post, and the amount of work they had to do, were serious hindrances to implementing any changes. So, despite this, it seems clear that the provincials were still wary of the imperial system and its administrators. Roman citizenship was not taken up outside the wealthiest classes. Many in the East who were Roman citizens were descended from men who had arrived in the region as citizens, being retired soldiers from the armies of the Republican civil wars, who were given land in a *colonia*, which was often a Greek city originally.

Roman citizenship was not a status many Greeks aspired to. In terms of participation in Roman political affairs, there was even less interest. In the century since Augustus achieved imperial control, only three men from the Asian province had achieved political office in Rome, and all three did so in Nero's reign, when the emperor's pro-Greek policies no doubt encouraged participation. This expanded, however, under the Flavian emperors, partly because Vespasian had depended to some extent on Eastern support in his bid for power. Considering the wealth of the province, though, the fact that only a dozen or so men reached the Senate in the quarter-century of the Flavian emperors implies a certain continuing reluctance. There was a greater willingness amongst the descendants of the Italian military colonists, who were mainly located further east in the *coloniae* of central Asia Minor. Becoming a citizen, and launching on a political career was, of course, a project limited to the wealthy; Trajan's requirement that senators should own land in Italy was another obstacle, though this probably soon lapsed;[12] so was the slow ascent through the *cursus honorem*, during which it could take twenty years to reach consul, which post would be held for perhaps three months. Unless one wished to govern provinces the effort may not have seemed worthwhile.

One of the men who had reached the Senate from Asia was from the island of Lesbos (which was included in the Asia province), and had been given Roman citizenship by Pompey the Great; a descendant of his re-entered the political stakes in Trajan's reign. T. Julius Montanus from Alexandria Troas climbed through the *cursus* process from Nero's time, and became consul in 81. From the same city, Sex. Quinctilius Valerius Maximus began his own climb under Nerva, and founded a political family which produced consuls until 180. Alexandria Troas was a Greek town which had been reconstituted as a Roman *colonia* under Augustus, and both of these men will have been of Italian origin, probably retired soldiers who brought their Roman citizenship, and their accumulated loot and retirement pay with them to the East. It was Ephesos, however, which produced the greatest number of Roman senators of any Asian city, but since it was not a Roman *colonia*, it did not begin to send men into Roman politics until Hadrian's reign.

The number of Roman citizens from Ephesos could well have increased because of the presence of the governors. Considering the whole list of Asians in Roman politics, which covers the period from Augustus' reign to the mid-third century, it is clear that most men who took part in Roman politics came from a very restricted number of families, again mainly of Italian origin, to whom political participation was both natural and a useful defensive gesture against local prejudice. The practice of seeking office – one had to go to Rome for entry into the system and start at the bottom and it was very expensive – did not seriously spread, though it continued to exist for local offices.[13]

When Frontinus was governor, therefore, he went to a province where there were relatively few Roman citizens and which had produced only a very few men who had entered on a Roman political career. On the other hand, there was a vigorous local political life in the cities, largely centred on holding civic offices and religious offices, and another centred on holding the priesthoods at the major temples or offices such as Asiarch, and there was also the competition between cities. As with Roman political and religious offices, civic posts were in effect open only to the rich, given that they had to finance the positions themselves and were expected to be generous while in office; in addition, there was a local pressure to participate in the cult of the emperors, and it was exactly in *Asia provincia* that the greatest concentration of altars and temples of the cult existed. They might not pursue Roman political office, but involvement in the imperial cult could ward off imperially produced disasters and displeasure.[14] There were other festivals associated with the cult and with temples of the more traditional type, with games and contests and races in the Greek, rather than Roman gladiatorial, style. And economically, the costs helped reduce economic disparity amongst the population.

The city of Aphrodisias has produced a substantial quantity of inscriptions running in date from the first century BC to the third century AD, in which are recorded the names of a number of Roman citizens and Roman officials; they are mainly letters to and from emperors, or triumvirs in the late Republic. Their survival is somewhat haphazard, depending on survival, recording, and the activities of the city – there are none, for example, between Augustus and Trajan, but many in the first half of the third century. Frontinus is not mentioned, but several governors have documents recorded, including one of his predecessors, the poet Silius Italicus, who had been governor of Asia a decade or so before him. This would suggest that there were other records of the first and second centuries which were not inscribed, or have not otherwise survived. But the majority of the records are of local activities and local personalities. The empire was acknowledged, it seems, when necessary, and often in the most extravagant terms – so extravagant that the words were transparently meaningless. The city was in fact mainly absorbed in its own affairs; the empire and its government were much less important.[15]

The Flavian emperors encouraged the promotion of Greeks in the Roman political system, though this took some time to be effective. It had been preceded by the philhellene Emperor Nero in the pre-Civil War period. The Flavians were less obvious in their encouragement, but did not stop it; Vespasian knew he had received significant help from Asian provinces in the Civil War of 69. This is not because he was a Hellene, but probably because the alternatives – Galba, Otho, Vitellius – were less than welcome in the East. The encouragement had therefore been imperial practice for a quarter of a century when Frontinus became governor, and it is reasonable to suppose its continuation was part of the instructions he had been given by Domitian before leaving Rome. The destruction of the 'Augustan Aristocracy' at imperial hands and in civil warfare left openings for men of talent and wealth to reach imperial offices in the same way as was happening in other provinces – Spain and Narbonensis first, and some from Africa, began producing numbers of senators, a phenomenon well remembered amongst historians.[16] It is hardly possible to detect Frontinus' own work in this area in the short period of his authority, but it may be relevant to note that he had begun his career as an *eques*. This may have made him more sympathetic to the policy than was the usual run of super-aristocratic senators, many of whom were absorbed in their own affairs. There are certainly a good sprinkling of Flavii, men who received Roman citizenship at the hands of a Flavian emperor, among the future Asian senators, though many of them did not reach the higher ranks until the third century – but to go from Roman citizen to praetor or consul in a century was no mean achievement, arguing as it does a consistent family drive to succeed. (Records of men who had been praetor are much fewer than those reaching the consulship; they could have been many more than are recorded, and most of them would be provincials.)

It is also not irrelevant to the local attitude to being part of the Roman Empire that exactly in the period of Frontinus' presence, the local intellectual world of Greece and the Greek East was in the process of revived activity. This is the period known to modern historians as the 'Second Sophistic', and included such important authors as Plutarch, Dio Chrysostom of Prusa, and through to Cassius Dio. One of the more unusual developments was the production of novels, of which it seems that Asia was now a major source, though not the only one. The Emperor Nero's pro-Hellenism has been instanced as a prime mover in this, but later emperors did nothing to damage it, and it had probably begun as early as Augustus' time, when the return of peace left room for intellectual activity once more.

The number of novels to be counted is not great, but Chariton was from Aphrodisias (*Chaereas and Callirhoe*), as was Antonius Diogenes, another novelist. These two were contemporaries of Frontinus and of each other in the late first century AD. (The genre had, of course, developed in the Hellenistic period, but was not valued highly enough later to provoke much preservation).[17] It may be pointed out, however, that this was just the time when St John was composing his book of *Revelation* on the island of Patmos, off the Asian coast, and this is clearly a form of novel. (Bowersock connects the development of novel plots with the fantastic story of supposed cannibalism and resurrection emanating from Palestine earlier in the century.)

The genre continued in popularity into the third century and it produced some near masterpieces, often set in past times or exotic countries, to the occasional confusion of later historians. Frontinus was in Asia in the midst of this intellectual revival, and as a man of curiosity and intellect he will certainly not have missed what was going on. (Aphrodisias is close to Laodikeia-ad-Lykon and to Hierapolis, both cities which he certainly visited and was generous to.) Novels may not have been to his personal taste, as his own work suggests, but the production of history certainly was.[18] He was interested in 'Homeric tactics', and may already have written his book on the subject; the *Iliad* and the *Odyssey* were clearly fictional, and perhaps he understood this. Troy/Ilion was in his province (next door to Alexandria Troas); one wonders if he visited the site; if he travelled overland to and from Italy he would pass it.

The general attitude of popular political indifference to the empire in Asia, albeit that it was clearly slowly changing under imperial encouragement and presence, particularly from the Flavians, was clearly a problem for the empire, or at least should have been. One result might be that a Roman governor could be encouraged into harsh measures because of the unnerving prospect of ruling so many indifferent people. Another possibility was that the attitude might lay the province open to dissidents. Nero's popularity in the Greek world might have been an early trigger which began to encourage political participation in the Roman system among the wealthy; it could also be seen that the scarceness of that participation (only three senators by AD 80), could provide an opportunity for anti-Roman sentiment to grow.

There had been an attempt in 69 to persuade political dissidents in the empire to take advantage of the confusion of the Civil War. A man, whose name is unknown, claimed to be the still-living Nero, and looked for support for his 'restoration'. He made no progress and, amid all the events of the time, his claim had little or no impact on events, though it was noted in Rome on 2 September 69, in the annals of the Arval Brethren, just before they made a record of the burning of the Capitoline temple, and the accompanying fighting in Rome, an event quite sufficient to drive any other issues out of Roman minds. One assumes he was rapidly killed.[19]

From then on, however, for a generation, it remained unclear to most of the population of the empire what had actually happened to the real Nero. There were, of course, rumours. Without credible details of his death, these alternative rumours of his continued existence persisted, especially in the Greek lands, where he had been popular (and where novels with plots including escapes from sacrifice, revivals of the dead, and other fantastic adventures were being produced). The restoration of Nero would be less amazing than the story of Christ. In 80–81 a man called Terentius Maximus, who bore a strong resemblance to the dead emperor, made another claim that he was Nero, still alive, and was coming to recover his throne. He was, it seems, from Asia originally, and no doubt understood the feelings of his fellow Asian Greeks – though his name suggests that he was a Roman citizen. He was said to have received some support, and, starting from somewhere in the Parthian lands, he reached the Euphrates crossing at Seleukeia Zeugma.

There was thus a wider international element in this. The Emperor Titus had failed, or refused, to recognize the kingship in Parthia of a usurper, Artabanus IV, who retaliated by sponsoring Terentius' adventure.[20] (Titus had negotiated with the Parthians in 70, as his father's envoy, and had succeeded in dissuading any Parthian intervention in the Roman troubles.) Terentius' origin, and whatever support he had from the Parthians, may have counted against him within the empire, and he seems to have made no progress beyond the Euphrates. There was a Roman legion, IV Scythica, stationed at Zeugma on the Euphrates, and it could well be that it was the first target of his persuasiveness, but it may have been moved to block his advance – it would certainly be the legion's responsibility to guard the Euphrates frontier, and if Terentius was to have any success, gaining the support of this legion would be his earliest priority. Terentius turned back into Parthia and there he became further involved in Parthian politics, which at that time, as Artabanus' usurpation demonstrates, was involved in its own succession crisis.[21]

It is thought that Terentius died in the Parthian troubles, though it is just possible that he survived and tried again. Another 'false Nero' turned up in 87, and made rather more progress than his predecessors. The secrecy, or silence, and confusion around the death of the true Nero, only encouraged the emergence of a pretender. The new pretender claimed the empire and gathered rather more support than his predecessors. Domitian's Dacian War was being fought at the time, and a conspiracy against Domitian was discovered in Rome, so this was an opportune moment, but it is difficult to accept that events in Rome, on the Danube frontier, and in Asia Minor were coordinated in any way. (Note that the earlier attempts happened in the Civil War of 69 and just after the death of Vespasian, periods which could be assumed to be politically unsettled in the empire.) Domitian survived these several crises, but the governor of Asia, C. Vettulenus Civica Cerialis, did not. He was exiled, probably for not reacting definitively or speedily enough to the threat of the false Nero's arrival.[22] The question for many, after all, in such attempts was always: 'what if he is successful and I have not supported him?' There seems no reason to assume any coordination of troubles, only the automatic reaction of enemies to the internal problems of the empire which had blown up from normal discontent to active dissidence.

None of these attempts occurred while Frontinus was in Asia, but he will have been familiar with the two first threats, so that one of the matters he had to concern himself with was to ensure that Roman control was maintained, not only in face of local indifference, but against external threats. He had to watch not only for the possibility of secession, or dissidence, or rebellion, in his province, but also the activity of the Parthians and any anti-Roman elements gathering support from them. As governor of Asia, an effectively disarmed province, he was hardly at the centre of events compared with, for example, the governor of Syria, with four legions at his disposal, or that of Cappadocia with two more. But it was the governor of Asia, Vettulenus, who was punished two years after Frontinus' term, probably for not reacting quickly enough to the false-Nero threat, or for being too credulous in the face of the pretender's claims. Frontinus may well have been aware of the third pretender two years before his arrival from intelligence gathered in Parthia. Certainly, the pretender must have been active in Parthia by his time. The Asian province, however, was not the best place to gather accurate intelligence (which may have been the difficulty Vettulenus faced). The first defence lay with the governor and legions of Syria, and the intelligence they could gather.

The attraction of Asia for these invaders was that it was Greek, and that it had shown, apart from the occasional elite participation in the imperial cult, little overt loyalty to Rome, and was virtually disarmed, and so that if the invader could get through the defences along the Syrian-Cappadocian frontier, there was nothing to stop him before Macedonia. Terentius Maximus was from Asia, and will have understood the situation there, the lack of enthusiasm for the empire, the limitations of the governor's period of office, even the romance of the Greek novels, which in some cases turn on unexpected successes by low-born men, in love, in politics, in war – and the Emperor Vespasian had been born an *eques*. Other provinces, behind the frontier defended by the legions in Syria and Armenia, were similarly largely unarmed. Stephen Mitchell has plotted the incidence of 'the Roman military presence in western Anatolia'. He counts four auxiliary forts in the Asian province, at Apameia Kelainai, Amorium, Sebaste, and Eunomeia – three of these forts were close together in the Apameian region, and Amorium was some way to the north. Apart from one fort at Ankyra in Phrygia, on the high road towards the Armenian frontier, and two in a curious position on the Lykian coast, possibly suppressing pirates, this was the total of regular forces in Anatolia west of the Parthian frontier – the governor's guard may be added, but it was probably not large. There were some *stationarii* (cavalry patrols) on the roads, but very few. If an invader fought his way through the fortified frontier, possibly persuading a legion or two to support him, there was little to stop him from reaching the Aegean and crossing into Greece.[23]

So the responsibilities of the governor were all interconnected. The degree of corruption had to be controlled, if it could not be eliminated entirely, because it was a danger to public order; similarly, the extraction of tax revenues had to be relatively moderate, but above all fair, or riots would result. And if unrest on these issues, or any others, came, there could develop a threat not just to the public order but to the imperial system in the province, since powers external to the empire automatically reacted, being enemies seeking any advantage.

The governor had to balance a series of roles and responsibilities. The Asian post may have been seen by some as a sinecure to which senior senators floated up by mere longevity and seniority, but any governor in Asia would have to work hard to keep control of the land; its problems bubbled away beneath the surface. The fate of Vettulenus which came only two years after Frontinus' stint in the same province was not only a punishment for negligence, but it was a clear warning to other Asian governors – and by extension, to those of other provinces – to be careful, diligent, and alert, and to react at once to perceived threats, even if they turned out not to be actual threats.

In 89 Trajan, commander of a legion stationed in Spain, marched his men all the way to the Rhine on the news of the rebellion of Antonius Saturninus at Mogontiacum – that was the reaction to a pretender which the emperor expected and required, and not just Domitian, but any emperor – the lesson of Vettulenus had clearly been learned. An emperor like Domitian was clearly willing to use his own powers to cut down any slack Roman aristocrat; by contrast Trajan became consul a year later and, of course, emperor a decade later.

Chapter 9

Nerva

We lose sight of Frontinus after his year as governor of Asia, which ended in 86. In the previous fifteen years he had risen from praetor through legionary commander in Gaul to consul in 73, and governor with the most active provincial campaign in the empire in Britannia, then to army command in Germany on campaign with the emperor (81 – 84), and then immediately to the senior governorship of Asia in 85/86. It was an unusually compressed and rapid political career. He was, in all likelihood, due a rest.

In the next dozen years, only a few disconnected notices exist to give some notion of his activity. There is the visit to him by the writer Aelian, who was intending to write a book on military conduct, but that took place about 97 or 98, by which time he can be located once more; Frontinus was at Formiae at the time of the meeting.[1] The poet Martial also visited him, this time at Terracina (Anxur), as he noted in one of his poems. This may have been the country retreat of Frontinus, though Martial was mainly intent on contrasting his busy life in Rome with the leisure he had enjoyed at Anxur and Baiae.[2] No date for this meeting is possible, but Martial implies that Frontinus was notably busy when in Rome. It is in this apparently blank period that Frontinus' daughter was married to Q. Sosius Senecio, at some point between 80 and 90.[3]

Senecio was a man clearly heading for the summit of Roman politics and society, intelligent, well-liked, and competent. He had had charge as *quattuorvir* of the care of roads, and then was military tribune in Legio I Italica, which was stationed at Novae in Moesia. He spent 85–88 in Achaia as quaestor – the same period that Frontinus was in Asia. Back in Rome he was tribune of the plebs from 90 to 92, and praetor in 92–94, in both cases as a *candidatus Caesaris*, that is selected for preferential promotion. Probably by 90 he was married to Julia Frontina, Frontinus' only child, but since she evidently accompanied her father to his postings in Germany and Asia, the marriage might have happened later. In 95 Senecio was sent to Bonna in Germania Inferior as legate of Legio I Minervia, the legion Domitian raised anew, clearly a post within the imperial view.

This was a rapid rise, especially for a *novus homo* and a man from the East. His origin is, however, uncertain, but Cilicia has become the favourite, with Hierapolis Castabala as a possibility; Phrygia, from one of the Augustan *coloniae*, is another. His early posting to Achaia might also indicate an eastern origin, since it had become a habit to ensure that Romans from the Greek East were given posts in that region. If he did come from Cilicia he was probably the first man from that province to enter the Senate; his family's citizenship might date back to C. Sosius, one of Mark Antony's commanders. Further reinforcing his probable eastern origin is that he was as a friend of Plutarch and attended the wedding of Plutarch's son Ambibulos, possibly while he was in Achaia; Plutarch dedicated some of his works, including some of the parallel lives, to him. He was also a friend of Pliny the Younger; this put him in the group of intellectuals inhabited by Martial and Frontinus; he was thus well at home in both Greek and Roman political and intellectual circles, a favourite of the emperor, and his post at Bonna was to prove a particularly advantageous one.

The same assessment could be made of Frontinus. He was one of the intellectual elite of Rome. However, he appears in the record almost always tangentially. Pliny was clearly reasonably close to him. He never addressed him in one of his letters, though he referred to him, and used him, as an arbitrator in a dispute.[4] Frontinus was an augur, a position it is suggested that he received in the context of his consulship in 73.[5] An augur was an ancient priestly office whose task was to discern the gods' approval, or otherwise, for political or military actions, and to advise the Senate (and the emperor) accordingly. It was, to a superstitious audience, a powerful office, and augurs clearly would have influence in foreign affairs; they were co-opted to the office and their imperial experience was no doubt part of their qualification. Frontinus several times nominated Pliny for an augurate, but it was only after Frontinus' death that Pliny gained the position, replacing his patron.[6]

In his letters Pliny refers to Frontinus three times, in the first concerning the augurate. The second mention is when Frontinus is roped in, as one of the most distinguished men in Rome, to help in a private judgment over a complex inheritance case; the third was when Frontinus is quoted as refusing to authorize that a memorial to him should be produced, though urged to do so by Pliny and others.[7] By that time, early in Trajan's reign, he had been consul three times, governor of three different provinces, and *curator aquarum*; his friends must have been sure that he deserved memorializing; he refused on the grounds that if his deeds did not constitute his memorial, no statue could.

If Frontinus habitually lived at Anxur or elsewhere in Campania, on the other hand, his participation in the intellectual life of the city would clearly be somewhat peripheral. And yet, it seems clear he was a regular attender at the Senate, and at Domitian's *consilium*, so he was hardly isolated. And Campania was hardly out of the way; some of his contemporaries and equals often lived in that area for part of the year.

Much of our information about Frontinus is therefore at second hand, or is a reasonable assumption based on Roman career patterns and social behaviour. No doubt Frontinus was busy in this time (86 to 96) composing his books on war, and the book on agriculture which is even more vaguely attested than his *Art of War*. But these references to him, in Aelian, Martial, Pliny, altogether do show that he was a constant presence, if generally unrecorded, in the city of Rome and central Italy – but then, we do not know the whereabouts of almost all Roman senators all of the time. Pliny liked and respected him; his daughter's marriage to Sosius Senecio linked him with one of the foremost coming men of the city, and no doubt Senecio welcomed the link; between them they formed part of a trans-empire political and social network which soon produced emperors (see Chapter 13). He was consulted by other authors. And, given his history with Domitian it is highly probable that he was a regular attender at the emperor's *consilium* – though he does not appear in any accounts of that group's meetings, but then there are few such accounts in existence. (He is not mentioned in Juvenal's political satire of the meeting, held, he suggested, to decide on the fate of a large fish; this absence, in fact, might actually be a compliment.[8])

One of the members of that *consilium* was M. Cocceius Nerva, whom Frontinus will have known from their joint presence in Rome at the time of the Civil War and after (Nerva was consul in 71, Frontinus praetor in 70, their offices were separated by Frontinus' campaign in Gaul). Nerva was the aristocratic scion of a family of lawyers and consuls going back to the 30s BC. He was adept at shifting his allegiance to whoever was in power, and in fact was highly skilful at identifying the location of power in moments of confusion. In 65 he had reported on the conspiracy of Piso to the Emperor Nero, with such important information that he was awarded triumphal insignia, almost a joke to a man who had never seen an army, nor ever left Italy.[9] At the time he was praetor designate for 66, though he probably did not take up the post.

In 71 he was appointed by the new Emperor Vespasian as ordinary consul, alongside the new emperor. This implies a swift and well-informed attachment to the new ruler; the honour awarded by Nero was not usually referred to after that emperor's death until he became emperor himself. What he had done in the time of the Civil War is unknown, nor what he had done to put the new emperor under such an obligation, though some signal service for Vespasian had clearly been rendered. (The same could be said of Frontinus, of course.) No doubt he kept quiet about his activities, and no one ever accused him of any actions or inactions in that time; nor was he ever accused of being a *delator* – an informer – for Nero, though that is clearly what he had been. But he was able with apparent ease to navigate the tricky political waters of the Civil War years, moving from conspicuous loyalty to Nero to conspicuous loyalty to Vespasian, by way of the Civil War. It took a master of duplicity, diplomacy, and intrigue to come out of the confusion so well. He continued to serve both Titus and Domitian in the same way. His value was probably as a man who knew all about opinion in the Senate and in society, and one who was fully prepared to report on it to the emperor, whoever the emperor was. He escaped being accused of being a *delator*, which, if the episode with Nero had become widely known, might have been inescapable, but this only shows how careful he was. Apart from their similar political orientation, he and Frontinus had in common that they were both augurs.[10] Nerva was also a *salius palatinus*, a position which involved a ritual dance of the city in March and October to mark the beginning and end of the war season, an ironic position for such a man.

Frontinus was probably another man with the political navigational skills to bring him to a safe haven in a dangerous time – the acceptance of the praetorship for 70, and his rapid ceding of the office to Domitian were cases in point, as was his apparent rise from *eques* to praetor during the Civil War. Then, and later in his time as a legionary commander in Gaul, he identified himself as a friend and colleague of the emperor's younger son, and this was no doubt of considerable assistance to his career. It seems probable that he had been adlected to the Senate before becoming praetor, and since he was an *eques* until the Civil War – so far as we know – he had perhaps entered the Senate under Galba's auspices, which would be a good mark for Vespasian. Alternatively, his patron was Vespasian all along, but since the emperor was out of Rome until late 70, it seems probable that the adlection was accomplished by Galba, if anyone. It does not seem likely that either Otho or Vitellius would have been responsible, though it must be recalled that Frontinus was probably in Spain in the 60s when both Galba and Otho were governing there (just as he had been in Africa when Vespasian was governor there). The favour of Vespasian certainly followed him in that emperor's reign. The suggestion may have been that of Mucianus, who, significantly, brought Frontinus with him on Domitian's Gallic expedition (which took place before Vespasian reached Rome) – but Frontinus clearly was able to steer clear of Mucianus later, who was perhaps identified as toxic at a fairly early stage in the reign.

Nerva was well rewarded by the Flavians. He was Vespasian's first colleague as ordinary consul in 71, he was a member of Domitian's *consilium* (and probably of Vespasian's and Titus' also); he had a second consulship in 90, courtesy of Domitian. He never commanded an army, probably avoided any military service, and, so far as we know, never visited a province.[11] His life was geographically limited to Rome and Italy up to a hundred miles around the city. He is a perfect example of a man who became important and a double consul simply by sitting still. His skill was in the knowledge of the political situation in the city, which he no doubt gained in incessant conversation, gossip, parties, and visits. He was a minor poet; he was presumably a good conversationalist.

His value, as Nero had discovered, was in the very fact that he was a habitué of Rome, with its circles of poets, gossips, intriguers, and politicians. He was, in other words, the reverse of Frontinus, and the two men had arrived at the same destination by completely different routes. Frontinus was happy to set off on his travels at the behest of the government system, visiting the East, Africa, Spain, Gaul, Britain, Germany, and Asia on official business, settling in Italy having been brought up in Gaul, marrying his daughter to a Greek politician, while Nerva never left Italy. There was another contrast: Frontinus was married and a father; Nerva was homosexual. The social relations of the two men are not known, there is no record of their meeting until after Domitian was dead, but they must have known and worked together, especially in the last year of Domitian's life.

It is the fact that Nerva was familiar with both Domitian's plans and the interconnections of life and politics and society at all levels in Rome that provides the essential basis for what happened in 96.

Domitian fought on the German frontier in 83–85 and 88–89 and on the Dacian frontier in 92–93, only just emerging with some sort of victory in each case, though the result in Germany was more than satisfactory, when he was able to create the two new provinces. There, he was able to extend the empire and create a much better frontier line, at least for communication purposes, but also to enclose a fertile region within the imperial boundary. This frontier line held for the next century and a half, with the one adjustment of the Antonine Limes, which must be counted a success. In the Dacian war, on the other hand, he was able to do little more than hold his own. The enemy was more secure in his defences, the region he was attacking was more difficult to penetrate.

But Domitian was politically and strategically creative, as the German episode showed, and he had come to think on a large geographical scale. He devised a new scheme by which he intended to do in Germany and northern Europe on a huge scale what he had already done on the southern German frontier, to extend the imperial boundary, enclose a large area into the empire, and solve the problem of constant frontier warfare on the north.

The major problem with the northern frontier of the empire was just that which he and his father had tried to deal with on the upper Rhine. The legions in their campaigns had ended up with just about the longest defence line it was possible to find in Europe. The German conquests had done something to reduce the length of that line, but the main problem remained. By 92, after fighting in Germany and Dacia, Domitian knew this probably better than anyone in the empire, having experienced it at first hand, more than any emperor for the previous fifty years; he was in fact the first emperor to fight personally on the frontier since Tiberius. After the German and Dacian campaigns he knew what had to be done about it.

There had been three separate areas of conflict in Domitian's reign, largely, it seems, arising out of the destabilization associated with the Civil

War, which included wars along much of the European frontier. Twice he fought the Chatti in Germany, pushing the frontier line forward; twice he fought the Dacians, without a clear result; and twice he fought on the Pannonian frontier. In each case he took overall command but acted with expert advice. We know he had advice from Frontinus in Germany and no doubt he had similar advisors in his other wars. We do not know what discussions took place in Rome in the periods between the wars, but that was when Frontinus, after 86, was in Rome and a member of Domitian's *consilium*. It may be presumed that his advice was available for the emperor, who clearly listened to him.

The sequence of wars on the northern frontier ended in 92/93, more or less in a draw. In the next years Domitian identified the strategic target as the tribes in Bohemia and Moravia, the Marcomanni and the Quadi. It is this decision, as much as his determination to attempt to solve the whole issue, which marks him as an original strategist. For he had recently fought the Dacians, and it would be natural to consider them the most important northern enemy. Later, Trajan certainly did. But in Germany Domitian had singled out the Chatti as the main enemy, because defeating them would permit the swinging eastwards of the frontier on the Upper Rhine. Now, defeating the Marcomanni and the Quadi and taking the Bohemian quadrilateral into the empire would give it a new and better frontier further north, acquire some fertile land which was also rich in minerals, and would outflank the Dacians. Control of Bohemia would open the rest of Germany to Roman influence and exploitation, and acquisition.

Since 93, therefore, Domitian, using agents, probably from the army, had secured a series of diplomatic alliances with a number of German tribes, with the intention of encircling the Marcomanni and Quadi in Bohemia and Moravia within this network. He also gathered a huge army in Pannonia, five legions plus the associated *auxilia*, and more of both in reserve, up to 70,000 soldiers or more, with the aim of conquering that surrounded group of tribes. By 96 all was in place.

The allies had been chosen with care. The Hermunduri in Bavaria, to the west of the Marcomanni and neighbours of the Romans in Raetia and the Agri Decumates, were his allies; this advanced Roman influence to the line of the Main River, between the Wetterau and the northern edge of Bohemia; beyond the Main the Chatti were pinned down by their peace treaty negotiated at the end of the Second War in 89. In the east were the Dacians, also pinned down by a peace treaty and so technically Roman allies; it is doubtful if anyone on the Roman side trusted that the Dacians would keep to the treaty, but if the attack into Bohemia was massive and swift enough the Dacians might well subside into quiescence. They would by then be outflanked on the west. On the other hand, they would surely understand that they were likely to be the next on Domitian's list of conquests, and might intervene in a Marcomanni War at a moment when this would have a serious effect. Beyond and north of the targeted tribes, the Semnones of Thuringia (neighbours of the Hermunduri) and the Lugii of northern Bohemia and Silesia were recruited as allies. They were already enemies of the Romans' selected victims. The Marcomanni and Quadi were thus surrounded by Roman allies or armies and could look to none of their neighbours for help; and they were about to receive an attack by the biggest Roman army assembled in one place for many a decade.[12]

Both Nerva, as a regular member of Domitian's *consilium* and Frontinus, as the emperor's friend and colleague in earlier military adventures and a probable *consilium* member, were aware of this projected campaign; indeed, it was probably common knowledge amongst senators. The appointed commander was Cn. Pinarius Aemilius Cicatricula Pompeius Longinus, the governor of Pannonia, and the adopted son of the German governor of 70–73 who had captured the Arae Flaviae area for Vespasian. He already had a distinguished career. Adopted by Pinarius Cornelius Clemens, who had been consul in 71, at a time when Vespasian was being exceptionally careful to choose active loyalists to take up consular posts (and so the consular colleague of Nerva), he had reached the consulship himself in 90, having governed the difficult province of Judaea for three years as praetorian governor. The son was therefore a consular colleague of Nerva in his second consulship. He went on to govern Moesia Superior in 92–94, after commanding in the preceding Dacian War. When appointed as governor of Pannonia in 95, therefore, he was already an experienced commander and was fully familiar with the problems of the northern frontier; he was undoubtedly fully aware of the emperor's plan and his diplomatic preparations for the war. He had been in Judaea, it may be noted, when the third 'false Nero' made his attempt (which had caused the condemnation of Vettulenus). He was not, it seems, called on to do anything, but men under Domitian gained points for displays of conspicuous loyalty, and by making moves of support in such crises; in Judaea Longinus had command of a legion, X Fretensis, stationed amid the ruins of Jerusalem. He may have moved some of his troops north in anticipation of trouble. He was certainly, like his adoptive father, a firm Flavian loyalist.

Another governor with a similar background of reliability and Flavian loyalty was M. Ulpius Traianus, governor of Germania Superior, Longinus' neighbour to the west. His father had been consul in 70, one of Vespasian's first selections, and had secured the annexations of Syrian client kingdoms in the early 70s. (He had been governor of Baetica in 57, and had no doubt met Frontinus in his surveying activity.) The son had been ordinary consul in 91, the year after Nerva's second consulship, having conspicuously marched with his legion from Spain to help suppress Saturninus' rising in the Rhineland two years before. (The legion was VII Gemina, the successor of the legion raised by Galba in his campaign against Nero, in which I have supposed Frontinus may have served during the Civil War.) The commanders of the expeditionary force were thus conspicuously loyal to the Flavians and to Domitian personally. Trajan was a Spaniard, from Italica in Baetica; his father had served with Vespasian in the Jewish War, then as governor successively of Cappadocia, Syria, and Asia in the 70s. Trajan thus had a hereditary loyalty to the Flavian dynasty. In 96 he was governor of Germania Superior, and was in effect Longinus' second-in-command.

The expedition no doubt took much arranging. Pompeius Longinus in Pannonia had five legions. XIII Gemina was at Vindobona (west of Vienna) and XV Apollinaris was at Carnuntum (Petronella, east of Vienna), both on the Danube and facing north. Elsewhere in the province there were: XIV Gemina at Musellae until it was moved forward to Ad Flexum, just south of the river; the two legions formed by Nero from the marines of the fleet, I and II Adiutrix, were at Poetovio and Mursa respectively, and they also moved forward to the river at Brigetio and Aquincum. All these were in Pannonia, a huge garrison for a single province, which must have made clear to all that an invasion was intended. The legions were backed up, as usual, by a large number of auxiliary regiments, six *alae* of cavalry and forty cohorts of infantry, at least. But this was not all. In the neighbouring province of Moesia Superior there were two more legions, IV Flavia at Singidunum and VII Claudia at Viminacium; and beyond them in Moesia Inferior were V Macedonica at Oescus and I Italica at Novae – all of which faced directly north from their bases on the Danube; those in Moesia Superior facing the Iazyges between the river and Dacia, and those in Interior facing Dacia across the Danube. They were supported by three *alae* of cavalry and twenty infantry cohorts.[13] There were also legions in the German provinces. Many of these forces were available if needed, either to reinforce the invasion of Bohemia or to deter intervention from Dacia.

This was a highly unusual concentration of Roman military power, which was usually deployed as a defensive force, and it was the first expeditionary force of such size since the Civil War – the conquest of Wales, an area half the size of Domitian's target, took one legion and a number of *auxilia*. Among the Romans it was known to the most senior politicians in Rome, but probably not, and certainly not in any detail, to the generality of the population. It was, however, probably well understood to the proposed victims. The strike force was the legions under Pompeius Longinus in Pannonia; those in the two Moesian provinces were there to watch the Dacians and the Iazyges in case they intervened. Legions were retained on the Rhine frontier as well.

The Roman calendar dictated the date of the invasion. The forces were concentrated in position by August, and would need to be launched soon, since by November the region would be too cold and snowbound for operations. The emperor intended, as usual, to be present to supervise, if not actually to command, but he had to be in Rome for a number of religious and secular celebrations in the middle of September. As a result, he would be living in the palace until 18 September at least, but he would travel north during the following days. His precise destination was unknown, but he was confident of victory.

If Domitian's commanders in the north were as successful as he expected, he would be the greatest Roman conqueror since Augustus, he would remove the stain of the defeat of Augustus' three legions in the German forest, and he would reverse the withdrawal from Germany ordered by Tiberius. The tribes he had allied with could be incorporated into the empire gradually. The empire would be extended north to the Baltic, and all Germany as far east as the Vistula would become Roman; in addition, Dacia would then be a straightforward conquest, as would Denmark; it was a hugely ambitious undertaking.

For a group of senators around Cocceius Nerva this result would be an intolerable situation. The Flavian dynasty had always had enemies, notably many members of the Senate, who had either survived the Civil War, or who were jealous of Vespasian and Domitian as emperors. Several of those enemies had been removed one way or another in the previous quarter of a century, and this meant that Domitian's domestic opponents did not put themselves in harm's way by open criticism; instead they spent some of their energy complaining about the tyrant; it also meant that they conspired in secret. A plot was almost ready in September 96 just as Domitian was about to join the army, but if they delayed their move Domitian would be out of the city and safely amongst his soldiers, where opposition was non-existent. The date of Domitian's departure from the city would probably be 18 September, since the conspirators could read the calendar as well as the emperor. The few days before then was the last chance the conspirators would have to dispose of him. For inevitably the plot had to begin with the assassination of the emperor.

Domitian, like every other emperor, regularly held an informal meeting in the courtyard of the imperial palace where he would be handed petitions complaining about perceived injustices, and where he could meet his senatorial colleagues. Unless a senator was ill or out of the city, he was expected to attend. The plotters fixed on 18 September as the day for their action.

This would be their last chance. If Domitian left the city for some time, the news of the plot would certainly leak – a good dozen or more men knew of the plot in detail – and he would descend on them in a fury. If he won his war he would be untouchable in victory; if he lost he would be doubly on his guard against domestic enemies. The plot had been forming for some time, and now the time for action had arrived. The plotters could not afford to wait any longer. They included the consul, Ti. Catius Caesius Fronto, whose assumption of office at the beginning of September was probably the catalyst, since he was in a prime position for the necessary moves which would follow the imperial assassination. The senators in the plot gathered on the morning of the 18th in the palace courtyard, where some at least were greeted by the emperor. The actual murder was carried out by a small group of palace servants, the chamberlain Parthenius in charge, and encouraged by at least one of the Praetorian Prefects. It was the junction of the palace plotters and the senatorial plotters with praetorian support, which allowed the plot to succeed.[14]

Domitian spent that morning hearing cases which he had to judge, and attending the informal gathering. He then ate a light lunch and intended to follow it with a siesta. On the way to his bedroom he was intercepted by Parthenius, who told him that Stephanus, a freedman of the emperor's niece Domitilla, had brought an important message from her; he had gone to the emperor's bedroom with it.

This was odd. Domitilla had been exiled to the island of Pandeteria a year before, when her husband, Domitilla's cousin and Domitian's designated successor, had been executed. Stephanus had been taken into the emperor's household, but was known to harbour anger at the way Domitilla had been treated. (Her exile was not necessarily a punishment; her relationship to the emperor meant that any man who married her would put himself into the line of succession, and Domitian wanted to avoid that – it was her husband's proximity to him which earned him execution.) Why was Stephanus bringing a message from her? She could just as easily have written directly to the emperor. Domitian may have had such thoughts. He certainly went off to his room to find out what was going on.

There he found Stephanus, who had been going round with his arm in a bandage for the last fortnight – which is an indication of how long the plot had been forming. Also in the room was a boy who was employed to tend the Flavian family shrine in the room. Stephanus handed the emperor a paper which was supposed to contain a list of men who were plotting against him, a subject which riveted Domitian's attention. But while Domitian was so distracted, Stephanus pulled out a knife hidden in his bandage and attacked. Domitian fought back, and shouted to the boy to get the dagger Domitian kept under his pillow, but this had been sabotaged. His cries attracted the servants, but the door between their quarters and his bedroom had been locked.

Stephanus' attempt at killing the emperor did not succeed. Domitian's resistance was too much for him. But four other men had been stationed at the main door to the room by Parthenius, and now came in to finish what Stephanus had started. These were a freedman called Maxentius, a soldier of the guard called Clodianus, an under chamberlain called Sagur or Sigellius, and a gladiator, whose name is unknown. Between them they inflicted eight stab wounds on the emperor; Domitian died.

Parthenius rushed in, ostensibly coming to the rescue but in fact to verify that the emperor was dead. Stephanus was forthwith killed, either by the other killers at Parthenius' instruction, or by Domitian's servants who broke through the locked door. Either way, Stephanus had been silenced, and any information he might have about the plot was lost. Parthenius then went out to the courtyard, where the senatorial plotters had gathered as part of the usual crowd of other visitors, and reported that Domitian was dead.[15]

Rumours had already leaked out, no doubt by way of the servants, while Domitian's shouts for help will have alerted people that something was going on. The designated new emperor was Nerva, and when a rumour suggested that Domitian had only been wounded, he nearly collapsed – so he was certainly in the plot. Parthenius' arrival and report reassured him and his co-conspirators, who were gathered around him in the palace courtyard. They set about ensuring that their plot went further than simply an assassination. This was a group of experienced politicians who knew that killing the emperor was not enough – most had memories of the events of 69; they had to seize power as well as removing the emperor.

Conducting a coup in an autocracy is straightforward – remove the autocrat, seize control of the armed forces, gather the legislature, suitably filleted, and announce that you are in power. This sequence is obvious to those who are familiar with the distribution of power and authority in any autocracy, but too often a coup leader believes that only the first of these necessities is sufficient. The plotters against Domitian knew what they were doing.

Nerva was the theoretical leader of the plot, but it is unlikely that he had organized it. That honour should go, probably, to Ti. Catius Caesius Fronto, one of the consuls in office since September 96. He was known as an anti-Domitian, a Stoic, and was the son of the poet Silius Italicus, who was an old associate of Nero, and also an anti-Flavian (though both men had accepted offices from Domitian). Fronto furthermore was from Patavium, a centre of the Stoic opposition to the Flavians (and to the imperial system). He was installed as consul by Domitian in an attempt to conciliate this opposition group – but it clearly did not work, or perhaps he was simply too late. Fronto had been consul for only eighteen days when he carried through the coup, so it is probable that the process had been under preparation for some time; that he would be in office from

September to December had been known since the year before, but it was only when he was actually in office as consul that they could act, since his participation in summoning the Senate was necessary. The other members of the conspiracy cannot be clearly identified, but the consular list drawn up by Nerva for 97 is full of old men who were being awarded second consulships, and it may be that they were involved – or possibly Nerva, a canny politician, was deliberately rewarding these old fellows to avoid rewarding, and so identifying, the plotters. Nerva was an old conspirator himself, back to Nero's reign. The plotters were all Nerva's old senatorial colleagues, so most likely he was indulging himself in honouring them while he still could.

Caesius Fronto as consul called the Senate for the next morning; he did so by notifying only those whom he knew were his supporters, the known anti-Domitians. There were enough of them to make a reasonable attendance – the dead emperor had been distinctly unpopular in the Senate. So next morning Nerva was officially installed as emperor.

The main force of the army was, of course, on the frontier, and did not need to be consulted, only notified when the formalities were over. Being presented with a *fait accompli* which had taken place several days before would take away some of the instinctive immediate military reaction; the soldiers would have supported Domitian had it been their choice. In Rome there were three military units, but only one needed to be involved: this was the Praetorian Guard, and that had been consulted through its two prefects, of whom one appears to have supported the plot and was possibly part of it; the other units were the Urban Cohorts under the *praefectus urbi*, and the *vigiles* under their own prefect; these latter two did not have the same political heft as the Guard, and could be ignored. In fact, of these three units, only the Praetorians, highly trained professional warriors, well armed and insistent on their rights, needed to be consulted.

It is a mark of the plotters' preparations that one of the Guard prefects had been squared in advance – the other prefect seems to have been ignored and been able to do nothing. It was also part of the plot that the soldier in the assassination group, Clodianus, was a *cornicularius* in the Guard, apparently a token representative at the deed and so intended to block complaints from the Guard that they had not been consulted, or alternatively that they were involved. The crucial individuals in the Guard were the two prefects, but only Ti. Petronius Secundus was brought into the plot in advance.

There was for the moment, therefore, a subdued welcome for the coup, since Domitian had not been popular in the city, and there was no overt opposition to it, yet the reaction of the army, of the several armies, was uncertain. Popular reaction would no doubt be subdued, and fearful that further trouble would come. In this reaction they would be correct. There proved to be several loose ends which soon tripped up those taking command. It was up to the new Emperor Nerva to watch out for and neutralize these dangers, but he was not the man to do this. He was an expert in the politics at Rome, and could scotch any Roman counter-revolution, but he was not knowledgeable about the army, the provinces, or the frontiers. This proved to be fatal to his regime.

So far as we know Frontinus had nothing to do with Nerva's *coup d'état*. Indeed, all that we know or can discover about him is that he was loyal to Domitian, and would probably count himself as the dead emperor's friend. There can be no doubt that he will have been shocked and grieved at Domitian's death. We can also be quite certain that had he known of it in advance he would have made sure that the plot was derailed and exposed. Whether he was in the city at the time is not known, but the Senate was in session, and it is probable that he was a regular attender.

And yet for the previous decade, since he had returned to Rome from his year as governor of Asia, there is no indication that Frontinus was publicly employed. There could be more than one reason for this. He was, after all, an author, and it is probable that it was in this time that his works on war were completed and published, also possibly the surveying volume and whatever it was that he was writing on agriculture. (And these are not necessarily the sum of his works.) In a time when such books were produced and reproduced laboriously by hand a decade is not too long for all this to be done, along with the research needed in every case. He was certainly around in Rome and Campania, as the incidental references in Martial and in Pliny's letters show. But this was exactly the time when Domitian's behaviour and political activity became worse. Frontinus was not subservient to any emperor, and yet he was certainly a Flavian loyalist; quietly immersing himself in his own work might well have been his method of avoiding both criticism of the emperor and participation in Domitian's activities.

This seems a reasonable interpretation of his political attitude, but there is another aspect to him and his reaction which emerges. He was certainly loyal to the Flavian dynasty, but this did not prevent him from accepting Nerva as his emperor, nor in accepting honours and a job from him. And for Frontinus, the real honour was to be put to work. He was quite prepared to work for Nerva even if he disapproved, quite possibly in public and out loud, of the way he had secured the throne. He was one of those senators who was loyal to the empire, no matter who was emperor. (For a long time this had been Nerva's position as well.) He might befriend the Flavian emperors, but he was perfectly willing to work for Nerva, or indeed Nero. In the result, however, it was Trajan whom he found most congenial.

Chapter 10

The New Regime at Work

Frontinus accepted Nerva as the new emperor, probably because he could do nothing else. He must have understood that as emperor the new ruler was in a very precarious situation. Nerva attempted to bolster his position by awarding second consulships to a series of distinguished men, but this only emphasized the lack of enthusiastic support elsewhere. He was in his late sixties and in poor health.[1] A man of that age and health becoming emperor was, to his rivals and enemies, one who would probably die soon. The contest for the imperial succession was even more obviously in the making than usual as soon as he took the throne.

There was also the question of the army's attitude. Domitian's death halted the planned offensive but did not prevent the army from sending out patrols across the Danube into the north, at least one of which, commanded by Trajan, resulted in a fight, but it seems that no orders came from the new emperor. The generals were left to wonder what was happening, relying on informal messages. The planned offensive could no longer begin, partly because the emperor apparently gave no instructions, but also because with Domitian's death the various peace and alliance treaties he had negotiated ended. An attack against the Marcomanni and the Quadi now risked bringing in the Dacians, at least. Nerva, as a former member of Domitian's *consilium* where all this had been worked out, will have understood the new situation – indeed, it was the timing of the attack which had determined the time of the coup.

The internal danger was of another civil war. A weak emperor in a precarious situation, in poor health, and with plenty of rivals seeking to replace him, was a situation not far from that of the last year of Nero, or perhaps of Galba's short reign. Looming over the whole position was that huge army, only a week's march away from Rome; and yet Nerva did nothing about that army.

What was actually happening in Rome was that the new regime was settling in, cautiously and carefully. The new consular list for the next year, 97, was drawn up, consisting of a number of Nerva's friends, plus the men who had been already designated by Domitian – it would not do to disappoint those who had been notified of their posts already. As a result there were to be a dozen consuls during the year (there had been six in 96, a figure regarded as large). A dozen was unprecedented since the constant replacements of consuls during the Civil War, when there were four emperors, each requiring his supporters in office as consuls – not a helpful precedent. The new rulers warily watched for reactions, particularly in Rome, but also from the provinces, and the army. It was, in a sense, an immobile regime.

The best way to avoid a hostile reaction was to be seen to be governing. This would distract the idle and preoccupy the busy. The consular list was one aspect of this, a means of conciliation and of roping in helpful friends. Then Nerva came up with plans for initiatives.

The emperor had to take a number of decisions on several official appointments. The city prefect, who had command of the urban cohorts, was T. Aurelius Fulvus, a safe man, already twice consul; he seems to have been left in post. The army Nerva ignored, but more from fear of upsetting the commanders than expecting its support. But the praetorian prefects were another matter altogether. One of them at least, T. Petronius Secundus, was dismissed. He had been involved in the assassination plot, and having been disloyal to one emperor and implicated in the assassination, he was clearly too dangerous a man to retain. The other prefect, Norbanus, a career administrator with no military experience, is not heard of again and may have also been dismissed. Even if he was not in the plot, his inability to prevent his colleague's actions certainly meant that his ineffectiveness merited dismissal. Nerva needed an experienced man in that post, so these men were quickly replaced by another former prefect, Casperius Aelianus.[2] This choice may have been made to conciliate the Guard who could well react badly to sudden replacements. The Guard was clearly a problem, potentially a bigger problem than the army. Note that the prefects were not in fact soldiers, but men who had risen to the top along the equestrian career *cursus*, which was parallel to that of men of senatorial rank. Secundus had risen to be governor of Egypt, one of the three senior equestrian posts; Norbanus had been governor of

Raetia; these were able men with much governmental experience. They had, however, little or no experience of the military, other perhaps than a year as military tribune; they had become essentially bureaucrats. For the moment, however, all went well under Aelianus. He also served another purpose. He had been Domitian's prefect earlier, and had been an early supporter of Vespasian in the Civil War; his reappointment may have been a gesture towards those who regretted the end of Domitian.

Any new regime needs to justify itself. For Nerva it was legislative enactments which were the obvious thing to do. Some projects seem to have been inherited from Domitian's time, and Nerva could take them up and implement them in his own name. Nerva anyway will have been involved in them before his accession and could now see things through into law. There were adjustments to the law on marriage, and to tax law, and others concerning games and public entertainments, all accomplished by the sort of tweaking and adjusting in a minor way which every government does more or less constantly. Regular announcements of such changes can make it seem as though the government is being busy and was having regard to the public interest, even if the measures were actually little more than bureaucratic fiddling. Most of the laws were, of course, largely ignored, in the absence of any enforcement procedures.[3]

An example of this was Nerva's prohibition of the practice of castration. This had already been forbidden, as recently as by Domitian, which Nerva now repeated. And yet the practice continued, and the product, eunuchs, also continued to be employed, not least in the imperial household. But the prohibition sounded good and caring. It presumably was aimed at preventing the operation being performed on citizens' children. Similarly, the prohibition of the marriage of uncles and nieces, a measure perhaps aimed at the memory of Domitian, since he was rumoured to have been planning to marry his brother's daughter. Again, the practice did not end, despite the legislation.

In the tax reforms, or alterations, a tax of two denarii per Jew which had been imposed after the conquest of Jerusalem had been abused by the tax collectors. (The product had been devoted, at least theoretically, to the reconstruction of the twice-burnt Temple of Jupiter Optimus Maximus, a task which was now just about finished.) Restitution was offered for the abuses; whether it was ever claimed or paid is not known. An inheritance tax dating from Augustus' time, which had always been especially unpopular, was adjusted to extend the range of exceptions, something already done two or three times. One reason for these tax adjustments, which would clearly bring in less revenue, was that Domitian had left a substantial reserve in the treasury, no doubt with a view to financing the planned campaign in the north. Nerva also reduced the tribute to be collected from the provinces, another reduction in revenue. All such measures are the sort of thing to be expected of a new emperor, especially one who owed his position to usurpation and assassination.

Domitian's memory had been condemned by the Senate, and his name was erased from many of the monuments and buildings which he had put up. Some were destroyed. Giant statues of him on a horse were probably no loss. On buildings his name was often erased from inscriptions, but this left an obvious gap, so obvious that it was painfully clear what had been removed, and so it simply emphasized who had been originally responsible. Some might receive Nerva's name instead, but the change was almost equally obvious. Some of Domitian's statues had their heads reworked into Nerva's features, often therefore showing him as a young man, whereas he was in fact old and ill; again this was hardly convincing, except that, especially in the provinces, no one knew what either man looked like anyway. It seems doubtful that anyone cared.

In addition to reducing the tax take, Nerva indulged in some extravagant spending. There was the donative to the army to be paid to commemorate the accession. There were buildings to be constructed or finished. There were games to be financed. There were plots of land to be acquired and then distributed to retiring soldiers – though with a new war imminent it is unlikely that there were many such retirees. This was budgeted at 60 million sesterces, which was about five per cent of Nerva's annual revenue.[4] There was a *congiarium* to be paid to the Roman citizens as a gift on his accession. All these could be afforded in the short term but would quickly drain away the surplus Domitian had left in the treasury.

Then there was a new scheme developed, apparently by Nerva himself, the *alimenta*.[5] This was a set of schemes to subsidize fathers with children. The aim was to encourage the production of children, the fear being that the population of Italy in particular was declining. This may or may not have been the case: it is highly doubtful if the perception of a decline was anything more than a widespread assumption. It was to apply to Italy only, since the perception was of a decline in the Italian population specifically, which it was feared would lead to a future lack of recruits into the forces; the legions in particular were still recruited very largely from the Italian citizen population.

This was not an entirely new idea. There were already in existence private schemes of family encouragement. For example, Pliny the Younger set one up for his home city of Comum in northern Italy.[6] Nerva's scheme therefore took the idea and extended it more widely to much of Italy, and made it into one funded out of tax revenues. (This of course would swiftly kill off any private schemes.) The development of the scheme has usually been ascribed to Trajan, but an inscription from Veleia in Liguria, dated to 98, which is Trajan's first year, shows that the scheme was already in operation when he took the throne.[7] It is reasonable to assume that it had commenced earlier, under Nerva. It is even possible, as some have suggested, that the scheme began with Domitian; certainly some of the private schemes did.[8]

The total of projected expenditure was clearly considerable, but also unpredictable. The Roman state's finances were, like all such essentially primitive states, very precarious, and only the money collected by taxation – physical cash in hand – (or by such means as loot) could be spent; deficit financing was not really possible, and emperors were at times compelled to resort to such devices as selling the imperial palace's furniture to refill the treasury. Nerva's generosity appears to have caused some anxiety in the Senate. His answer to the problem and to the anxiety was a typical politician's move – he handed the issue over to the Senate, which appointed a commission to study the issue.[9]

It is at this point that we may reintroduce our man Frontinus, whose activities have been only conjectured since his governorship of Asia ended more than ten years before. He was appointed to be one of the financial commission – though he had already shown his willingness to support Nerva's regime. Like many military men he was a Flavian loyalist in politics, if anything. But after September 96 there were no Flavians left who were eligible for power; there were two nephews of Domitian, still only children, and Domitian's divorced wife, now his widow, but none of these was capable of acting as an heir to the dead emperor. So, since it seemed that, after six or seven months, Nerva was fairly in command, loyalty could be attached to him. We may assume that this was Frontinus' decision, as it was with others.

Alternatively, if Nerva seemed to be threatened with overthrow, it might seem best, even if a man was unhappy about his exercise of power, or about his process of reaching the position of emperor, to support him, at least until a viable successor was located and appointed. A second imperial coup within a year would be almost guaranteed to incite trouble in various places. Nerva had neatly dealt with one plot against him within a few weeks of his own coup. C. Caecilius Piso Crassus Frugi Licinianus plotted to kill the emperor at the Plebeian Games in November 96. The problem for the plotters, a group of young and wealthy men, was that they had talked publicly about their plans, and many senators, Nerva himself, and the Guard commanders knew all about it. Nerva, attended by Guards at the Games, was actually in no danger, but he made a show of confronting the chief plotter, Crassus Frugi, and dared him to strike. With a couple of Guardsmen nearby the potential assassin dared do nothing. He was pushed off into exile in Tarentum in southern Italy, no great hardship.[10] He apparently believed that with a longer aristocratic lineage than Nerva, he was entitled to be emperor.

Other problems emerged in the summer of 97, including the realization that the emperor's generosity over taxation had seriously depleted the treasury. This was the reason for the senatorial commission's appointment, which was to investigate the taxation problem and was to consist of five senators. We only know the names of two of them: T. Vestricius Spurinna and Sex. Julius Frontinus, though L. Verginius Rufus refused to accept nomination, possibly through age and decrepitude (and in fact he died later in the year).[11] This commission appears to have been set up in the second quarter of 97 – the dating is approximate only – and eventually reported back about six months later, by which time events had moved on; there is no indication that it had any effect.

At about the same time as the appointment of the commission, or perhaps somewhat earlier, Nerva appointed Frontinus as *curator aquarum*, the official in charge of the maintenance of the water supply of Rome. It was his acceptance of this charge, and then of the appointment to the senatorial commission, which marks Frontinus' public acceptance of Nerva's rule. He was now in charge of a complex of nine aqueducts, the associated plumbing systems, and a substantial workforce (see Chapter 12). He was replacing Manius Acilius Aviola, who had held the post for over two decades, and was now over eighty years old (he had been consul in 54). Aviola was a member of a family of the highest Roman aristocracy, descended from a consul of the 190s BC. The family is probably the longest-lived aristocratic family in Roman history, and can be traced into the fifth or sixth century AD, each generation holding public office. This longevity, however, does not mean that the members of the family were particularly active or efficient, only that they were well born and adept at avoiding involvement in awkward political situations. (One was suggested to be emperor in the crisis of 193, but successfully slid out of it; this seems to be the only point in the family's history when they came close to real executive power.) Aviola himself appears to have been lazy and careless in his post as *curator*, probably leaving the actual work to his slaves and freedmen, and to some experts already employed by the office. His age probably meant he had been unable to perform his duties in any serious way for the past decade.

This is not necessarily why Aviola was replaced by Nerva with Frontinus. It is not known exactly when the appointment was made, but Frontinus had been silent and out of sight until appointed to the post of *curator aquarum*, and the senatorial commission appointment probably came not long after. And at that very time the emperor faced a whole series of major difficulties which forced a major change in direction for his rule and compelled him to make a decision on the succession. The coincidence of the emergence of several senior senators in new and visible posts with a major threat to Nerva's life and position was probably no accident.

In summer 97 the succession issue, which had dogged the Nervan imperial regime from the first, became suddenly more serious. Nerva was a bachelor, had no children, and his only near relative refused absolutely to be considered as his heir or successor. (This was M. Salvius Otho Cocceianus, Nerva's nephew; he was also the nephew of the former Emperor Otho; Otho's grandson, M. Sergius Octavius Laenas Pontianus, a descendant of Otho's marriage to Poppaea, also adamantly refused to be considered.) Either of these would have provided an easy solution to the succession problem, since Roman society was deeply imbued with the hereditary principle. But they were clearly too sensible to even consider it. No doubt both had lived too close to power to be attracted.

One reason the adult and elderly members of the Senate accepted Nerva as emperor was that they expected him to die soon, so one of them might become his successor; a series of elderly and brief emperors was thus in prospect, and it was not a prospect others saw as attractive. In summer 97, however, the governor of Syria, P. Cornelius Nigrinus Curiatius Maternus, began giving out signals that he was eligible and available as an imperial successor, and making moves which suggested he might emulate Vespasian in making a play for the empire from the eastern provinces. This was a man who had four legions in his province, and three or four more within reach (in Egypt, Palestine, and Cappadocia). This was exactly the power base from which Vespasian launched his bid for the empire, though the military balance had shifted since then. It might be that the legions and the legionary commanders were attracted by the thought of a campaign to install an emperor, and the associated opportunities for loot and plunder which would thus be available, but a brief calculation of the positions and concentrations of the other legions no doubt deterred at least the officers. Curiatius Maternus was really too far away from the centre of power in the empire for such an attempt to be seriously considered. But his moves brought the issue, which had been hovering in the air since Nerva's coup, to the fore at last.

Curiatius Maternus was rightly seen as a threat by Nerva, and he sent a message to the legionary commanders of the Syrian legions, who deposed Maternus, and another to the governor of Asia, who sent his quaestor M. Larcius Priscus to Syria with orders to take over the command of Legio IV Scythica at Seleukeia Zeugma, and then became temporary provincial governor.[12] Priscus was startlingly junior for such a position, brief and temporary though it was, but using a man of quaestorial rank would clearly deflate the legionary commanders and perhaps alarm them; it would certainly show Curiatius Maternus what Rome thought of his performance and pretensions.

Once again the politician in Nerva had identified a neat way of solving a potential crisis without serious trouble. Maternus returned to Rome with the promise of a second consulate, and was put on the list for the next year. So, no bad feelings again, and the crisis had been scotched rather cleverly. But this was the third time the issue of the succession to the empire had arisen – with Crassus Frugi, with Nerva's nephews, and now with Curiatius Maternus, all in perhaps nine months, and no solution had emerged. It would arise again unless Nerva pre-empted further attempts. Nerva could clearly solve these relatively minor crises, but the question would keep coming. He could only solve the problem by dying, which could well result in another civil war, or by choosing an acceptable successor, which might persuade the chosen man to move quickly to seize actual rather than potential power, in advance of the emperor's death, just in case Nerva changed his mind.

It was thus in the midst of, or in the aftermath of, the Syrian crisis that the Senate's financial reform commission was set up, with Frontinus and four others, all aged senators again; Frontinus had been appointed as the new *curator aquarum* even before this – his re-emergence was thus Nerva's doing, in search of wider support. Nerva had already appointed a new praetorian prefect, Casperius Alienus, whom he must have expected to be loyal, and had confirmed the city prefect, Aurelius Fulvus, another old senator, in office. His *consilium* was composed inevitably of senators of his own generation, including those men who had been in the plot to make him emperor. He appears to have been sensibly surrounding himself with loyalists who were partly his fellow plotters. In part also he was recruiting others, like Frontinus, by putting them into useful offices, which they owed to him. Frontinus had been out of any office for a dozen years, but he was an active man who wanted to work – hence, in many ways, his books – and putting him in charge of a technical problem, such as the water supply, was to put him primarily into just the sort of work he enjoyed and did well.

Nerva was clearly aiming to find men who could be fitted into posts in accordance with their careers and interest; his political aim was to attract such men, and so make them loyal. He was also evidently keen to avoid creating hatred, as with his conciliatory treatment of the two men who had made moves to displace him, Crassus Frugi sent to Tarentum (he could well have been executed), Maternus brought to Rome and promised a future consulship (rather than being exiled to a small island). It was all policy of the same type: satisfy men and use them profitably, do not make eternal enemies of others, a typical Nervan policy of smoothing over difficulties, and a vivid contrast to Domitian's more brutal methods of dealing with opponents. These men were variously calmed down, or given useful jobs, but, as with his generosity with the money in the treasury, this was a policy which had only a limited life.

And still the overall problem of the succession was not solved, and the issue would not disappear until he made an acceptable choice – and he must have known this after the repeated crises on the problem. Nor had the equally serious resentment of some at the death of Domitian gone away.

The signs of continuing loyalty to the dead Domitian were several, and increased in importance as time passed. Soon after his death the altar boy who had witnessed the murder left the palace, without difficulty, and went to visit Domitian's former nurse, Phyllis, who was angry enough at what he told her to take action. She found the emperor's body (in the public morgue) and arranged for its cremation and for it to be placed in an urn in the Flavian temple, alongside his brother and his father and other family members.[13] That was one sign of respect. Perhaps the slow response of some senators to respond to Nerva as emperor might indicate their reservations about him – Frontinus' absence from the record for nine months could indicate such a reservation; or it was perhaps a due caution to see what else would happen. That he emerged into public life at the time when the emperor was facing increasing difficulties over his authority and the crisis of the succession, suggests that he appreciated that Nerva needed support in holding on long enough to name that successor in an orderly way; it may also mean that he wanted to be involved in the choice, and to help oversee the transition. It was not necessarily overt support for the emperor, only a wish to calm affairs down.

The main problem emerged as the Praetorian Guard. These men were supposed to protect the emperor, and yet he had been murdered, one of the prefects had been in on the plot, and one of the Guard had participated in the murder. The two Guard commanders had been dismissed by the new emperor, who had been the principal beneficiary from the murder, but their replacement was, from Nerva's point of view, hardly an improvement. Casperius Aelianus had assisted Vespasian in 69, and had been praetorian prefect for a time under Domitian; he could obviously be counted as a Flavian loyalist. The Guard, hardly hindered by their new prefect, gradually built up a feeling of anger, a feeling that justice should be meted out on the murderers; it seems that Aelianus encouraged this feeling, for his own purposes.

It seems that the murderers' identities were known; there had been too many men involved, as plotters and murderers, to keep their names secret for long. Stephanus, who had wielded the knife at first, was already dead, probably an attempt by Parthenius and the others who were present to make him the scapegoat. But too many men were involved for this ploy to work. In summer 97, a section of the Guard decided to take action; Aelianus was with them. They surrounded the palace and demanded that the emperor punish the murderers of his predecessor. This was the Guards' revenge. It is possible that Aelianus put himself in the lead to head off worse violence, but he seems to have enjoyed his role too much for such an easy explanation.

The demands of the Guardsmen were limited to the actual murderers, either because they thought the deed was the plotters' idea alone – a palace plot, in other words – or because this was to be the first stage in a campaign to seek out everyone involved, which would include the senators, and must end sooner or later with Nerva himself. If it was the first, Nerva was on the spot, because he was sheltering Parthenius and Petronius Secundus in the palace; if it was the second, Nerva personally was in imminent danger as the man who had profited most and most obviously from the murder, and Nerva's action in protecting two of the men involved did clearly indicate his own involvement. One might detect the incipient demagoguery of Aelianus in the early limitation of the soldiers' demands; if they succeeded, they would surely return with increased demands.

Nerva came out of the palace and told the soldiers that he personally was guaranteeing the safety of the two men, whom the troops had identified as murderers. If he had been able to count on armed support this might have worked, as with Crassus Frugi at the games; but his Guards were now his accusers, not his protectors. They persisted in their demands. Nerva melodramatically bared his throat and claimed he would defend the men with his life. (Again, one may recall his equally melodramatic scene at the games when he confronted the sword-wielding Crassus Frugi.) The soldiers did not cave in to this bluff; they simply ignored the hapless emperor and some of them pushed past him and went in to search the palace; they dragged the two men out, then proceeded to kill them themselves. Petronius was killed cleanly, as a Guardsman, but Parthenius, a freedman, was first castrated then slowly strangled. (The castration was perhaps a deliberate comment on Nerva's decree which prohibited the practice – that is, it was a further display of contempt for the emperor.)[14]

The emperor survived, shaken and humiliated, but with a grievous loss of authority. The Guard had carried out a partial *coup d'état*. If they found a further cause for complaint – another murderer to be punished, or a further episode of Aelianus' slow seizure of power, or a shortage of their pay – they might not stop at simply showing contempt for him. For the moment tempers cooled, and no other issue arose. But time was now up. Nerva was old, probably unwell; this crisis cannot have improved his health, and it would now not take a major event to kill him.

The emperor was, in Rome, effectively defenceless if he could not rely upon the Guard. It was necessary, therefore, to find a defender, an armed force which could overawe the Guard, and the obvious source, indeed the only possible source, was the army in Pannonia, still without orders to go to war, left in suspense for the past year. The price of any support from that army would be to name a successor, and it would have to be a military man with an army at his back. The army in Pannonia was the only one which was reasonably close to and within reach of Rome. One problem with using it, however, was that it was commanded by a set of generals appointed by, and conspicuously loyal to, Domitian. It would take a clever politician/intriguer to navigate this situation. But that is what Nerva excelled at. Naming a successor was the one power Nerva still possessed, that and his innate cunning.

Surveying the list of candidates Nerva will have had certain qualifications in mind. The man must be of mature age, late 30s or 40s would be best. He must have been consul. He must have governed one or more provinces and shown some initiative – in so far as such was acceptable to emperors – and to have displayed an administrative capability. It would be good if he had commanded armies. Only by appointing a Domitian loyalist would he be able to calm many of the dissidents. These qualifications automatically ruled out all the ageing supporters of Nerva in Rome and the Senate, who would have been hoping to take their turns as emperors, though perhaps he did not tell them that; and yet they were in as great a danger from the angry guard as Nerva, and they must have known this. Another quality would be that the candidate should be at least a second-generation aristocrat, and possibly of patrician rank. Nerva was as much of a snob as other Romans, such as Crassus Frugi.

The two or three months following the Guard riot, which took place probably in July or perhaps August, were spent in searching out and sounding out a successor, and plotting a method by which he could be announced. So Nerva was organizing a plot which would save him from punishment for organizing and profiting from an earlier plot. The selection of the successor was probably made by September and the plot was laid. Several of the senators were informed and were brought onside, and approved the choice; those who could not approve were kept out of the secret. Nerva's experience of the men in Rome and the Senate was no doubt invaluable in sorting out those who could be informed from those who must not be. Quite possibly Nerva, in his element, enjoyed the whole process.

It seems very likely that Frontinus was involved in all this. He was trustworthy, he was a military man, and he knew the generals in Pannonia, and he had access to the emperor. (He was also too old to be considered as a candidate.) It is quite possible that he was Nerva's choice of messenger to the Pannonian commanders, not perhaps in his own person, since his disappearance from Rome at such a moment would feed suspicion, but he will have known men, or perhaps had slaves, whom he could trust to carry such messages. Q. Sosius Senecio, if he was in Rome at the time – he had been commander of the legion at Bonna from 94 to 97, in contact with the generals, and had probably returned to Rome during 97 – was as Frontinus' son-in-law ideally placed to be a message conduit. He was bright, well-connected, of patrician rank; and he was certainly well rewarded in the early years of the next reign. The consular lists for the years 99 and 100 were partly composed of men who had assisted in the succession, just as those for 97 and 98 were littered with the names of Nerva's supporters.

The timing was arranged. The sequence of events was worked out. The chosen man was informed, as were his military colleagues, some of whom were no doubt jealous, though the obvious man, the overall commander Pompeius Longinus, was not the man chosen, and made no complaint; this will have prevented any serious complaints by others. In October, therefore, 'a laurelled letter', as Pliny the Younger later described it, arrived by special messenger from the great army which Pompeius Longinus commanded in Pannonia. It announced that a victory had been won on the German frontier. (This may even have been true, but if so it was probably a manufactured victory, to enhance the chosen successor's reputation.) Nerva took the letter to the Senate and announced the good news, and at the same time named the victorious general and arranged that this man, Marcus Ulpius Traianus, consul in 91, was to be adopted as Nerva's son, and so would be the imperial successor.[15]

Chapter 11

Traianus Imperator

The attempted coup by the Guard commander Casperius Aelianus in summer 97 – if that is what it was, or perhaps it was the preliminary to a more decisive one – did not succeed. Nerva stood his ground, accepted responsibility, was humiliated, but was not killed. He was unable to protect two of his fellow conspirators, who were killed in front of him and in public. His authority was badly damaged by this, but he remained emperor. As an experienced political operator, he developed the new plot which involved recruiting the commanders of the great army which Domitian had assembled in Pannonia as his supporters. In exchange the army in effect insisted on nominating his successor, choosing M. Ulpius Traianus (cos 91), a conspicuous Domitianic supporter.

The choice of Trajan must have been unexpected to the Senate and to the Romans. He had been moderately prominent in the Saturninus affair, but no more than that; his father had been consul, and had annexed Eastern kingdoms, but was never prominent in Roman politics. Nerva undoubtedly knew him, but hardly well; indeed, he had probably known the father rather better. The son had spent much of his time in office governing provinces or commanding armies; he perhaps spent little time in Rome. All this means that it is unlikely that Nerva himself made the selection, and it is more likely that he was nominated by the senior commanders of the army in Pannonia. But again, how it was that he was their choice is impossible to see. He was a moderately good commander, but there were plenty of those, for the Roman army operated almost automatically in war, and commanders often had little effect except on occasion, say in bringing the army to the point of battle. On the face of it Pompeius Longinus would have been a more likely choice, though he was perhaps ten or more years older than Trajan. It may be that it was his and his father's loyalty to the Flavian emperors which was decisive, the army commanders making it clear that it disapproved of Nerva's coup. However he was chosen, Trajan had to be accepted in Rome, by *force majeure* if by no other way. Nerva had no choice but to accept.

That is, Nerva found himself saddled with a successor who was dedicated to reversing whatever new directions in imperial affairs Nerva had instituted – and the most obvious change he had insisted on so far was to suspend the planned war against the Marcomanni and Quadi in the north; perhaps 'insisted' is not quite accurate – he actually seems to have ignored that planned invasion, which could not go ahead without an imperial order. The fact that the war remained suspended could be explained by the lateness of the season when the new political situation in Rome was finally arranged.

There were plenty of reasons for keeping the army immobile until the winter of 96/97 closed in; the alliances with the German tribes had lapsed, and would need to be renegotiated, and Nerva's indifference was an obstacle; the Dacian peace would similarly need to be renewed, if possible. The strategy, military and diplomatic, had to be rethought. There is no sign that anything was done. It was Nerva's responsibility as emperor to negotiate new agreements. There is no indication that he did.

Then in 97 there were recurring crises in the empire and in Rome. But perhaps the main reason was that Nerva was profoundly unmilitary and sending the army to war would be to hand too much power to the generals. The several challenges to the emperor over the succession were thoroughly unsettling, and were made worse by the way the problem repeatedly re-emerged. Nerva cannot have felt safe at any time, and sending off the army to campaign would render him even more vulnerable. It was not until October of 97 that matters between the emperor and the army were settled, and Trajan was appointed heir. By then it was again too late to begin a new campaign, if there was to be one. In a month winter would have clamped its grip on Bohemia and the army might be trapped.

It may well have been clear also by this time that Nerva did not have long to live. He died, in fact, on 27 January 98, shortly after surrendering his fourth consulship to his suffect Domitius Tullus.[1] His death was no doubt hastened by the strain of being emperor, and by the experience at the hands of the Guard five months before.

One of the things which had to be arranged between the dying emperor and his successor in those months between October 97 and the end of the year was the list of men who would take office as consuls for the coming year. No doubt there were also other matters to arrange, including the continuing matter of the projected war, but in Rome one of the most urgent was the consular list. And the list for 98 is very curious.

Nerva, on coming into the office of emperor in 96, fairly late in the year, had found a list of consuls for the year 97 already drawn up by Domitian, and those on the list had already been informed. This was the usual practice in order that the men nominated would have time to prepare, and sometimes to get to Rome if they were out of the city or out of Italy. Nerva was able to insert himself into the first place on Domitian's list, as *consul ordinarius* for January and February. He also brought in his old friend M. Verginius Rufus as his partner – both men holding the office for the third time; Rufus had refused the urgings of the German legions to take the throne in 69, thereby attempting to prevent a civil war; he failed then so his reappearance as consul was a timely reminder that Nerva had taken the throne without more than the moment of violence against the assassinated emperor; the change had not resulted in a civil war, and Nerva had successfully deflected threats of further fighting by blocking Curiatius Maternus, Crassus Frugi, and even the Guard. The appointment of Rufus might also therefore be a warning to any other aspirants to power.

The rest of the year's consuls as a result would have to serve shorter terms. In fact, it looks very much as though he brought in another pair of men, Cn. Arrius Antoninus (for his second term) and Calpurnius Piso – the latter perhaps included deliberately as a memory of his relative's choice as heir by Galba in 69, and then quickly murdered. These, like Rufus, will have had his own supporters and nominees. So, instead of Domitian's list of eight consuls, each pair serving three months, Nerva's list was twelve men, each of whom served for two months – ten would not divide the year easily into equal sections. So those who had been tapped for consul by Domitian for 97 took up the office as proposed, but for two months instead of three, and the new emperor did so as well, as was expected, together with three of his pals. One of the consuls later in the year was Curiatius Maternus, no doubt inserted by Nerva, as one of the two added to make up the twelve. The last man on the list was Cornelius Tacitus, probably also added to make up a more convenient number.

But the same problem arose for 98. It was necessary that the emperor's partner, as Trajan really was, to receive a second term as *consul ordinarius*, and yet Nerva had already drawn up his own list for the year, with himself as *consul ordinarius* again, and these men could not be disappointed, for there was no point in needlessly antagonising the group of senior senators he intended to honour. So the list was shuffled again. Nerva would open the year once more, with Trajan as his partner, both serving as ordinary consuls. No one could object to this. But Trajan, just to emphasize his new importance, and to point out that he was really now in charge, would serve for no less than six months, an unprecedented term for many years for any emperor, or indeed for any consul. Nerva's pals, four men each serving a second term, then followed as his own suffects, but served only a single month each, partnering Trajan one after another during the new emperor's six months. Not only that, but Trajan would serve as an absentee consul, for he intended to stay with the army in the north the whole time.

Then, in the second half of the year, the office would be taken by six more consuls, who were probably nominated by Trajan (though this is not certain), each serving for two months. Nerva's one-month-at-a-time suffects were all serving their second terms, and all of them were of his own age, in their 60s or older. It may have been intended originally that they would serve longer terms, perhaps three or four months, since there were only four of them, and certainly the last group, of six, served two months each. It is a very oddly constructed list indeed.

One of Nerva's suffects, serving his second term as consul, was Sextus Julius Frontinus, taking up the office for February, only four days after Nerva's death.

His name appears in the list of what must have been Nerva's choice of suffects, holding the office in February. Nerva died late in January, and Trajan, the other ordinary consul, was in Germany. Once again, therefore, as in 70 as praetor, Frontinus was in effect left in charge. (The immediate successor for Nerva, Domitius Tullus, was consul for only two weeks.) This placement of Frontinus so high in the list, cannot have been accidental. Nerva's death was no doubt expected for some time, and to have a man like Frontinus, cautious and careful and a Domitianic loyalist, but also friendly with both Nerva and Trajan, left in command in Rome was possibly very satisfactory to all involved.

Nerva had in fact abdicated his consulship on 13 January, to be replaced as suffect by Cn. Domitius Tullus (in his second term) for the rest of that month. The news of Nerva's death was sent to Trajan at Colonia

Agrippinensis (Cologne). His cousin Hadrian, who was serving at the time in the army, managed, so he said, to beat the official messenger to bring the news to Trajan. Meanwhile in Rome there was a pause while the Senate waited for instructions. They came, for the funeral, and for the necessary process of legitimizing the succession, all carried out during February, the month Frontinus was consul. It gradually dawned on the senators that the new emperor had better things to do than travel all the way to Rome to attend some ceremonies, which were presumably competently composed and conducted under Frontinus' supervision. Trajan stayed on the frontier.

The danger during an imperial accession was twofold, a coup in the city, and invasions over the frontiers. It is clear that Trajan felt no fear of any problem in Rome. He was all too clearly the chosen successor to Nerva (however it was arranged), chosen publicly by the old man and acknowledged as a sort of joint emperor for several months already; at the same time, he was the successor to Domitian, to whom he had long been conspicuously loyal; he was pursuing that emperor's policies, and was recognized as doing so. There was little danger of a Roman coup either by Nerva's partisans or by those of Domitian in the circumstances, and with the succession of a group of jointly chosen, and very senior, consuls in charge in the Senate for the next months he could be sure that any threat could be detected and quickly suppressed.

So the real danger came on the frontier, hence his presence at Colonia, the headquarters of Germania Inferior, with four legions close by. The large army in Pannonia was to be partially dispersed, but Trajan had his own plans, as Domitian's successor. However, the danger at the frontier came not just from the possibility of invasions from outside, but from a coup from within the army. Trajan had been, when chosen to be put forward as Nerva's successor, just one of a group of senior commanders. He was a long-experienced legionary commander, and at the time of his selection he was governor of Germania Superior; he had also been active in preparing the invasion of the Marcomanni lands. Indeed, the report of a victory he is said to have gained was instrumental in provoking Nerva to proclaim him as heir – or so it was said. So he was a senior commander in the great army, but he was only one amongst a set of equals. The danger clearly existed that he would be assassinated or otherwise removed before he could get set. It was a recurrence of the main problem of Nerva's reign.

He had to avoid a frontier war for the moment, since the empire was likely to be unsettled by the events in Rome for some time, and he had to demonstrate his authority. Fortunately there was a group of victims to hand.

The praetorian prefect Casperius Aelianus was summoned to attend the new emperor at Colonia Agrippinensis, along with a selection of those of his men who had participated in the Guard riot threatening Nerva the year before. They went willingly, apparently convinced that their action was approved (they had, after all, avenged Domitian's murder and the action had inadvertently led to Trajan's promotion); they clearly thought they were to be congratulated or promoted or rewarded. But this was a clear failure of imagination on their part, most surprising in an experienced politician like Aelianus. It was comparable with their original action, which was also extremely short-sighted. Aelianus had perhaps been praised for the action by Trajan to lull his suspicions. But the continuation in power of men who had performed such an action was an obvious threat to any emperor, a condition which would not be tolerated by any emperor, for it might set off similar attacks. The Guard had dominated Rome ever since; the city was not a safe place for an emperor. It did not matter that they had claimed to be avenging Domitian; what mattered was that they had threatened, humiliated, and defied an emperor. When they reached Trajan, Aelianus was executed and the others were 'put out of the way', as a later historian puts it.[2]

No doubt this upset the Guardsmen who were still in Rome. A new prefect, Sextus Attius Suburanus Aemilianus, was appointed. He had long experience throughout the empire in a series of procuratorial posts, including governor of Alpes Cottiae, and his last post, procurator of Gallia Belgica, will have brought him into contact with Trajan and the army.[3] His first task was to impose his authority as Trajan's appointed prefect on the Guard in the city. Executing a prefect and removing those who had been involved in the humiliation of Nerva was bound to annoy and upset some of the men, though no doubt others will have approved – only part of the Guard had been involved in the humiliation of Nerva. What Suburanus actually did to restore discipline to the Guard is not known, though some expulsions, and possibly executions, no doubt took place. He remained in office for several years and was rewarded by Trajan – he was adlected to the Senate in 101 and made *consul ordinarius* in 104 – so it may be assumed that he was successful, at least from the emperor's viewpoint.[4]

Here, of course, was another good reason for the new emperor to remain outside Rome for the moment; until the Guard – the main military force in the city – was under control and was clearly returned to loyalty, his presence in Rome might put him in danger; this was the obvious lesson from Nerva's experience. The Senate was busy attempting to demonstrate its loyalty by offering him extravagant titles – 'Augusta' for his wife and his sister, *pater patriae* for himself, which he clearly found distasteful – and such sycophancy might be another reason for him to stay away.[5] When the consular list for 99 was drawn up, he refused to be *consul ordinarius* again, on the curious ground that he would be out of the city still, which had not prevented him from taking up the post – the extraordinary consulship for six months – in his absence in 98.

The main reason for staying away from Rome, however, seems to have been that he needed to devote attention to the army and the frontier. His first residence at Colonia Agrippinensis during 97–99 allowed him to attend to the German army, in both the Inferior and Superior provinces. What exactly he was doing is not known, but just being present may have been enough to reassure the army. He moved to the Danube frontier later, about the end of 98, where it seems that the army was restless and had been losing discipline.[6] No doubt this was because it had been in camp awaiting orders to invade Bohemia for two years, while Nerva ignored it. The arrival of the new emperor, whom many of the men already knew, no doubt solved the discipline problem, and increased morale – two donatives in two years will have helped – but what the army wanted to do was to fight.

It appears that Trajan appreciated that the situation on the frontier had changed, and that it was no longer possible to launch the great attack on the Marcomanni and Quadi which Domitian had planned. This change was the result of Domitian's murder. With his death the treaty with the Dacians lapsed, and Nerva did nothing to renew it – or perhaps Decebalus, the Dacian king, refused to renew it. This had been one of the cornerstones of Domitian's aggressive plan, that the Dacians would remain quiet, pinned down by their treaty, while the Marcomanni and Quadi were dealt with. (All the other treaties, with the Hermunduri and others, also lapsed, but it is likely that Trajan would have been able to renew these fairly easily.) The absence of a treaty with Decebalus meant that it was too dangerous to take the army into Bohemia with a possibly hostile Dacia on his flank. Therefore, given that a war on the northern frontier would have to be fought to scotch the usual threats, Dacia had become Trajan's priority. Pliny, in his *Panegyricus* (of AD 100) describes a confrontation across the frozen Danube between the Roman army, drawn up in battle array, and a threatening barbarian tribe, which may be a set of Dacians; the confrontation ended with the tribe going home, having surrendered hostages.[7]

Trajan's appreciation, therefore, was that Dacia would need to be his first conquest; only when that land was conquered and neutralized could he consider attacking Bohemia. (That he did not in the end do so is probably due to the difficulty of conquering Dacia in the first place, and the subsequent need to impose a large garrison in the new province (or, later, provinces), which would leave him short of the necessary manpower – it was a new version of the problem Frontinus had left for Agricola in Britannia, with a large part of the British forces locked in garrisons in Wales.) Meanwhile he gave orders for major construction works to prepare for the Dacian War, by improving the tow path along the Danube, and by the excavation of a canal to bypass the rapids and cataracts of the Iron Gorge; Apollodorus of Damascus eventually built a great bridge over the river. These inspections and plans took the first half of 99. Leaving the work to be done over the next year or so, the emperor could then travel back to Rome at last, but still without hurrying, arriving in September (three years after Domitian's murder, eighteen months and more after Nerva's death). By all accounts his arrival in the city and his conduct there brought great approval and much public adulation, and perhaps some relief.

In the absence of the emperor the Senate had exercised much authority, and one of the emperor's first acts on arriving in the city was to greet the senators with affection and praise. The actions of Frontinus in this period of imperial absence are not known in specific detail, but certainly they included his second consulship in February 98, during which he was partly responsible for the arrangements for Nerva's funeral, and supervised the ceremonies by which Trajan's imperial authority was enacted into law. He was, of course still *curator aquarum* (unless it had been necessary to give up the post on becoming consul – he could be reappointed, of course). This will have taken up some of his time, as will attendance at the Senate. He was now one of the most senior senators, and was known to have Trajan's confidence, so that his personal authority was therefore much increased.

No doubt also his workload was much greater. The Guard had to be watched, and Suburanus supported; plots in the city had to be watched for and countered; there were at least two men in the Senate – Curiatius Maternus and Crassus Frugi (returned from his enforced exile in Tarentum) – who had manifested an active desire for Trajan's position. (Maternus was consul late in 97, but this consolation prize from Nerva will scarcely have quenched his ambition. He had by then been brought to Rome, where he was no longer in command of a set of legions; a very neat Nerva-type solution.)

It is also likely that Frontinus was involved in the construction of the consular lists for 99 and 100, since the emperor was away until well after the list for 100 would need to be published. This may be one of the reasons why Frontinus' own son-in-law, Q. Sosius Senecio, was consul in 99. He was not only consul, however, but *consul ordinarius*. So far as we know Senecio was a *novus homo*, with no known senatorial ancestors, and he probably came from Cilicia, so his ordinary consulship is either a result of Frontinus' exercise of nepotistic influence, or a result of Senecio's success in his earlier career. He would be the first from the Greek lands to become ordinary consul. He had commanded Legio I Minervia, stationed at Bonna, which was the legion Domitian had raised, while the crisis in Rome was happening, and while the grand army gathered in Pannonia; Trajan's arrival as governor of Germania Superior made them colleagues, and Senecio's next post, as governor of Belgica, was equally close. The suggestion that the Senecio-Frontinus connection was perhaps a major instrument in sorting out the succession crisis has already been noted.

There is enough here to have alerted Trajan to the fact that Senecio was a valuable man who would be worth promoting.[8] To do so would also be a compliment to Frontinus, whose influence and role in steadying the ship at Rome was no doubt appreciated, and a compliment to him would be a pleasant bonus.

There is a further dimension to this appointment, however. Senecio's partner as ordinary consul was A. Cornelius Palma Frontonianus, and these two were to be prominent as commanders in Trajan's Dacian Wars (and in the preparations for the Parthian war later). It seems that one of Trajan's motives in promoting these two men was to enhance their reputations in preparation for command in the planned war, which was now to be against Dacia, and they both received second consulships a few years later. There are thus quite enough reasons here for these two appointments; Frontinus' influence was perhaps marginal, though it will have existed nonetheless.

Trajan nevertheless demonstrated his gratitude for Frontinus' support in the next consular list, for 100, when Frontinus was *consul ordinarius* alongside Trajan himself, both of them in their third term. Frontinus was now an old man, almost 70, but it is unlike Trajan to make a man consul simply because he had survived for a long time. (Domitian had made Manlius Valens consul in 96 at the age of 90, to considerable derision.) Gratitude, however, was a credible reason, and Frontinus' third consulship may be seen as a gesture of thanks for his work in holding things together in 97–99 while the emperor was busy on the frontier. It is also a mark of esteem that Frontinus and Senecio were consuls in three successive years. When Trajan returned to Rome in 99 'he greeted the senators who awaited him with a kiss', and, in strong contrast to Domitian, he 'walked to the palace with the same modest demeanour as if it had been a private house'. All good public theatre; Trajan had learned fast.[9]

Chapter 12

Water, and Another Book

When Frontinus was appointed *curator aquarum* in 97 by Nerva, there were perhaps several agendas in operation. One was the obvious one that the previous curator, M. Acilius Aviola, had held the post for more than twenty years, having been appointed by Vespasian in 74. Even then he was in his 60s, had been consul in 54, and was probably born about AD 10. It was his death in 97 which opened the post to the appointment of a successor, and so to Frontinus – who, as it happened, was much the same age as Aviola had been when he was appointed. The post was at the disposal of the emperor, but was always given to a senior consular (a man of consul status, usually an ex-consul), apparently for life. (One of Nerva's ancestors had been curator seventy years before.)

It has already been suggested (in the previous chapter) that Nerva was seeking political support after the rocky start to his reign. He had already faced two, perhaps three, direct threats to his tenure, and Frontinus, as a prominent senatorial supporter and friend of Domitian, could be a very useful supporter for the new emperor to recruit, if he could be enticed out of retirement. Appointment as *curator aquarum*, the sort of technical job he enjoyed and was good at, was probably not unwelcome, therefore, and it was then followed also by his appointment to the financial reform commission set up by the Senate. Thus Frontinus was satisfactorily snagged as a supporter for the new regime.

Aviola's long tenure of the office had probably occasioned both surprise at his longevity and complaints at growing inefficiencies. Frontinus in his usual busy way instituted an inspection of the aqueduct system and, of course, he found much that needed to be done in the way of maintenance and repairs. No doubt any large-scale system such as the Roman aqueducts, even if his predecessor had been exceptionally diligent in supervising the work, would always require a series of repairs which would be revealed by a close inspection, and would show imperfections. There is thus no obvious fault in Aviola's curatorship.

Frontinus, nevertheless, was able to cast the blame for what he found wrong with the system back in time. Certainly, he felt that much needed to be done to upgrade and improve the system, which was in some parts several centuries old – improvements both in administration and in maintenance. It must always have taken a continuous effort by those working in the department to keep up with damage and wear and other problems, even without coping with exceptional difficulties.[1] Frontinus was in his element in this sort of work.

The work was done, of course, in the emperor's name, and Frontinus was reasonably diligent in giving praise to Nerva and Trajan, just as he had been in similar work under Domitian, and as he was in doing the work itself. Any improvement in water supply and quality would therefore be ascribed to the emperor, thus enhancing his popular reputation, but there would be praise enough left over for Frontinus, certainly amongst 'those who counted', the Roman opinion-makers, at least when things went well where it counted, that is in the imperial administration and the Senate.

Giving Frontinus this job was placing him into a congenial occupation. Nerva clearly knew his man, and successfully lured Frontinus out of his semi-retirement and his annoyance at the murder of Domitian – he'd had six months to get over any pique at the murder of his friend – and back into a position where he had to give active support for Nerva's rule. The emperor was thus able to use him, when the time arrived, as his envoy to Trajan, or perhaps as Trajan's man in Rome, to ease the way for Trajan to be adopted as Nerva's successor. The precise sequence of events is not recorded, but Frontinus was certainly involved in much of what went on between the Guard riot in August 97 and the return of Trajan to Rome in late 99. Nerva may not have envisaged these developments, but having Frontinus, with his military background (to reassure Trajan and the army), his long displayed diplomatic skills, his high standing in the Senate, and his long association with Domitian (again to reassure the army) was to have a man available for such work if and when he was needed. The Guard riot, orchestrated by Casperius Alienus, emphasized the need for a man like Frontinus to be on the spot and onside.

And Frontinus, busy though he no doubt was in the last year of Nerva's reign and in Trajan's first years, also wrote his book on the Roman water system, *de Aquis*.[2] As usual he proceeded systematically in his account, first with a description of the aqueduct system in its historical development, then on to a variety of issues he had identified, including identifying crimes, faults, and the legal framework. His aim was partly to rectify problems, such as leaks and illegal extractions, and expose the corrupt activities of the water men, but also to point out these difficulties for the benefit of his successors, whom he assumed would be as diligent as he was – which seems unlikely. What he ignored was that the curators were normally Roman aristocrats at the end of their political careers (as he was), doing the job negligently by relying on the work gangs of illiterates and slaves, or not at all. Contempt for his predecessors is barely suppressed at times.[3]

Frontinus, as noted, was well over sixty years of age when he was appointed as curator, and the aqueducts were, in total, over 500 kilometres in length.[4] Therefore it is highly unlikely that he inspected them all. And, in fact, in his description, analysis and criticism he only rarely indicates that he went and looked for himself. It follows that his account is less personal and much more a matter of research. The first section in fact is clearly the result of a consultation with the archives, giving a list of the aqueducts, their lengths, capacity, and problems, and so on; the book as a whole suggests that much of the content was in fact copied from archival accounts; in other words, it bears clear affinities with both his collection of *Stratagems*, and the technical account of surveying.

The description of the aqueduct system with which he begins leads on, in book II, to a discussion of the capacity of the various elements of that system, and here for once is a record that Frontinus himself was active and involved. The Aqua Julia, like other aqueducts, delivered its water into a central basin, but it was unusual in that it received its water from another aqueduct, the Claudia, and sent part of its water into a third, the Tepula, making the gauging of the capacity difficult to judge. (It is, however, also clear that Roman methods of calculation were not adequate to determine accurately the aqueducts' capacity and the flow of water.[5])

The Aqua Virgo was similarly awkward, since it received water from several sources, namely springs. Frontinus claims to have succeeded in making an accurate gauging of the flow, though this seems unlikely. He was comparing the capacities as noted in the records he had access to with what was actually being delivered, and found considerable variation, both greater and lesser, than expected and recorded.

He searched for the reasons for the differences, and found a wide variety of problems. The system of calculation was inadequate to the task, a matter he himself had reported; then there was the dishonesty of the workers, who diverted water to be used by private householders, presumably having been bribed to do so, and the even-less-official diversions by private citizens 'just to water their gardens'. In fact the fault clearly lay with the age and decrepitude of the administrative system (just as the age of the aqueducts themselves created many problems). The system was repeatedly interfered with by the tendency of emperors to grant rights to take water for private use, rights which, contrary to the intention, continued to be exercised long after they should have expired. In the result, the system of water use had become very complex, with numerous exceptions, rights, and exemptions, over the century or so since Augustus had first regulated it, and probably no one now knew who was entitled to what, thus giving some cover to those extractions which were manifestly unauthorized and illegal. And this was in addition to the plainly illegal thefts of water.

Frontinus records next the improvements made, and indicates what had still to be done. He makes it appear that the work done at his behest had decisively improved the lives of the inhabitants: 'the appearance of the city is clean and altered; the air is purer; and the causes of the unwholesome atmosphere which gave this area of the city so bad a name with the ancients, are now removed.' He ascribes these improvements to 'the care displayed by the Emperor Nerva', which is of course a means of self-praise, since he has spent the previous section explaining how hard he has worked to bring about the improvements he lists. This scarcely disguised self-praise is something new in his writings, perhaps an aspect of the high position he had gained in imperial and senatorial politics in these last years of his life. If he spoke like this to his fellow senators he may well have been insufferable, not that any Roman senator could be described as reticent.

He details some of the changes, particularly to the Old Anio, New Anio and Marcia aqueducts. He has heaped scorn on the Alsietina, whose waters were, he claimed, unwholesome. This was supplying the trans-Tiberiana part of the city; a new aqueduct named after Trajan which was finished in 109 to supply the same region of the city, but it had probably been begun under Nerva. Designed for the same destination, it was much longer and tapped into a purer source.

Frontinus points out the need to sort out the legal situation, much altered by additions and alterations since Augustus, and by the practice of granting out water rights, which was by his time clearly muddled and thus generally unclear. This leads him, inexorably, into a discussion – in effect another list derived from the records – of the previous curators, with extensive quotations from their decisions. And he attempts to set out the legal situation, but it is clear, though he does not say so in so many words, that the basic problem is that the emperors are always liable to grant out water rights to their favourites and to petitioners without consideration of the effect on the general supply. That is, the Roman Empire was an autocracy, ruled at the whim of the emperors, even down to the level of taking water from the public supply. Any attempt at orderly administration was therefore out of the question; codification of the system was required.

He ends by laying out the necessary work regime, the problems which should be dealt with, the restriction of thefts, the supervision in a much more detailed way of the work gangs, the need to be constantly vigilant in restricting the diversions of water by illegal private thefts. He explains the need to carry out repairs without interrupting the flow of water, and therefore to do so in winter, when the weather is cooler, and so on and on, in at times very fussy detail. The list is so long and requires supervision of such detail that it is clear that he considered that the task of *curator aquarum* was too much for a single man. It is therefore notable that only two more curators are known. It would seem that Trajan, or perhaps Hadrian, took note of this difficulty and altered the system.

This book is therefore a typical product of the man, bearing a clear relationship to his technical-cum-legal treatise on surveying, and on his systematizing attempt on warfare in the *Stratagems* (and presumably also in the lost *Art of War*). He allows rather more personal opinions to intrude than in his other books, contrasting private illegality with the provision of water for the public good, and allows his anger to show through at times; his interventions may be an aspect of an ageing irascibility.

It is a curious fact that this technical manual has provoked a plethora of associated studies, many of them even more impenetrable than some of Frontinus' technical passages.[6] There is even a 'Frontinus Symposium', based at Louvain/Leuven, which produces lengthy volumes of essays often of little relevance to the man's own work. In so far as studying *de Aquis* stimulates the understanding of Roman aqueducts and water systems generally, this seems reasonable. Studies have also reached out to techniques of building aqueducts (Hodge) (an issue which Frontinus scarcely considered) and the practices of Roman administration (Bruun, Peachin), within which Frontinus was clearly immersed. Bruun even takes the subject and extends it to a consideration of 'Roman imperial administration', perhaps forgetting that the issue is a supply of water to a single city.

Frontinus, of course, did not himself encourage this proliferation, which takes the student well away from his particular subject. He was engaged more by the theft of water, by the corruption of the water men, and the deterioration of the system, and he deliberately quoted a series of Roman laws aimed at suppressing these problems, in other words he was combatting maladministration. He even ended with a clear threat in his final paragraph (130). He had attempted, he said, to persuade the thieves to cease their illegal practices, or to confess and seek imperial forgiveness, in exchange for his secrecy about their activities, and so not exposing their misdeeds. His final sentence, however, promises that he was not inclined to be so restrained in future (which implies that he would continue as curator until the end of his life, or his resignation, even if he had been compelled to surrender the office when he was consul). His threat was clearly directed at those who felt that they were safe from his threats and disdained his methods.

It is characteristic of the study of his work, not merely in the quoted list of modern works but in other works also, that every student of this final paragraph has understood it differently. For some it is menacing, or 'severe, almost sinister' (Baldwin); others find in it a gentle warning, with emphasis on imperial forgiveness.[7] Throughout the work, however, Frontinus has endeavoured to insist that the aqueducts are a public service delivering water to the whole of the Roman population, and it is the derogation from this which sparked his anger, and produces the final menacing threat.

So, despite the apparent restrictions of his title, Frontinus has started enough hares, no doubt incidentally, to set historians off on a series of chases, often diverging from one another. These can be aimed at illuminating the ways of Roman administration, corruption and thievery in ancient Rome, and in investigating the aqueduct policies of other provinces and cities. But at the same time his emphasis is on holding a public office which is aimed at providing a public service, and therefore there is a need to ensure that the office's reputation is of the best, that it sets a clear example, one which is partly derived from Cicero and Seneca, but which echoes to this day in public vigilance against corruption and scandal.[8]

His precise purposes, however, tend to be elusive. The book may be a handbook for himself and future curators, giving the necessary information in a reasonably well-ordered way; it may be a polemic against bad administration and thievery; it may be a notebook for his own use – though there is certainly some evidence that copies were made and either given out or sold; Peachin has detected a hint in Martial that he had a copy with him when he returned to Spain.[9] Or, most likely of all, it is a mixture of all of these. It is called 'perplexing', and 'devoid of any literary pretensions or eloquence', though why a technical treatise should show such 'eloquence' is not clear;[10] it is by contrast also regarded as 'completely reliable',[11] though that surely only applies to the technical elements of the book; there are personal comments which may well be less than reliable.

Confusion has been created by his referring to 'Nerva', which has been interpreted as meaning Trajan, who acquired the name 'Nerva' through his formal adoption by the older emperor, or at times he refers to either Trajan or Nerva, clearly unambiguously, but the only clearly unambiguous references designate Nerva as 'deified' and therefore dead, and to Trajan by name. It seems best to assume that 'Nerva' means Nerva, unless there is a compelling reason to believe he meant Trajan. But Frontinus was inevitably compelled to refer to both emperors in sycophantic terms; his references to the 'Emperor Nerva' tend to be less so than those to Trajan, suggesting that he was writing after Nerva's death, perhaps in the period between Nerva's death in January 98 and Trajan's return to Rome in September 99, and before Nerva was deified by the Senate.

He was still writing this book in Trajan's reign, even referring at times to that emperor's attitudes in a way which is rather reminiscent of Pliny the Younger's letters to Trajan from Bithynia.[12] Frontinus is, of course, rather unpleasantly subservient and obsequious, in the same way that authors were in Domitian's day. On the other hand, he was clearly being encouraged in his work by Trajan, who was not short of suggestions, and Nerva also appears to have encouraged him to be rigorous in opposing illegalities. Trajan went on to fund the construction of another aqueduct, the Aqua Traiana, which was completed by 109. It is not beyond the possibility that it was Frontinus' advocacy which persuaded Trajan to undertake the work – he must have been involved as curator – and it is very likely that he was involved in the planning, perhaps during Nerva's reign. It is therefore curious that in the book he shows no interest in this aqueduct, nor in planning and building aqueducts, and that his references to the new aqueduct are few and indistinct.

There is no point in going into greater detail on the contents of the book. This has been done by numerous others. It is, at least superficially, a straightforward description of the aqueduct system of Rome, its problems, and the means of maintaining it. It was a technical manual, and as such it was clearly designed both for his own use and for the edification of later curators and for anybody interested in the subject. It was thus not a literary production, 'eloquent' though it is on the problems of the aqueduct system; it does have its moments of literary flair, and it has a certain eloquence in personal opinion which is unusual in Frontinus' works.

Above all it has a series of similarities to the other works bearing his name. It is well organized, it is technically competent, it is written in straightforward language, and, if it is not especially readable because of the content, then at least it is clear. It has survived, even if in only one original copy, kept at the Monte Cassino monastery. These similarities reinforce the attribution of the *Stratagems* to Frontinus (not that this is in any doubt), but also to the ascription to him of the pamphlet on surveying contained in the Agrimensores collection. The style, language, and approach of all these are so alike that only a single author can be imagined for all of them.

Chapter 13

The Narbonensian and Other Connections

Two assumptions underlie this chapter. The first is that our man, Sextus Julius Frontinus, came from the province of Narbonensis. There is, in fact, no direct evidence for his origins (which is assumed, and argued, in other places in this account), but there are certain indications. The name Julius Frontinus was more common in Narbonensis than in any other single province, and by a considerable margin.[1] This is hardly decisive, but it is certainly indicative, and so a man called Julius Frontinus is already more likely to have originated from Narbonensis than from anywhere else.

The second assumption is that Cn. Domitius Corbulo also came from Narbonensis, but this rests on even flimsier grounds; his *cognomen* looks to be Gallic, and the Domitius *nomen* is relatively common in Narbonensis, deriving from the governorships of more than one of the Domitius Ahenobarbus family in the Republican period. But the hills of Apennine Italy, notably the land of the Vestini, is also a possible origin for Corbulo, and is supported on very similar grounds.[2]

A further aspect to this is that a series of undisputed Narbonensians rose through the senatorial ranks from the time of the Emperor Tiberius onwards, and Frontinus and Corbulo again fit that process very well. These were men from several towns or cities in the province; not, in fact, from the Roman *coloniae*, such as Narbo Martius (Narbonne), but from the Gaulish population. The *coloniae* received an Italian population of legionary veterans when the men were retired and pensioned off in part by a grant of land in a *colonia*, a process which mainly took place in the discharge of soldiers at the end of the Republican civil wars, though it continued on a much smaller scale into and beyond Frontinus' lifetime. The land provided was sufficient to support them, even perhaps allowing them to buy a slave or two to work the plot, or rent it out and live on the proceeds. But none of these veterans were rich, and it would take two or three generations for a family to accumulate enough wealth to aspire to a Roman political career, and most never did.

The first-century senators from Gaul were much more likely to be men descended from the chieftains of the Gallic tribes who had converted their tribal eminence into the ownership of large estates, slaves (or serfs), and wealth, and were possessed of Roman citizenship, indicated by their *nomina*, derived above all from the Ahenobarbi (Domitii) and from the Caesars (Julii), but also from Valerii and Pompeii (the four most common *nomina* of Narbonensians.

Gaulish Consuls

The earliest of the Gaulish consuls were chiefly noted for their great wealth. Thus Cn. Domitius Afer (cos 39), who came from Nemausus (Nimes),[3] adopted the brothers Cn. Domitius Lucanus (cos 79) and Cn. Domitius Tullus (cos ?80, II 98; Nerva's first suffect in that year, with Frontinus following him).[4] They advanced to the consulship and several govenorships in tandem, having inherited Afer's riches. Nemausus was a Latin *colonia*, that is, it was granted *ius Latii*, probably by Julius Caesar when he was proconsul in the 50s BC; the locally elected city officials became Roman citizens on election, which quickly spread Roman citizenship through the local elite. Before that the city had been an inhabited site since the Bronze Age, and a tribal centre and trading town of the Volcae Arecomici for several centuries before the Roman arrival.

The Via Domitia was organized to go through the town in the 120s BC, providing an imperial link between Italy and Spain, by way of Nemausus and Narbo Martius, but noticeably avoiding several of the other older cities, including Massilia. As a result, Nemausus' importance automatically increased, as did the city's wealth, and so therefore did the opportunities for gaining still more wealth. That is, its population was always largely Gallic, fairly quickly Romanized, and the likelihood is that the Domitii of the city were in origin Gallic.[5] It did receive an infusion of colonists from Egypt, of all places, according to its coinage, but no Roman veteran soldiers were imposed on it, unlike Narbo and other places.

Another town which was connected by the Via Domitia was Ruscino (Chateau Roussillon), where the Pyrenees dip down to the Mediterranean. This had, like other places in Narbonensis, long been populated, and was particularly prosperous in the first century AD. It was at a strategic location, on the end of the Pyrenees, and commanding the road from Gaul to Spain. (It was where a group of tribes assembled their warriors in 218 BC to block Hannibal's progress, unsuccessfully). The town declined somewhat, but slowly, during the second century. It had the patronage of P. Memmius Regulus (cos 31), who had a career mainly in the eastern territories of the empire and left a connection with Sparta.[6]

The city of Tolosa (Toulouse) was the home of Antonius Primus, the bad boy of the recent Civil War. He was successful on Vespasian's behalf in invading Italy, but was quickly pushed aside, and then retired to his home city, probably wealthy. There is no sign that he established a family, though this is very probable, nor did the city produce other notable men who went into politics.[7]

The First Consuls

The first man from Narbonensis to reach the consulate was D. Valerius Asiaticus, a notable orator, a very wealthy man, and a Gaul (cos 35, II 46).[8] He was from Vienna (Vienne), on the Rhone south of Lugdunum (Lyon).[9] Like Nemausus the city was granted *ius Latii* by Caesar, but was promoted to a *colonia Romana* by Caligula when Asiaticus was noticeably powerful; this would considerably increase the number of Roman citizens in the city. It had an assertive governing regime, which had expelled some Roman citizens (who were not Gauls) to Lugdunum at the time of Caesar's assassination, and in 69 it supported Julius Vindex in his rebellion, quarrelling in the process with Lugdunum.[10] Apart from Asiaticus, Roman consuls from the city included Asiaticus' younger brother (consul at some point between 39 and 45), L. Pompeius Vopiscus (cos 69), M. Julius Vestinus Atticus (cos 65), and C. Bellicius Natalis (cos 68). This was a remarkable record – five families wealthy enough to put a son (or two) through the Roman political *cursus* from one city – especially for a provincial city inhabited largely by Gauls. It argues a strong concentration of wealth in those few families, and a conspicuous Roman loyalty – but then Tacitus claimed that the whole of Narbonensis was a conspicuously loyal province, especially towards the Senate.[11] In the case of Vienna, therefore, we have five consuls from the city between 35 and 69; there were more of them later.

The descendants of some of these Viennan consuls were particularly notable. The two Valerii held three consulships between them between 39 and 46; the son of the elder, another D. Valerius Asiaticus, was consul in 69 (one of many in that fraught year), and a later adoptee, D. Cottius Paetus D. Valerius Asiaticus Saturninus, was consul in 94 and 125.[12] Pompeius Vopiscus, without sons of his own, adopted C. Arruntius Catellius Celer, from Volsinii in Etruria, who became consul in 77; his grandson had a busy career and was consul twice, in the 140s and 150s.[13] The only one of the mid-first-century group without descendants was Vestinus Atticus. His father had been a friend of the Emperor Claudius, and the son was a known wit; he expended some of that wit at the expense of the Emperor Nero, and was gathered in for execution during the Piso plot in the year of his consulship; he was probably completely ignorant of the plot, but it seems that Nero did not appreciate jokes at his expense.[14] Nero had also stolen away, or had stolen, Vestinus' wife, Statilia Messalina, another good reason, in the emperor's twisted mind, to get rid of the ex-husband.[15] Bellicius, on the other hand, launched a senatorial dynasty in which his son, two grandsons, and a great-grandson were all consuls (in 89, 118, 124, 143, and 148); he was consul in the last part of 68, probably appointed therefore by Galba (which would induce Vespasian to favour him).[16]

Domitius Lucanus' daughter Domitia Lucilla inherited both her father's and her uncle's fortunes (she was adopted by Tullus after her father's death). She was married twice; her first husband was P. Aelius Hadrianus Afer, and they had a son who became the Emperor Hadrian (cos 108; Emperor 117–138); they also had two daughters; Lucilla's second husband was P. Calvisius Ruso (cos 79), who was probably from Narbonensis, and their daughter married M. Annius Verus (cos 97, II 121; III 126), whose son became the Emperor Marcus Aurelius (161–180).[17] The wife of the Emperor Trajan (98–117), Pompeia Plotina, is generally assumed to have come from Nemausus.[18] Arrius Antoninus (cos 69, II 97) another imperial ancestor, also appears to have originated at Nemausus.[19]

There are a number of connections amongst these men, both in Narbonensis and with other parts of the empire, and it is these connections which are of particular interest here. Narbonensis linked with Spain in the person of Domitia Lucilla married to Hadrianus Afer, and Pompeius Plotina married to Trajan; Pompeius Vobiscus from Nemausus was linked by his adoption of Arruntius Celer with Etruria, a link which would be later strengthened; Vestinus Atticus' forebears probably came from the Vestini country in Umbria, which may have been the original homeland of the Corbulones. This sort of attachment became increasingly important, not just in the western provinces, but in other areas as well. The stages were, first, a series of intermarriages and adoptions within a province, then, second, as the wealthiest men made their ways to Rome and a political career, the same process joined provinces to one another; eventually there was a wide interconnection linking large areas of the empire. It was one of the main sources of imperial strength.

Two Problem Cases

Two men were possibly Narbonensian, but the evidence is difficult. Cn. Domitius Corbulo was one of them, based, as noted earlier, on his characteristically Narbonensian *nomen*, and his probable Gallic connection. It may be noted that his daughter married Domitian before he became emperor, though they soon divorced, but the connection remained. The second of these awkward cases is C. Memmius Regulus (cos 31), who, as already noted, has been suggested to be from the province; he is recorded as the patron of the small city of Ruscino, though his career was largely in the eastern provinces, as governor of Achaia, Macedonia, Moesia, and Asia, and his marital connection was probably there also. The connection with Ruscino, however, is so anomalous in all this that it rather implies that he may have originated there, while the connection with Greece is apparently a result of his governorship of Achaia or Macedonia; several people in Sparta received their Roman citizenship from him, according to their citizen *nomina*. He is a puzzle. If he was from Narbonensis, which the connection with the Ruscino would suggest, he was the first consul from that province, beating Asiaticus by four years; his son was consul also, in 63; he was also one of the earliest to form a link between the western provinces and Greece.[20]

City Origins

Three other Narbonensian places produced consuls in the first century AD. The home of C. Julius Agricola (cos 77) was Forum Iulii (Frejus), on the Provencal coast; his father had risen to be a senator and praetor, but he was killed by Caligula, while Agricola's mother was killed when her estate at Intimilia (Ventimiglia) was sacked by Otho's troops in the Civil War.[21] Agricola was encouraged in his career by Seneca, partly because of the death of his father, and reached the consulship in 77.[22] He married Domitia Decidiana, the daughter of a Gaul who had risen to be *quaestor aerarii* in Rome; their daughter married Cornelius Tacitus, biographer, historian, and consul in 97.[23] Also from that town was Q. Valerius Paulinus (cos 107), none of whose ancestors or successors reached so high, though the father (or grandfather) was procurator in Narbonensis, and a friend of Vespasian.[24]

Arelate (Arles), the only Roman *colonia* in this province to produce a consul at this period, was the home of M. Pompeius Paullinus (cos 53), son of another *eques*, and whose daughter married Seneca.[25] The city also produced the Mettius family, beginning with M. Mettius Modestus, procurator in Syria in Claudius' reign. He had two sons, M. Mettius Modestus, who reached the consulship in 82, but was later exiled by Domitian in his paranoid later years. His brother, M. Mettius Rufus, proceeded along an equestrian career and rose to be prefect of Egypt and *praefectus annonae* in Rome. The sons were senators, M. Mettius Rufus, proconsul of Achaia (and so he had reached the rank of praetor) in about 90, and C. Trebonius Proculus Mettius Modestus, consul in 103, governor of Lycia-and-Pamphylia before then, and eventually governor of Asia. Another Mettius Rufus became consul in 128. The family therefore held offices of major importance for four generations. However, they seem to have made no mark in their home city; perhaps the family shifted to Rome once they became so political. They were unusual amongst the emerging consuls in the province in that the family was descended from an Italian immigrant of the Republican period, as indicated by the family *nomen*.[26]

Vasio (Vaison) produced two or three consuls. Sex. Afranius Burrus was Nero's mentor along with Seneca (who himself was married to Pompeius Paullina, daughter of Pompeius Paullinus from Arelate). L. Duvius Avitus was consul in 56;[27] again, neither of these men had any discernible descendants. It has been argued that the historian Cornelius Tacitus was also from Vasio. He married the daughter of Agricola, and was consul in 97, having avoided, or been denied, the honour under Domitian. He was generous to Burrus in his *Annals*, and to Seneca, which may suggest personal sympathy for both of them, based on their joint origin. His origin is never actually stated, but Agricola was clearly a link with Forum Iulii. In the absence of clear evidence, however, the issue is moot, but tends to favour Vasio as his origin.[28]

Vienna may have produced those senatorial families discussed above, and the ancestors of emperors, but Nemausus was even more productive of senators. The several Domitii have been noted, and after Domitian the family extended into three senatorial generations with the son of Domitius Tullus (cos 100). In addition, there was T. Aurelius Fulvus, double consul, founder of a three-generation senatorial family; he was Domitian's *praefectus urbi* for a time, retained by Nerva and Trajan, and an ancestor of both Marcus Aurelius and Antoninus Pius.[29] The latter emperor was also descended from Cn. Arrius Antoninus, another two-time consul; like Fulvus, he was from Nemausus.[30]

At a less-exalted social level, but only just, P. Marius Celsus (cos 69) was another from Nemausus.[31] One of his consular colleagues in that difficult year was Cn. Caecilius Simplex, who was, it seems, also from Narbonensis.[32] Celsus' son (cos 86 and 105) married Caecilius' elder daughter; they had two sons, one of whom was consul in 122 while the other reached the praetorship in 106, but died soon after.[33] A second daughter of Simplex married L. Julius Marinus, consul in 93, who was from the *colonia* of Berytus in Syria;[34] their son, consul in 101, married into the great Asian network of (former) royal families and wealthy Italian immigrant colonists.[35]

Alliances and Connections

Originating from the same town or city is one connection which could exist between these consuls, but there are others, and putting them all together rather suggests a fairly formidable network of influence, not just in the province but increasingly throughout the empire. Some early links between Spain and Narbonensis, and Narbonensis and Italy, have already been noted, but there were more.

It may be assumed that consuls from the same city would tend to operate in alliance, at least when in Rome and the wider world, even if, as seems quite likely, they were rivals at home. So the two men from Forum Iulii, C. Julius Agricola and the father of Q. Valerius Paulinus, may be considered as allies, with the former then assisting the progress of the latter's son. He reached the consulship in 107, supposing a start, at age 18, in the early 80s, so he will have begun his climb up the process while Agricola was governor of Britannia, or possibly earlier.

The two men from Vasio who were active in Nero's reign, Burrus and Paullinus, may well have assisted Cornelius Tacitus in his early career stages – Tacitus is notably kind about Burrus in his *Annals*.[36] And Tacitus (if, of course, he was really from Vasio) married Agricola's daughter. This would count as the beginning of a part of the network within the province, linking Vasio and Forum Iulii.

The line of Valerii from Vienna – the Asiaticus father, son and grandson – could be expected to be allied, when in Rome at least, with Pompeius Vopiscus, Bellicius Natalis and Julius Vestinus, all from the same city. Vopiscus, as noted, adopted Arruntius from Etruria, Bellicius established a senatorial dynasty lasting several generations; only Vestinus failed to father a successor or form a marriage alliance (so far as we know), though his *nomen* implies a possible family origin amongst the Vestini in Italy (who could have produced Cn. Domitius Corbulo), and his father was a friend of the Emperor Claudius, which could have helped his career; it may also have given him the self-confidence to joke about Nero, resulting in his early death.

The group of consulars from Nemausus were all more or less contemporaries, and may be assumed to have assisted each other where possible. T. Aurelius Fulvus and Cn. Arrius Antoninus were linked by the experience of 69 (Fulvus' influence from his post as governor of Moesia helped persuade the governor of Dalmatia to join Vespasian with his legion; Antoninus was consul for a time in Rome in that year); Fulvus' son married Antoninus' daughter and their son became the Emperor Antoninus Pius. Domitius Lucanus' daughter married Hadrianus Afer, and they produced the Emperor Hadrian. Pompeia Plotina married Trajan. (Narbonensis was thus ancestral for every emperor from 98 to 192.) The connection with Trajan, who was from Baetica, was reinforced by the marriages of Lucanus' granddaughter Domitia Lucilla with Fulvus' son – their son was Marcus Aurelius. His father was Calvisius Ruso, almost certainly from Narbonensis, possibly from Nemausus.

The Spanish-Narbonensian connection was thus highly significant in terms of the imperial succession, but it was also important in other, more widespread, connections of natives of Narbonensis who forged links with other parts of the empire, and in the time of Frontinus it was the latter aspect which was important. In the reign of Domitian no one could have predicted that this group of (relatively) obscure provincial consuls would be the progenitors of a line of emperors. Only with the emergence of Trajan as emperor did this Narbonensian connection become imperially important, and it seems that Trajan was the army's nominee to succeed Nerva.

In another link, Marius Celsus' son (cos 86), and Caecilius Simplex's daughter married and their daughter married L. Julius Marinus from Berytus (cos 93), who brought in a link with the elaborate network which was simultaneously developing in Asia Minor amongst the descendants of Italian colonists and migrants and of the local kings, who ruled a variety of temporary kingdoms from Judaea to Pontus and Thrace before they were gradually annexed to the empire. Memmius was linked with Greece, as governor of Achaia and Macedonia, by giving his names to a family of Spartans who took their Roman citizenship from him, as well as acting as patron of Ruscino. In diagrammatic terms, these links are the outline of a network, but it is still in a number of discrete sections (See the diagram on page 201).

The Corbulo Connection

On top of, or alongside, this series of marital links, was another connection, that of the legates of Domitius Corbulo in the Parthian War.[37] There are multiple indications that these men formed a close relationship because of their long service under Corbulo in that war. Corbulo has been asserted, with some evidence, to be from Narbonensis. Several of his commanders, including legionary legates, also came from Narbonensis. These included T. Aurelius Fulvus, who commanded Legio III Gallica, which was moved to Moesia; there he defeated a major invasion by the Rhoxolani, for which he was awarded consular insignia by Otho, though he soon came out for Vespasian.[38] He then persuaded the governor of Dalmatia to join Vespasian, a crucial addition in both force and geography to Vespasian's cause. Vespasian and Domitian both made him consul, in the early 70s and in 85.[39]

M. Ulpius Traianus (the elder) was from Baetica; he commanded Legio X Fretensis, and probably accompanied Vespasian when he moved to Egypt, a crucial moment in the slow coup the latter was conducting; he was made consul in 70, after being praetorian governor of Baetica before the succession crisis developed. He was made consul for 70 even before Vespasian reached Rome, no doubt to reinforce the Flavian support in the city; between 72 and 78 he governed Syria, Cappadocia-and-Galatia, and Asia. A. Marius Celsus commanded Legio XV Apollinaris, under Corbulo, was consul in 69, and governed Germania Inferior in the early 70s.[40] Then, of course, there was Frontinus, who was perhaps with Legio VII Galbiana in Pannonia. The legionary legate of this legion had been contacted from Syria on Vespasian's behalf, and as a unit raised by Galba, it would almost inevitably support Vespasian against Otho, Galba's murderer.

Both Vespasian and Mucianus in Judaea and Syria from 66 (when Corbulo was ordered to commit suicide) were acquainted with the great commander, and were affected by the affection his commanders exhibited. Others of Corbulo's legates came from Italy – Vettulanus Cerialis (cos 77), Cn. Pompeius Collega (cos 71), Rutilius Gallicanus (cos 78 and 85), commander of Legio XV Apollinaris, had governed Cappadocia for nine years while Corbulo campaigned in Syria and Armenia, a vital backstop position for the main campaign.[41] These men, perhaps a dozen in all, Narbonensians and Italians, formed a close-knit group who were outraged at the treatment Corbulo had received. Note also that Corbulo's daughter had married L. Aelius Lamia Plautius Aelianus before she was taken from him by the young Domitian – Aelianus showed no annoyance at the seduction, no matter how he had really felt.[42]

Narbonensian Senatorial Network.

Lay this group of senior warriors over the several fragments of the marital network in Narbonensis, and the whole begins to cohere. The links between the Narbonensians and Spaniards are reinforced, and the network of the west is extended into Italy; indeed the Corbulo links may have been the origin of this whole networking system, and the basis of support for the Flavian dynasty is revealed.

The Narbonensian and Other Connections 201

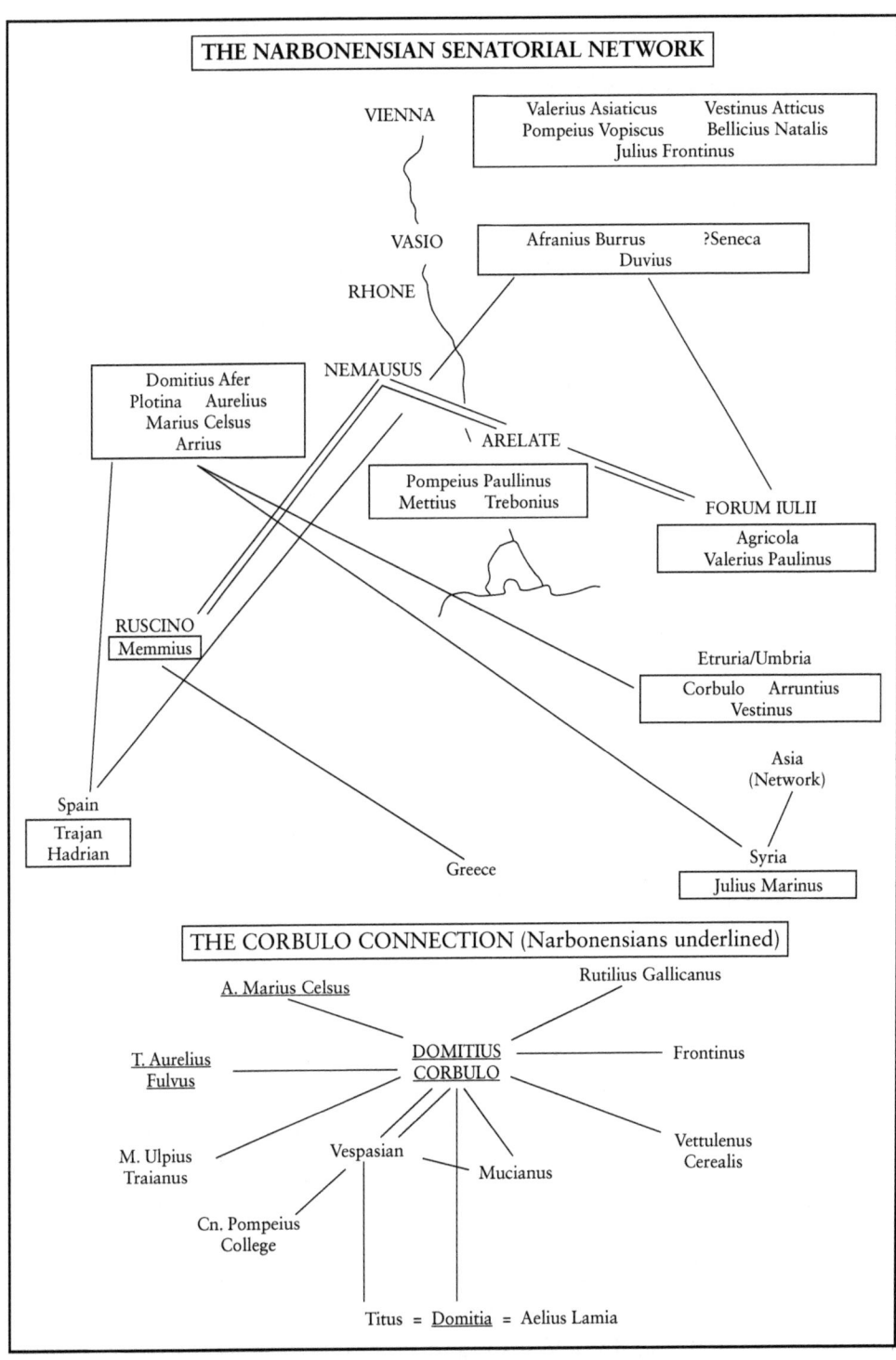

The Year 68–69

There is a further link, which overlaps both of the previous ones. During the Civil War, Bellicius Natalis was consul in the later part of 68, and Pompeius Vopiscus, Arrius Antoninus, Marius Celsus, and Caecilius Simplex were all consuls in 69, the period between the suicide of Nero and the arrival of Vespasian in Rome, though appointed by different emperors. Here, therefore, is another link, one forged by the danger produced by the rapid imperial turnover in the city of Rome itself. That they all survived might be a factor in their later association, and their joint origins from Narbonensis may have been another factor in their survival.

There were several elements in all this which remained separate from the central part of the network, which was the Nemausian–Spanish connection which led to the imperial power, but it seems reasonable to conclude that Narbonensians helped Narbonensians when in the intrigue-ridden great imperial city. Burrus and Seneca certainly assisted Agricola and Tacitus, while the shared experience and outrage of the Corbulo group, and the presiding influence of Vespasian, all imply a loose-knit but effective aristocratic network at work.

Frontinus

The question arises how, or if, Frontinus fitted into this network. He was, of course, first of all perhaps, a Corbulo man, if of a lower rank than all those legionary commanders, and at the time of only equestrian status. But by the time he emerged as praetor in 70 he had certainly become a Flavian partisan, by way of Galba in 68 (like Bellicius). He was in all probability a Narbonensian, and by the 70s, as senator, he was on terms of social and political equality with the others from the province and from Spain, though many were older than he was, and precise connections with the others cannot be detected other than a common provincial origin, and perhaps friendship. His command in Britannia will no doubt have brought him into contact with Agricola, who both preceded and succeeded him in the province, if he had not met him earlier.

Further, it will be argued later, in the final chapter of this study, that Frontinus probably came from Vienna, along with the Valerii, Bellicii, Pompeii Vopisci and Iulii Vestini, and in family terms he had other connections. If that is correct, he was therefore part of a highly influential political and governmental group, one which emerged afterwards as one of the most influential of all.

This is all rather amorphous at times, but it was perhaps similarly less than obvious to others outside the network at the time – somehow that is typical of Frontinus' whole career. It may perhaps be put down to his equestrian origins, which may have induced a certain social timidity in his early career, but perhaps the main reason would be his practice of writing. He produced perhaps six books between 70 and 100, though only three of them survive (and six may not be all of his production). If the three survivors are typical of his output, the others will also have required much research, which probably in turn required a great deal of time and travel to accomplish. And if these two elements were operating in tandem, the isolation of writing would reinforce and emphasize his societal reticence. But his increasing eminence as an adviser to at least three emperors between 80 and 103, and especially his importance in the last six years of his life, would certainly put him at the centre of the Narbonensian network.

Chapter 14

The Man

The record of Frontinus' life and career is difficult to sort out, as the previous chapters have shown. The problem is the same with his origins: his birthdate, parentage, and birthplace are all as difficult to discern as his career. They are worse, in fact, since there is only inference and indirection to go on. This is why this chapter is concerned with items which really should be considered first in a conventional biography: his family, relations, descendants, together with his work, and his contribution to the empire he was loyal to. It has seemed best to leave this most difficult part to the last and so concentrate on his work and career, which is less controversial, and, of course, more important.

Family

There is no record of Frontinus' parentage, though it is probable that, in line with the usual Roman system of nomenclature, his father and he had the same name. This is a reasonably firm basis for what now follows. Nor is the name of his mother on record, and it is only known that Frontinus himself was married because he had at least one daughter, Julia Frontina, who married Q. Sosius Senecio. The name of his wife is not known; it seems likely that she died early. There is no sign that he remarried.

This is the extent of our knowledge of his family, a poor harvest, but one which helps in discerning his descendants, which will be discussed later in this chapter. There are, however, two more men who had the name Julius Frontinus added to their other names as extra *cognomina*. These were P. Calvisius Ruso Julius Frontinus and Q. Valerius Lupercus Julius Frontinus. The first of these has occasioned considerable comment and theorizing.[1] The second has produced little of this, and he has been generally ignored in the discussion, but his existence opens the way to the following interpretation.

We have suddenly, therefore, all at the same period, in the second half of the first century AD, three men pursuing political careers, all bearing the name Julius Frontinus, one with that name alone, the other two with these names as *cognomina*. Leaving aside for the moment their varied careers, and ignoring the possibility of coincidence (never to be adduced as an explanation without convincing proof) the obvious interpretation would be that Julius Frontinus the elder had three sons, two of whom were adopted into the families respectively of Calvisius Ruso and Valerius Lupercus. This is what their compounded names imply, and it is best and simplest (applying Occam's razor) to assume that this is the explanation for their names. No doubt the adopters were both wealthy families – one became consul in 53 – and the adoptees would have a greater chance of a useful career with their wealth behind them than if the father's wealth had to support all three careers. The elder son, presumably our Julius Frontinus, therefore pursued a career in equestrian posts, no doubt supported by his father, who was relieved of the burden of providing for three sons.

This interpretation does away with the need to invent two other people, which has been done: a sister for the elder Julius Frontinus, who is supposed to have married the elder Ruso, the consul of 53,[2] and an invented brother or half-brother for the Ruso Julius Frontinus, who is also supposed to have pursued a political career in parallel with these others.[3] The existence of the third Julius Frontinus, who attached the name to Valerius Lupercus makes this interpretation, of course – the abolition of the invented extras – much more likely; it is noticeable that this third man is generally ignored in all the earlier discussions, whereas his existence, added to that of the two other Frontini who were his contemporaries, provides the best explanation for the Frontinus in the Ruso family and for the whole family for that matter.

We therefore have Julius Frontinus as praetor in 70, consul in 73, and his subsequent career. Calvisius Ruso Julius Frontinus had a head start by being adopted by a man who had been consul in 53; the adoption will have taken place before his political career got under way. Partly as a result of his new family the adopted son was adlected as patrician in Vespasian's great adlection of 73/74. He had already occupied a number of junior offices, and had served as legate, though where or in what capacity is not known since the inscription is broken at that point. He was quaestor by imperial designation next year, and consul in 79.[4]

This speed of ascent has occasioned surprise, even consternation, but Vespasian's reign was hardly the most conventional of periods for pursuing the *cursus* – Julius Frontinus himself was an example – and Ruso Frontinus had already served in several offices before his adlection. Vespasian had been adlecting others even before reaching Rome, exercising his prerogatives as emperor, and it would not be beyond conjecture that he was favouring a relative of his successful protégé Julius Frontinus, just returned from Britannia, when Ruso Frontinus became consul. Ruso's career continued to be somewhat unconventional. He was consul in 79 and governor of Asia in 92/93. His career was therefore running several years behind that of Julius Frontinus – six years behind as consul, seven years behind as governor of Asia, even as a patrician – which suggests that he was at least six or seven years younger. He went on to govern Cappadocia-and-Galatia in 106/107, a considerable time after his consulship – but then there had intervened the events of 96–99, another period in which the even flow of men into offices was disrupted.[5]

His son was P. Calvisius Tullus Ruso, whose mother was Domitia Lucilla, daughter of Domitius Tullus, a wealthy Gaul. He was consul in 109, thus born (as a patrician) about 75, when his father was probably in his 30s. The career of the two Rusones clearly overlapped, but can be easily sorted out as father and son, when the adoptions are accepted. This interpretation is far more straightforward than all the twistings and turnings of earlier theories.

The third brother, Q. Valerius Lupercus Julius Frontinus, was perhaps the youngest of the three, and was adopted by Valerius Lupercus, whom we know was from Vienna (which may be a clue to the home of the Frontinus family).[6] This brother also began a senatorial career, reaching the rank of *praetor designatus* but apparently went no further; the fact that he did not take up the post as praetor having been already designated suggests that he died at that point. He had descendants. A man called Valerius Lupercus, on a very cramped inscription, is recorded as the commander of the II Lingones auxiliary regiment in Britain in the 120s.[7] The dating suggests that he was a grandson of the praetor designate.

His family *cognomen* is of interest, for it argues some connection with the priestly college of the Luperci in Rome, and so we may assume that the family was descended from a Roman citizen who arrived in Gaul as an immigrant from Rome, perhaps two or three generations earlier.

This, if accepted, provides a home base for our man. Q. Valerius Lupercus Julius Frontinus was from Vienna, and it is likely that it was amongst the families in that city that the adoptions were arranged. To be sure, this only indicates the home city of the adopting father, Lupercus, but it is likely that the adoptions reflected continuing relationships between the three families, Calvisii, Julii, and Valerii, all of whom might thus be from Vienna, or at least from Narbonensis. (The Calvisii, however, show no evidence of any particular origin, other than, presumably, somewhere in Italy originally.)

The senior and wealthiest of these three was the Calvisius family, whose P. Calvisius Ruso was consul in 53. If it can be assumed that the three Frontini were brothers, they were born in the 30s or 40s AD. P. Calvisius Ruso Julius Frontinus, consul in 79, had been adopted well before that date, no doubt in his teens, when the adopting father realized he would have no sons of his own, and so in the 50s; his career had been founded on the wealth of the Ruso family, which then and earlier had been of a senatorial standard. He may well have been the eldest of the brothers, but it is perhaps more likely that Frontinus *pater* would seek to promote his eldest son first. So let us assume that our man was the eldest, and since he had an equestrian career until 69, and then a senatorial career, his consulship in 73 was probably at the legal age for the post, 41 or 42, making his birth occur in 31. (It has often been assumed, or guessed, that it would have been later: 35 and even 40 have been suggested, but the earlier date is the better basis than these guesses; as a father with one child he would be able to become consul earlier but the times were upset, so exact dating and sequencing is unlikely.)

The Calvisius adoptee had been adlected as a patrician – though his father remained plebeian, if he was still alive – a promotion which probably took place in Vespasian's mass upgrading in 73/74. This would mean the adoptee was entitled to be consul at the age of 32, which may have been his age in 79, putting his birth at between 47 or thereabouts, unless his consulship was somewhat delayed, which is quite possible. This birthdate seems rather late, however, and one would be happier with his date of birth up to ten years earlier; of course, the age of patricians becoming eligible to the consulship is only a first date, there is no need to assume that they all went on directly to the consulship at 32, and an adoptee could well reach the post several years 'late'.

The circumstances of Vespasian's anxiety to maintain control had led to a very deliberate and careful choice of men as consuls during his reign. This reflected Vespasian's political priorities, and any man not fully part of his clique was liable to be pushed aside, at least for a time. This may well have been the case with almost anyone. Calvisius' birth therefore may then be placed some years before 47. The Valerius brother is undatable, and his adoptive father is otherwise unknown, but it does appear that his home was the city of Vienna in Narbonensis. This, by the argument laid out above, should mean that the other two families were probably from that city as well.

Frontinus and Calvisius Ruso Frontinus pursued rather contrasting careers, both in their consulships and in their varied other duties. The Calvisius Ruso brother had been legate after his praetorship, though exactly what responsibility he had is not known. He apparently did not move out of Italy until his governorship of Asia, nor does he seem to have held a military command.[8] After his consulship he curated a road in Italy. He was governor in Asia in 92/93, and governed Cappadocia from 104/105 to 106/107, rather a stretched-out career. He lived several years beyond Frontinus, which may be another hint that he was younger than our man.

Ruso's senatorial career was clearly unusual, with major offices only taken up after his stint in Asia, though in this he was like Frontinus, for his governorship of Asia was thus not, as it was with so many other senators, the end of his public career. It would appear that he was regarded as just as valuable a man as Frontinus himself, if in a different way and less prominently so, and willing to undertake such tasks in his old age. He married Dasumia, from a very wealthy Spanish family, which put him as a cousin of the future Emperor Hadrian and, more distantly, of Trajan. Their son P. Calvisius Tullus Ruso, *consul ordinarius* in 109, and possibly with another stint as consul later, married Domitia Lucilla and so became an ancestor of Marcus Aurelius.

Descendants

Sextus Julius Frontinus' descendants have been sorted out, in an interesting article in which the sequence of his descendants has been developed from the last member, by study of their names.[9] Here a chronological sequence will be attempted. Frontinus' daughter married Q. Sosius Senecio, consul in 99 and 107, in each case as *ordinarius*, as already noted. They had two children, both daughters. Sosia Frontina did not marry, so it seems, but Sosia Polla married Q. Pompeius Falco, consul in 108, who was the grandson of the Roscius Coelius who had carried out the coup in Britain in 69 which ousted the governor Trebellius Maximus; his consulship had been somewhat delayed during the reigns of Vespasian and Titus, no doubt as a result of his questionable action, but Domitian seems to have relented.

Sosia Polla is recorded in the inscription from Laodikeia-ad-Lykon in Asia Minor which notes her father's generosity towards Hierapolis.[10] Her husband in fact had a long career, beginning as military tribune in Legio X Fretensis, stationed in the ruins of Jerusalem, and legate of Legio V Macedonica after his praetorship. He was governor of Lycia-and-Pamphylia in 102/103 to 104/105 (and so when Frontinus died), then returned to Judaea as governor of the province and commander of his old legion X Fretensis. He was consul in 108, the year after his father-in-law Senecio, and then was governor of Moesia Inferior during Trajan's Parthian war, 115/116 to 117/118. (Her father Senecio died in about 115.)[11]

Pompeius Falco was transferred to Britannia directly from Moesia, apparently at the direct personal instruction of the new Emperor Hadrian, because of an insurrection, or invasion, in the province. He was presumably a military man, having served in military and difficult provinces on all occasions, including in Judaea while a Roman expedition was taking control of the Nabataean kingdom, just next door, always an unsettling process. There was some trouble in Britannia after Trajan's death at the same time as the Roman withdrawal from Parthia – an obvious defeat – which was no doubt the reason Hadrian sent him there. While he was there it is likely that the planning for the construction of Hadrian's Wall began – it has been suggested that the actual construction began as early as 120, and so during Falco's governorship, which ended in 121/122;[12] it certainly seems very likely that at least the planning and the initial surveying was undertaken well before construction began. This may be seen as a curious appendix to the career of his grandfather Frontinus, whose provincial policy had consisted of a mixture of conquest and assimilation. One notes that one of the inscriptions recording Falco's career is from Terracina, the Roman Anxur, which was one of Frontinus' estates while he lived; probably it was inherited through his mother.[13]

Meanwhile, P. Calvisius Tullus Ruso became consul in 109, so that the extended family had consuls in three successive years, just as in 98–100. The descendants of Frontinus *pater* and his descendants had thus held six consular offices in Trajan's first ten years. And the ascent continued. Pompeius Falco was a notable governor and politician and was long-lived.[14] He could also see his Ruso cousins ascending even higher up the political ladder, until Tullus' grandson became the Emperor Marcus Aurelius in 161, while his cousin Annia Faustina was married to the Emperor Antoninus Pius, who lived far longer than anyone anticipated, until 161. He had been born in Domitian's reign and had been consul for the first time back in 120.

The Sosia/Falco line did not climb quite so high, but did last longer. Pompeius Falco and Sosia Polla had two children. The son was Q. Pompeius Sosius Priscus, who held early offices in the Roman city cavalry, and as a *monetalis*, then went through the usual offices of quaestor and praetor, but there is no record of his governing any active province nor of commanding any legion; he was consul in 142 and governor of Asia in 163/164.[15]

His sister Pompeia Falconilla apparently did not marry. (The *cognomen* Falconilla indicates her descent from Asian royalty.) Priscus himself married twice, first to a lady called Claudia, and then to Didia Severina. Claudia may have been the daughter of a branch of the Bellicius family (from Vienna), but the name is not distinctive enough for certainty; Didia Severina was a member of the family which eventually produced the brief Emperor Didius Julianus in 193. The son of Priscus, who distinguished himself by gathering up all his ancestry into a long string of *cognomina* which he carried around all his life – thirty-four *cognomina*, at least – was consul in 169. He governed Asia in 183/184 under his distant cousin, Commodus. His sister married M. Pontius Laelianus, consul also in 169, son of a consul of 144; their son was consul in about 170.

The consul of 169, Priscus, married Ceionia Fabia, the daughter of L. Aelius Caesar, the almost-emperor and successor of Hadrian, who died in 138, and contributed the *cognomen* Commodus to the Antoninus royal family. They had two children. The son, called Q. Pompeius Sosius Priscus Falco, was consul in the fatal year 193, and was scouted as one of several possible emperors in the complexity of the events following the Emperor Commodus' murder; his sister Sosia married C. Julius Erucius Clarus Vibianus, another of the consuls of 193. The family therefore counted two consuls and a briefly-reigning emperor all in the same year, and was flying close to real power; but if this was a family project, they were trumped by the power of the Pannonian legions and the ruthlessness of Septimius Severus.

Q. Priscus Falco's first wife was Sulpicia Agrippina, who was the daughter of C. Sulpicius Pollio, a senator, though any offices he held are not known. His mother, however, was Claudia Ammiana Dryantilla, the descendant of a long line of men who were Lyciarchs in southern Asia Minor and occasional consuls in Rome. The Sulpicius family was also therefore probably from the East, no doubt descended from one of the Italian migrant soldiers who settled in the cities which became Roman *coloniae*. The men were members of the Arval Brotherhood in Rome through at least three generations in the second and early third centuries; Sulpicia's brother in turn was governor of his mother's province of Lycia-and-Pamphylia for three years from 198. (Her granddaughter was married to yet another brief Emperor, Regalianus.)

This is a formidable record for the descendants of the *eques* from Vienna in the early first century. Frontinus had half a dozen emperors among his descendants, even if some of them lasted only for brief inglorious reigns. The family, however, died out after 180. The Calvisius branch ended with the Emperor Commodus. (The Valerius branch seems to have expired with the commander of the auxiliary regiment in Britannia in the 120s, or with the Bithynian quaestor in the 160s.) The Sosius branch ended with, I suppose, Regalianus' wife, a rather distant descendant. All too many of these briefly-reigning emperors died violently – Didius, Regalianus, Commodus – in which case one may say that the family participated fully in the triumphs of the Roman Empire in the second century and in its disasters in the early third century – which makes it a typical aristocratic family of the period.

The Author

Whereas Frontinus may have loomed large in the political landscape of the Roman Empire at times, notably during the crisis of the imperial succession in 96–100, his later reputation stands mainly on the basis of his literary production. (This is probably to reverse his real importance, but without his books we would probably not notice his political importance.) He therefore deserves some consideration as an author. However, to examine the work of an author without knowing more than half of his output, and with a somewhat speculative understanding of his life and not knowing where or when he was born, where or when he died, without knowledge of his parentage and upbringing, and what exactly he did for much of his life, may be counted a hopeless enterprise. And so, of course, it is. Add to that the fact that his surviving books are less than enthralling; two of them can be described as technical manuals, and the third a compilation of items culled from other authors.

There is thus not a great deal to venture as a discussion of his work as an author. It may be said that he was thorough, and that his aim was to provide guidance for his fellow surveyors, soldiers, and aqueduct managers, and that none of his work was directed at anyone other than fellow professionals, and so any criticism of the texts on the basis of literary quality is misplaced. And yet, since these three books have survived, were copied and re-copied, it seems reasonable to suppose that he evidently succeeded in his aim, at least in the Roman world. It is worth noting, however, that the books on surveying and the Roman water system survive in single ancient copies, preserved as much by accident and the negligence of mediaeval monks as for their intrinsic value. Beyond that, his work is now mainly a useful quarry for historians of his time.

Perhaps more notable than the quality, technical or literary, of the books, is the fact that in many ways they were pioneering works in their genres. This is not to say that no earlier works in surveying, military methods or the study of aqueducts and the water supply of Rome were produced, but it is to point out that earlier books were partial – books on siege warfare, for example, not on the military art or collections of military stratagems – and both the works of surveying and on military stratagems were followed by a series of later books on the same subjects, usually amplifying Frontinus' texts rather than superseding them.

One might wish that he had used his technical expertise to describe some of the work he himself did, such as the conquest of Wales, or the fortification of the German frontier, but it was probably too dangerous politically to do so while Domitian lived. (Tacitus did not produce his work on Agricola, or on the history of the empire until that emperor was dead, and his dynasty extinguished, nor did Suetonius.) Still more would we like to read his own account of the events at the end of his life, from the murder of Domitian to the establishment of Trajan as emperor. But by then he was old, possibly weary – he was probably aged 70 in 101 and died two years later, and no doubt was constrained by his political dependence on Trajan as he had been by his relationship with Domitian, if far less threateningly.

No one would read his books for pleasure; they are now used as historians' quarries, with the commentators complaining at the author's lack of style, and the tediousness of his lists. The *Strategems* is a useful book of anecdotes from which to supplement broader accounts of events, and sometimes a source of unexpected or otherwise unknown events. His book on surveying – little more than a pamphlet really – is especially helpful in giving clues to his own life (as is the *Stratagems* in a few anecdotes), and in that it evidently provided a template for later surveying accounts. The only items in the *Agrimentores* collection earlier than Frontinus' work is a law, the *lex Mamilia*, on the subject, and brief fragments from a Carthaginian and an Etruscan work (or so it is claimed); it looks very much as if Frontinus' survey manual was so useful that earlier accounts, probably in languages other than Latin, ceased to be used, and vanished. It was certainly the basis for many of the other books in the collection, which supplement or expand his. The unreadable book on the aqueduct system of Rome has been a quarry for discussions of political attitudes and studies of administrative methods, which may be more the results of those of modern historians' preoccupations than they were part of Frontinus' own beliefs or intentions. The fact that extensive remains of the aqueducts he described still exist, so that their lengths and construction and capacities can be subject to modern measurement and surveying techniques, and mean that his account can be compared with the ruins – it stands up reasonably well, of course, to such scrutiny.

He also wrote at least three other books, now lost, which might have modified this conclusion. *Tactics in Homer* would be an interesting exercise in enquiring into the differences between the conduct of war in the Roman Empire – fortified frontiers, disciplined regiments and legions – as against an unbelievably long siege of a single 'city', by a bunch of unreliable, quarrelling, greedy and headstrong warriors. The fact that the war probably never happened, the city was little more than a village, and the Mycenaean Palace system of the invaders had collapsed years before the supposed war began, would have rendered the whole enterprise one of unreality, as discussions of the Trojan War today are, in effect an exercise in no more than literary criticism.

Rather more interesting and useful for later historians would have been his books *Art of War* and *The Practice of Agriculture*. Apart from Caesar's *Commentaries* – actually more a political tract than a reliable military description – little survives from the pens of practising soldiers to give us some notion of methods and tactics in Frontinus' time. He is often paired with the much later Vegetius, a fourth-century writer who similarly attempted to systematize military processes, but he was a bureaucrat, with the bureaucrat's passion to organize and ignorance of reality. Another author with whom Frontinus is sometimes paired is Vitruvius, another systematizer, but at least he seems to have been a practical architect, just as Frontinus was a practising surveyor, soldier, and administrator. Other than this practical experience of the subjects they wrote about, and being bracketed together as technical authors, the two men have little else in common. Perhaps the greatest loss is Frontinus' book on agriculture, which was in a long tradition of writing on the subject, back to independent Carthage, Cato the Elder, and Columella. But whatever his purpose was in writing the book, his particular viewpoint was almost certainly much the same as in his other books. From the evidence of his extant work, he wrote (as did the elder Cato) for the benefit of the managerial class, which in agriculture would be the owners of the great estates in the empire. This, of course, was a class into which he had been born, and in which he lived all his life.

His great-grandson Q. Pompeius Falco entertained the Emperor Antoninus Pius at his estate to an exhibition of his work experimenting in arboriculture.[16] This was derided by Sir Ronald Syme, but was a suitable retirement occupation for a descendant of Frontinus, author on agriculture; it may also have taken place on an estate inherited from Frontinus – it was thus perfectly fitting that Frontinus' practical bent should include, while writing on agriculture, remarks on his own experiments.[17]

At this distance in time it is impossible to provide an estimate of Frontinus' character, and it would be presumptuous to do so. But one can say that he was ambitious, and so typically Roman, loyal (not such a typical Roman characteristic), an accomplished organizer, and a man on whom a series of emperors relied with confidence. He was a conqueror, yet his achievements in this area were deliberately ignored and belittled by the pre-eminent historian of the day, which says more about Tacitus than about Frontinus. His work with Domitian in Germany established a stable frontier for a century and a half, just as his work in Wales, and perhaps in the North of England, lasted even longer, for over three centuries. He founded three, perhaps four, legionary fortresses, two of which are cities to this day. In a vast organization such as the Roman Empire, where even emperors had difficulty in having a serious effect, this was highly unusual, and a notable achievement.

Chapter 15

Frontinus and the Roman Empire

For half of his life, Frontinus was a minor functionary in the imperial military and political bureaucracy. That he used his experience in surveying to produce a technical manual on the subject should not blind us to that fact. The book might have survived without his later fame, though that is perhaps unlikely. But the second half of his life, from the Civil War of 69 to his death, shows him in a new light, as a major political figure in the empire, if intermittently. In this it was the fact that from 69 he had access to whoever was emperor which provided him with a modicum of power. And that power, in his hands, was always limited by the brooding presence of imperial oversight. To estimate his effect on the empire and government, therefore, it is necessary first to discover just how he managed to remain on good terms, even friendship, with such a very diverse set of emperors as those who ruled from Nero to Trajan.

Relations with Emperors

Frontinus was well acquainted with the emperors in his own time. He lived through the reigns, or parts of the reigns, of a dozen emperors, from Tiberius to Trajan. Of these, he knew or spoke with at least five of them, and possibly several more. It is possible he met Nero, who appointed him as surveyor after his service as military tribune in the East, though it is more likely that the appointment came to him through the machinery of the imperial bureaucracy. In the East he may have encountered either or both of Vespasian and Titus, though he had probably met the former in Africa rather than the East, and had probably been in Spain when they were fighting the Jewish War. In Spain he can have met Galba and Otho (and Trajan's father, who was governor of Baetica in the late 60s, and also the future emperor, who was still young at the time). As an important official it is very likely that he would have been expected to announce himself to the governors of any of the provinces he worked in. Of these men only Galba was likely to have had some effect on his life – though Nero had possibly done so if he had taken an active part in appointing him as surveyor. It is possible that Galba was his commanding officer in the march from Spain to Italy. In which case he will have met Otho, who was also on that march, while he still aspired to be Galba's successor. He would also have met both men while working in Spain. With the murder of Galba, however, his acquaintanceship with Otho was also probably severed. If he was part of the Legio VII Galbiana he was probably moved back and forth with the legion. It may be assumed that he was actually in Rome in the latter part of 69. (He does not figure in Tacitus' account of the war, the *Annals*, but Tacitus has done his best to write him out of history except when it was impossible to avoid it.)

He may, as noted, have met Vespasian during the latter's governorship of Africa, but otherwise not until Vespasian's arrival in Rome in 70, but it was the new emperor who appointed him to the key post of praetor at the beginning of that year, so some knowledge of Frontinus' character and activities must have reached him. He must also have done this from a distance, without a direct meeting, since Frontinus was clearly in Rome at the beginning of 70 (and for some time before the New Year), yet Vespasian was still in the East until later. He followed this with the assistance to Domitian in the Lingones campaign, in which the prince learned a good deal about military matters, and Frontinus will have gained high marks from Vespasian for ensuring a peaceful and lasting submission by that tribe, as well as tactful relations with his volatile son. The result of these relations was – though this is not attested – his appointment as governor of Britannia in 73, and the cementing of his relationship with Vespasian by his success, and of his reputation among the men who counted in Rome.

All three Flavian emperors clearly trusted him and employed him, in Britannia, in Rome, and in Germania, so that in effect from 70 to 86 he was fully employed there and finally in Asia. Even in Rome he was often part of the imperial *consilium*. The governorship of Asia, when he was aged 55 or thereabouts, must have seemed, for him, as it usually was for other senators, his final posting. No doubt he enjoyed his time there, for it was a congenial post for a man of culture who spoke Greek as well as Latin. And after that post he returned to Rome and Italy, to his estate at Anxur (and others elsewhere, no doubt). But he was still valuable, and available.

It is in this period that he no doubt completed his book *Stratagems*, since some of the Domitian anecdotes are included, and when he wrote the vanished books on the art of war and on agriculture, but he also attended the Senate, and was a member of Domitian's *consilium*.

His relationship with Domitian was, after that with Vespasian, the most important of his life. From all indications they were friends, perhaps since events in Rome in 69, certainly since the confrontation with the Lingones the next year. It is all but certain that it was Domitian who made him *comes* in the German campaign, though his appointment as governor of Germania Inferior seems to date from 81 (though, like so many dates in his life, this is uncertain). He then sent him to govern Asia, rather earlier in his life and career than might have been expected, perhaps after his illness in Germany, which is commemorated in the inscription, though Asia was hardly the most healthy of postings. It may well have been difficult for anyone to maintain good and friendly relations with Domitian in the last few years of the reign, when he was becoming increasingly suspicious (with good reason) and murderous, but it seems that Frontinus had the diplomatic skills, and knew Domitian well enough, to negotiate the difficulties, and perhaps to stay out of the way when necessary; his political timing was always good. We can assume his presence in the Senate on a regular basis, and in the *consilium*, but there is no record of anything he did or said in either place.

In that time he also got to know Nerva, who was also a member of the emperor's *consilium*. In fact they probably knew each other from the time of the Civil War, when, at least in 70, both were in Rome and active in working to stabilize the new regime (Nerva was consul in 71). If we can be sure of anything we can be certain that Frontinus disapproved of the murder of Domitian, and may well have been privately scornful of the idea of Nerva as a Roman emperor, which was certainly liable to be a disaster, and seemed to be heading that way after only nine or ten months. He was consequently absent from affairs for the first months of the new reign (though, to be sure, he had hardly been obvious in public affairs for a decade before 96). The wobbling of Nerva's rule in 97, however, seems to have persuaded him to return to political affairs, marked by his appointment as *curator aquarum* and to the financial reform commission set up by the Senate – this is an unanticipated aspect of his life, but he was presumably believed to have some financial expertise. He was also active in securing the succession for Trajan, which was organized by October 97. It may be assumed that he supported Nerva in the last months of the emperor's life.

After Nerva's death in January 98, it was Frontinus who, as consul in February of that year, received the instructions from Trajan in Germany concerning the obsequies for the deceased emperor, and arranged the proclamation of the accession of Trajan as sole emperor. Since Trajan stayed away from Rome for the next eighteen months, Frontinus was clearly one of the governing group of senators who ran the city and perhaps much of the empire in that time. His reward was to be made *consul ordinarius* for 100 (his third time as consul); his son-in-law Q. Sosius Senecio had held that post the year before; Senecio had no doubt also assisted in the government. Nerva's cronies were allowed to hold their second consulships (for only a month each – Frontinus was one of them), but they were dying off at the same time. (Had Nerva survived much longer he might well have found himself without any friends, and so would have been even more vulnerable than in 97; his choice then of successor would be even more difficult than it had already been.)

While Trajan was absent from the city, and so well away from any threats, especially from the Praetorian Guard, Frontinus and his colleagues organized, in effect, the transition from Nerva's uncertain reign to the new regime and the restoration of the Flavian system under Trajan, who was described in one source as '*Domitiani continuator*'. This may well have been a consolation to Frontinus for the death of Domitian, his friend. It would not be appropriate, however, to import much sentiment into this concluding period of Frontinus' life. This was Roman, and imperial, politics, and if there was ever any process which was less than sentimental it was that; an example was the treatment meted out to Nerva's praetorian prefect, who was summoned to the emperor clearly believing he was about to be praised (and how did he get that idea?), only to be executed instead; Frontinus and his colleagues in Rome were no doubt co-conspirators in this deception.

Frontinus had worked with Vespasian, Titus, and Domitian, all hard men, with success; he had eventually supported Nerva in his increasingly shaky position, and he had eased the accession of Trajan, another hard man. In all this there was little sentiment, nor any room for it; the operative necessity was to ensure that the governmental system of the empire worked, and, since it was an autocracy, modified slightly by the presence of the Senate and the bureaucracy, the key to a successful regime lay with the emperor, and the need for an effective one. This was likely to have been Frontinus' priority.

Frontinus and the Empire

It is always difficult for a single citizen to have a decisive effect on greater events. Only those with great power can move events; all too often individuals last in the public eye for 'fifteen minutes' only. Frontinus could be said to have been imperially effective, however, twice. The Roman Empire was, and was intended to be, an immobile political system. Only at the very top and at the edges could change take place, in the form of decisions by the emperor, and by way of expanding imperial territory. This was where Frontinus first had an effect. His experience and activities before and during the Civil War, whatever they were, are now invisible, only to be conjectured, though his emergence as praetor in 70 suggests that he had achieved something which brought him to the positive attention of the winning party in the Civil War and of its leader, the new Emperor Vespasian. Experience in the Eastern war, and in the government of Africa and Spain (as well as knowledge of his homeland of Narbonensis) will have also counted.

The successful subjugation of the Lingones, without noticeable violence or casualties, was a strong contrast to the simultaneous and violent, even confusing, campaign pursued by Petillius Cerialis along the Rhine, though it may have been the knowledge of the violence of Cerialis which persuaded the Lingones to submit to the quieter approach of Frontinus (and Domitian). This surely had its effect in Rome, for not only Domitian but also Licinius Mucianus was present and could both report approvingly to the new emperor. It was, perhaps, the more remarkable in that there is no indication that Frontinus had commanded any unit larger than an auxiliary regiment until then. He had clearly displayed large amounts of confidence in persuading his seniors of his methods, as well as in negotiating with the Lingones.

Warfare was the most obvious way by which a Roman could make his mark, for this was, after all, a military empire, in which the emperor based his power and authority on his command of the army. To shine, therefore, any man had to achieve command of an army first, and that meant going through the political *cursus* and catching the eye of the emperor. This Frontinus achieved by 73, unexpectedly early, since he had been an *eques* no more than four years before. By then, however, he had not only the experience of not fighting the Lingones, but had spent some uncertain length of time in the East as a military tribune, where he had observed the methods of Domitius Corbulo, and even longer in command of a group of soldier-surveyors as well. Similarly, the Civil War had lessons for any observant military man. In terms of the Roman army, which imposed boys of eighteen as military tribunes, and put consuls who had no military experience in command of armies, he was well trained, and had undeniable and varied experience of command. His peaceful approach to the Lingones also marked him out from the often-automatic violence of Roman armies and commanders, who tended to go in fighting, confident of victory in command of armies, but careless of the consequences of their violence – Cerialis was such a commander. He was clearly capable of judging a situation's requirements and adjusting his approach accordingly; he had shown that he was keener on results than gaining renown through violence. This was a particularly useful approach in the aftermath of the Civil War which had caused very large casualties amongst the Roman forces. For once, saving Roman lives was a political necessity.

This all came to fruition in his governorship of Britannia. Frontinus' conquest of Wales, both south and north, was achieved with little fighting, probably because of his marshalling of such an overwhelming force that the Silures and the Ordovices, the main tribes making resistance, were persuaded to surrender fairly quickly; they had been softened up partly by the former fighting, and partly by being neighbours of peaceful and prosperous Roman territories for a decade and a half. To ensure their continued submission he then organized the network of roads and forts which was stretched over the conquered territory, particularly in the land of the Silures, but also by surrounding (rather than occupying) that of the Ordovices. He then made a start on a similar campaign in the north of England, but restricted his ambitions to the land south of the Ribble and the Tees. This meant that Agricola, more intent on acquiring a warrior's reputation, could quickly complete the occupation of the northern half of the land of the Brigantes, where the suborning of tribes who may have preferred Roman to Brigantian suzerainty made his advance straightforward, but then he collided with the tribes in the Highlands, who had little experience of Rome. These, unlike those in Wales and Northern England, had not been softened up by a generation of contact with Roman civilization, and resisted, compelling Agricola to fight. But Frontinus' methods had secured Wales and much of the North; Agricola occupied the Southern Uplands and the Central Valley fairly thinly – continued hostility from further north compelled him to be ready to fight, and be less extravagant with his garrisons. After his military victory in the Highlands, his methods progressively failed until the land he had supposedly conquered was slowly abandoned; the retreat ended only by building Hadrian's Wall, a desperate measure by any standards, replacing aggressive victory by stolid defence. It is notable that whereas Agricola's conquests were failures, those of Frontinus were held and retained.

This achievement duly made Frontinus' reputation, to the extent that Tacitus refused to mention it in any detail because it contrasted so strongly with his hero Agricola's geographically more extensive, but politically lesser achievement. Frontinus was soon re-employed by Domitian in the German campaign, which again brought a considerable accession of territory to the empire. (Ironically the withdrawal of forces from Britannia for the Chattan War brought Agricola's campaigns to a halt, and Agricola, supposedly victorious, was not employed again.) In Germany his fort-and-road system had to cope with a linear frontier, and he was able to adapt his method to the different conditions. The German frontier was arguably more effective than the Wall, which was the scene of repeated warfare, abandonments and re-occupations for the next century.

He had significantly extended the empire, almost doubling Roman territory in Britannia, and in Germania he had fashioned a defence line which calmed the frontier, and lasted for a century and a half; these were concrete achievements, since one of the most pressing issues of the empire was the constantly increasing requirement for military recruits, and a successful conquest and a firm defence line were essential to allow manpower resources to be deployed effectively.

One might also point out that the books he wrote were of significant value for the empire. The pamphlet on surveying stimulated a series of follow-up pamphlets, elaborating on his work, until they were all collected together, presumably for continued availability and use, in the fifth century. The book of military stratagems has remained in use for a variety of reasons and for a changing set of purposes, ever since, though, to be sure, we do not know of anyone ever consulting it to get ideas for a campaign. The book on aqueducts set out what should be done to maintain the water supply of Rome and it may have persuaded Trajan to build a new one, the Aqua Traiana. Both the works on surveying and aqueducts were designed for use by his successors, hence were clearly valuable.

Frontinus' final achievement was to steady the ship in the aftermath of the murder of Domitian, a potentially extremely unsettling situation, as the repeated attempts to upset Nerva's regime showed. Domitian had been a much more effective emperor than Nerva could ever be, and the presence of the conqueror of Britannia beside the weaker emperor may have been politically necessary to survive his problems. Frontinus successfully oversaw the transition to Trajan as emperor after the strongest threat yet, from the Guard. Trajan was another effective ruler, a revival of the methods of Domitian, at least in foreign affairs, and willing to leave the Senate to its own affairs. This was clearly a busy time for him and his colleagues in Rome, while Trajan was preoccupied with the situation on the northern frontier, but the temporary emperor-less administration in the city between January 98 and autumn 99 was successful enough that Trajan could make his way slowly and leisurely through Italy to the city, when he had finished his immediate tasks on the frontier. And he could later leave the city in order to conduct wars over several years – which Domitian had aimed to do when he was killed. It may have been some consolation, if Frontinus had lived another few years, to see that in his conquest of Dacia, Trajan in many aspects used the methods he employed to control Wales – roads, garrisons and forts, all imposed in a suppressing network.

The Man

The career of Sextus Julius Frontinus is a remarkable case of a man rising from a fairly obscure provincial origin and from the middling class of the empire, to a position where he was in effect virtual deputy emperor for a couple of years. This is, of course, a process which can take place in any society, where capacity and intelligence are valued, but in imperial Rome conspicuous loyalty was required, which all too easily slid into obnoxious obsequiousness. He is an example of how a man could rise by exploiting the possibilities in an autocracy, and in disturbed times. Seizing one's chances and exploiting imperial contacts, but at the same time achieving notable results at the difficult tasks imposed on him, was the stuff of his success – partly imperial favour, partly native abilities, partly social position and wealth (an *eques* was wealthy; a senator was very rich), and partly an ability to seize the moment, all contributed. One must admire his timing, being on the spot in Rome in late 69, so that he could do Vespasian's and Domitian's bidding by resigning his praetorship – quite probably a position he had been eager to reach for some years – was the decisive step from a minor military role to a position of imperial power – and, that achieved, it led on to all the rest.

Partly, of course, it was also luck, in that he was on campaign in the East under Corbulo, and he was in Spain when Galba set out on his long distant *coup d'état*. But he clearly went to the East because that was where the possibility existed of becoming noticed and gaining promotion. Spain, on the other hand, could not be regarded as anything but a backwater when he went there, so exploiting Galba's ambition was riding his luck with a vengeance; had Galba lost in his bid for empire, Frontinus was liable to lose his head, and even if he survived, he would never have been heard of again.

And yet this was also exploiting his own personal resources, for he was clearly from the start a capable organizer, and always prepared to undertake tasks – surveying, for example, or surrendering his hard-won praetorship after only a day – which his less enterprising contemporaries would probably shun or refuse. Partly it must have been due to his conspicuous loyalty to the empire. This is the best explanation for his repeated support of those in power, from Nero and Galba (probably) to Trajan, though Otho and Vitellius he probably spurned. This loyalty could be exploited by the emperors, of course, but he could also use it to bring him to as high a situation in the empire as anyone who was not an emperor could attain – effectively an imperial regent while Trajan remained on the frontier.

So he was a man with a sense of political (and probably military) timing, able to exploit his luck, capable of serving a variety of emperors with skill (and such a varied lot they were, Nero and Galba, Domitian and Nerva), adept at diplomacy, and without loss of pride. The autocrats who ruled the empire relied on loyal men of personal independence and integrity to support their precarious position, and to work hard to maintain the empire. Frontinus was such a man.

As I pointed out in the previous chapter, to define his character is as impossible at this distance as it is to imagine his personal appearance. There is no representation of him in existence, and probably, owing to his distaste for being commemorated in stone, there never was. His character may only be outlined by considering his actions, but to define character by a man's actions is never sufficient. One can say he was loyal, to the empire, to whoever was emperor, to the Roman system, to his friends, and to his family. He died full of honours and was probably mourned by a fairly wide circle of friends – though that is yet another thing about him we do not know.

Notes

Introduction
1. Examples are Pliny the Younger, the subject of two recent biographies: Roy K. Gibson, *Man of High Empire* (Oxford, 2020), and Daisy Dunn, *In the Shadow of Vesuvius* (London, 2019); note also Gilbert Charles Picard, *L'Ascension d'un dynastie Gauloise, la Gloire des Sedatii* (Paris, 1990), a three-generation family biography; all three of these subjects were Frontinus' contemporaries, but none of them are in the same league of importance as Frontinus.
2. Note particularly, Brian W. Campbell, *The Writings of the Roman Land Surveyors* (London, 2000); R.W. Rodgers, *Frontinus, De Aquis* (Cambridge, 2004), and G.E. Bennett, in the Loeb edition of *Stratagems and De Aquis* (Cambridge, 1925).
3. Anthony R. Birley, *The Fasti of Roman Britain* (Oxford, 1981).

Chapter 1: Early life: an Exercise in Speculation
1. Tacitus, *Histories*, 4.39.1–2.
2. Just as his commanders reported back to him – e.g., Antonius Primus (Tacitus, *Histories*, 3.53) and Mucianus (3.52), and other commanders.
3. See next chapter.
4. Tacitus, *Histories*, 3.52.
5. Ibid, 4.4.
6. *Corpus Agrimensorum Romanorum*, ed. C. Thulin (Leipzig, 1913); I have used the edition of Brian Campbell, *The Writings of the Roman Land Surveyors* (Society for the Promotion of Roman Studies, monograph no. 9, London, 2000).
7. Campbell, *Writings*, 3 and 9, both idiosyncratic references, which might be based on personal experience.
8. The conclusion that he was *eques* was reached by Sir Ronald Syme by a different route, *Tacitus* (Oxford, 1958), p. 790.
9. Campbell, *Writings* 3 and 9.
10. *Urbicus* 43/Campbell, *Writings*, 352; *Urbicus* 43/Campbell, *Writings*, 351.
11. See the story of an expert private soldier, chapter 2, note 5.
12. Tacitus, *Annals* 14.23–24.
13. Frontinus, *Stratagems* 2.9.5; Tacitus, Annals 14.23–25.
14. Pliny, *Natural History*, 30.16–17; Tacitus, *Annals* 15.24; Suetonius, *Nero*, 30; Cassius Dio, 63.2.
15. Tacitus, *Annals* 13.35.
16. Frontinus, *Stratagems* 4.1.21.
17. *Ibid*, 4.1.29.
18. *Ibid*, 4.2.3.
19. *Ibid*, 4.7.2.
20. Or even 'c.40' in the Wikipedia article, 'Sextus Julius Frontinus'.

21. Anthony R. Birley, 'The Governors of Roman Britain', *Epigraphische Studien* (1967), pp. 63–102, in effect retracted in Birley, *The Fasti of Roman Britain* (Oxford,1981).
22. Campbell, *Writings*, li – lii, for a discussion on surveyors.
23. Paul Leunisson, 'Direct Promotion from Proconsul to Consul under the Principate', *ZPE* 89 (1991), p. 236.
24. Yet he is not mentioned in any accounts of the civil war, not by Tacitus, nor by Plutarch.
25. Birley, *Fasti*, 70, note 4, says that there were 36 Sex. Iulii and nine Frontini in *CIL* XII; Ronald Syme, *Tacitus* (Oxford, 1958), p. 790, makes a similar point.
26. Syme, *Tacitus*, appendix 83, p. 788.
27. A further argument on Frontinus' origin in is in Chapter 14.
28. Syme, *Tacitus*, appendix 79.
29. *Ibid*, appendices 78 and 79.
30. For Narbonensis see A.L.F. Rivet, *Gallia N nsis, Southern Gaul in Roman Times* (London, 1988); for the languages see Alex Mullen, *Southern Gaul and the Mediterranean, Multilingualism and Multiple Identities in the Iron Age and Roman Province* (Cambridge, 2013).
31. *Ibid*, 2.1.17; Eusebius, *Chronographia* 114.3.
32. *Ibid*, 4.6.4.

Chapter 2: Frontinus on Surveying
1. Campbell, *Writings*; Frontinus' pamphlet is on pages 2–15; see also O.A.W. Dilke, *The Roman Land Surveyors, an Introduction to the Agrimensores* (Newton Abbot, 1971).
2. Paul MacKendrick, *The North African Stones Speak* (London, 1980), pp. 28–37, with helpful maps; a list of the locations of Spanish centuriation can be found under 'Centuriation' on Wikemedia.
3. Frontinus 3/*Commentum* 65/Campbell's notes 318; see also *Liber Coloniarum* at pages 184 and 424.
4. Frontinus 3/*Commentum*, 53–55.
5. Dilke, *Roman Land Surveyors*, p. 107.
6. Frontinus 11/Campbell 326, note 28; Campbell refers to it as 'obscure', meaning location unknown.
7. Frontinus' text was presumably produced during or shortly after his term as a professional surveyor, and so by about 70, when he moved on to a more political career; it is thus misleading to refer to him as 'the distinguished senator' (Campbell, *Writings*, xlviii) when discussing this work; on the other hand he undoubtedly did not later disown this work.
8. For an example, see Serafina Cuomo, 'A Roman Engineer's Tales', *JRS* 101 (2011, pp. 143–165). The engineer was a private soldier who had made himself an expert, and was called on several times to build such things as aqueducts.
9. Dilke, *Roman Land Surveyors* examines the sort of training the surveyors might have received (Ch 4), but there is little information, which would suggest that it was not a concern and that their training was essentially informal.
10. Campbell, *Writings*, xlv, points out that the second century BC playwright Plautus used technical surveying terms in *Poenulus* (48–49), and clearly expected his audience to understand them.

11. Campbell has an appendix listing 'Epigraphic Evidence of Land Boundaries and Disputes' (Appendix 3), and one giving a 'List of Cadastral Stones' (Appendix 2), though not of centuriation projects of imperial date, for which see the chapter in Dilke, *Roman Land Surveyors*, Ch 10; a short but incomplete list of western European examples is on Wikipedia, 'centuriation'.

Chapter 3: Rise to Consul

1. Tacitus, *Histories* 4.73.1.
2. For a summary account and references, see Birley, *Fasti*, p. 90, note 9; and C.E. Bennett in the Loeb edition of *Stratagems*, pp. vii-xxiv.
3. *Stratagems* 4.3.14.
4. Tacitus, *Histories*, 4.85.
5. B.W. Henderson, *Civil War and Rebellion in the Roman Empire* (London, 1908), pp. 242–244; the incident is passed over by more modern historians, who are obsessed with fitting all events into a single year.
6. J.B. Ward Perkins, 'The Career of Sex. Iulius Frontinus', *Classical Quarterly* (1937) (suggesting II Adiutrix); *PIR* J 322 (suggesting XXII Primigenia, which had fought for Vitellius).
7. Rene Goguey, 'Legionnaires Romains chez les Lingons: la VIIIeme Augusta a Mirabeau (Cote d'Or)', *Revue Archeologique de l'Est*, 57 (2008), pp. 227-257.
8. G.B. Townend, 'Some Flavian Connections', *JRS*, 51 (1961), pp. 54–61.
9. The same favouring of old friends as consuls will be found in 97 and 98, at the start of Nerva's reign – see Chapters 9 and 11.
10. Barbara Levick, *Vespasian* (London, 1990), Ch 6.
11. *PIR* R 67; Tacitus, *Histories* 1.60.
12. Tacitus, *Histories* 75.3; *PIR* Q 39; his son commanded Legio IV Scythica under Trajan.
13. *PIR* C 84; M.-Th. Raepsaet-Charlier, *Prosopographie des Femmes de l'Ordre senatorial (Ie – IIe siecles)* (Louvain, 1987), pp. 152-154; see also Chapter 13.
14. I have taken as my basic consular list that published by Wikipedia, 'List of Roman Consuls', claimed to be revised to June 2017, together with the supplementary 'List of undated Roman consuls'.
15. Josephus, *BJ* 3.289; *PIR* U 864.
16. Tacitus, *Histories* 2.67; *PIR* A 637, and P 654.
17. *Ibid*, 3.50; *PIR* L 33/C 104.
18. *PIR* R 248; *ILS* 9499; Statius, *Silvae* 1.4; Brian W. Jones, *The Emperor Domitian* (London, 1992), p. 56; Syme, *Tacitus* 593; I take it that the Q. Iulius Cordus in Wikipedia's list is actually this man; John Henderson, *A Roman Life, Rutilius Gallicus on Paper and in Stone* (Exeter, 1998).
19. His post-civil war career mirrored that of Frontinus, who was also usually employed from 70 to 86.
20. *PIR* C 1425.
21. Evan W. Haley, *Baetica Felix, People and Prosperity in Southern Spain from Caesar to Septimius Severus* (Austin TX, 2003), pp. 93, 137, and 217 note 8.
22. Tacitus, *Annals* 16.28–34; *PIR* E 84; his first consulship, in 62 had lasted one day; he was eventually tried for conspiracy against Vespasian, and committed suicide.
23. *ILS* 986; *PIR* P 480; Tacitus, *Histories* 4.5 3.3; Birley, *Fasti*, pp. 357-358.

24. Kenneth Wellesley, *The Long Year, A.D. 69*, 2nd ed (Bristol, 1989), 77–78, 81–82; Jones, *Domitian*, pp. 44–47.
25. *PIR* V 542; Juvenal, *Satires* 4.82 – 93; Frontinus, *de Aquis*, 102; Pliny, *NH* 19.4; *AE* (1939), p. 60.
26. Tacitus, *Annals* 15.72; *ILS* 273.
27. Ronald Syme, *Tacitus* (Oxford, 1958), p. 1.
28. Suetonius, *Vespasian* 4.4.
29. J. Crook, *Consilium Principis: Imperial Councils and Counsellors from Augustus to Diocletian* (Cambridge, 1955).
30. *PIR* V 41; Tacitus, *Agricola* 45.1; Juvenal 4.94 and 113; the quote is from Syme, *Tacitus*, p. 594; Jones, *Domitian*, 57.
31. *PIR* P 213; Crook, *Consilium Principis*; he is not mentioned in Levick, *Vespasian*.
32. Tacitus, *Histories* 2.98 and 4.49–50.
33. *PIR* V 73; his governorship of Asia is uncertain.
34. Juvenal 4.89; Tacitus, *Dialogue* 8.3; B.W. Jones and R. Develin, 'M. Arrecinus Clemens', *Antichthon* 10 (1976), pp. 79–83.
35. The post was his presumably because of the family connection; he was also the son of an earlier guard prefect, of Gaius' time.
36. *PIR* F 269 and 186.
37. *PIR* D 167; Pliny, *Epistles* 8.18.1.
38. John D. Grainger, *Nerva and the Roman Succession Crisis of 96 – 98* (London, 2003), Ch 7, 'The Aristocratic Networks'.

Chapter 4: Governor of Britannia, I: The West

1. Graham Webster, *The Roman Invasion of Britain*, revised ed (London, 1973), Ch 47; Peter Salway, *Roman Britain*, (Oxford, 1981), pp. 95–98; the Fosse Way line may have been mainly a pause for consolidation, not intended as a permanent frontier.
2. Tacitus, *Annals* 12.31–40; Salway, *Roman Britain*, pp. 100–107.
3. Graham Webster, *Boudica* (London, 1978).
4. *Ibid*, 2.66.
5. Birley, *Fasti*, pp. 59–62.
6. *Ibid*, 2.57.
7. Tacitus, *Agricola* 14, *Histories* 1.60.
8. Tacitus, *Histories* 2.57.
9. Tacitus, *Histories* 3.1.
10. *Ibid*, 2.65.
11. Tacitus, *Histories* 2.45; Statius, *Silvae*, 5.2.55–56.
12. A.L.F. Rivet and Colin Smith, *The Place Names of Roman Britain* (London, 1979), pp. 301–302 (Carvetii), pp. 322–323 (Corionototae), pp. 456–457 (Setantii and Setantiorum Portus); pp. 470–474 (Tectoverdi); the Lopocares is a fifth possibility, but they are neither locatable nor well sourced.
13. Keith Branigan (ed.), *Rome and the Brigantes; the Impact of Rome in Northern England* (Sheffield, 1980), referring especially to the surveys by Herman Ramm and Nick Higham, on the settlement east of the Pennines; Tom Garlick, *Roman Lancashire* (Whitehaven, 1977), Ch 1.
14. Salway, *Roman Britain*, pp. 45–46.
15. Statius, *Silvae*, 5.2.140–149; *PIR* V 407 for Bolanus' son, Crispinus: 'this is the corselet he took from a British chief'.

16. Birley, *Fasti*, p. 68; the precise relationship between Vespasian and Cerialis was worked out by Townend, 'Some Flavian Connections'.
17. P.A. Holder, *The Roman Army in Britain* (London, 1982), pp. 113–114.
18. *Ibid*, pp. 107, 108–109, 111, 118.
19. Tacitus, *Agricola*, 8 and 16.
20. Patrick Ottaway, in Patrick Nuttjens (ed), *A History of York* (Pickering, 2007), pp. 6–8, does not venture a date, but in his later *Roman Yorkshire* (Pickering, 2018), p. 118, he states AD 71 as the date for the fort's foundation.
21. N. Hodgson (ed), *Hadrian's Wall, 1999 – 2009* (Kendal, 2009), pp. 140–144.
22. Ottaway, *Roman Yorkshire*, p. 131.
23. Frontinus' consulship is assumed from his appointment as governor, invariably a post for a recent consul; its date is not therefore certain, but 73 is widely accepted.
24. Ottaway, *Roman Yorkshire*, p. 134; Alison Konig, 'Frontinus' cameo role in Tacitus' Agricola', *Classical Quarterly*, 63 (2013), pp. 361–376.
25. Tacitus, *Agricola* 16.
26. Salway, *Roman Britain*, p. 135.
27. Barry C. Burnham and Jeffrey L. Davies, *Roman Frontiers in Wales and the Marches* (Royal Commission on the Ancient and Historical Monuments of Wales, Aberystwyth 2010), pp. 187–193 (Usk), 230–232 (Cardiff), 264–265 (Monmouth), 237–238 (Clifford), 248–249 (Hindwell Farm), 229–230 (Canon Frome), 196–198 (Abergavenny), 304 (Chepstow).
28. Tacitus, *Agricola* 12.40 for this assessment of Venutius.
29. Tacitus, *Agricola* 17.
30. Salway, *Roman Britain*, p. 136; Christopher Houlder, *Wales, an Archaeological Guide* (London, 1978), pp. 137–138.
31. John Wacher, *The Towns of Roman Britain* (London 1974), pp. 375–389; Burnham and Davies, *Roman Frontiers*, p. 302.
32. Wacher, *Towns*; 'straitjacket' is on p. 376.
33. Burnham and Davies, *Roman Frontiers*, pp. 91–98 (the route system), pp. 315–322 (gazetteer of roads).
34. *Ibid*, pp. 172–181; earlier, temporary, forts have been discerned on the site.
35. *Ibid*: pp. 224 (Caerphilly), 245–248 (Gelligaer, an earth-and-timber fort which was replaced by one in stone on a close-by new site), 275 (Penydarren).
36. *Ibid*: pp. 240–241 (Coelbren), 291 (Hirfynidd fortlet), 298 (Rheola Forest fortlet).
37. Burnham and Davies, *Roman Frontiers*: pp. 161–170 (Caerleon), 230–233 (Cardiff), 200–204 (Brecon Gaer), 253–255 (Llandovery), 251–252 (Llandeilo).
38. See the 'Roman Britain' reports in *Britannia* (2018), and (2019), for example.
39. Burnham and Davies, *Roman Frontiers*, pp. 298–299 (Y Pigwn), 276 (Pen y Gaer).
40. *Ibid*: pp. 276–280 (Pumsaint), 260 (Dolaucothi).
41. 'Roman Britain in 2014', *Britannia*, 46 (2015); the date of the origin of the fort is put at c.50, but this is highly unlikely, unless it was a local Demetan exploitation taken over by the Romans later – which is very possible, of course.
42. Roger White and Philip Barker, *Wroxeter, Life and Death of a Roman City* (Stroud, 1998); Burnham and Davies, *Roman Frontiers*, pp. 193–196.
43. Burnham and Davies, *Roman Frontiers*, pp. 243–244 (Forden Gaer), 205 (Pentrehyling), 224–229 (Caersws).
44. *Ibid*: pp. 307 (Llanfair Caereinion), 295–296 (Hafan), 297 (Pen y Crocbren).

45. *Ibid*: pp. 260–262 (Llanio), 286–289 (Trawscoed), 268–270 (Penllwyn), 292–293 (Erglodd).
46. *Ibid*: pp. 211–212 (Caerau), 234–237 (Castell Collen); the fortlets are at Abererbwll (302), and Penmicae (296).
47. *Ibid*: pp. 282–286 (Tomen y Mur), 217–219 (Caerhun), 291–292 (Brithdir), 206–208 (Bryn y Gefelliau).
48. *Ibid*: 212–214 (Caer Gai), 256–260 (Llanfor).
49. *Ibid*: pp. 220–223 (Caernarfon), 270–272 (Pen Llystyn); 'Roman Britain in 2017', *Britannia* 49 (2018), for Tai Cothiau.
50. Orosius 9.1; Barbara Levick, *Vespasian* (London, 1999), attributes the occasion to Cerialis' campaigns, which may have been included, but the emperor still waited until 75 to carry out the ceremony, by which time Frontinus had added still more territory.

Chapter 5: Governor of Britannia, II: The North
1. Burnham and Davies, *Roman Frontiers*, pp. 172–181.
2. W.S. Hanson, *Agricola and the Conquest of the North* (London, 1987), pp. 26, 52–53.
3. White and Barker, *Wroxeter*, Ch 2.
4. Tacitus, *Agricola*, 17 credits Cerialis.
5. Rivet and Smith, *Place Names*, pp. 456–457.
6. Tacitus, at *Agricola* 8, called Bolanus' regime 'gentle', but in *Histories* 4.37 he writes of several battles being fought.
7. Hanson, *Agricola*, figs 4 and 8.
8. Herman Ramm, *The Parisi* (London, 1978), makes no effort to discuss the political inclinations of the Parisi and ignores the highly suggestive placing of the line of forts, as does Peter Halkon, *The Parisi, Britons and Romans in Eastern Yorkshire* (Stroud, 2013), who ignores several of the forts.
9. Hanson, *Agricola*, p. 61 and map on 59; Patrick Ottaway, *Roman Yorkshire* (Pickering, 2018), pp. 118–120, 125–134.
10. Tacitus, *Agricola*, 17.
11. R.E.M. Wheeler, *The Stanwick Fortifications* (London 1954); W.S. Hanson and D.B. Campbell, 'The Brigantes: from Clientage to Conquest', *Britannia* 17, pp. 73–89.
12. The routes of these roads vary with the researcher, but the forts are clearly aligned.
13. Hanson, *Agricola*, p. 64.
14. P. Abramson, D.S. Berg and M.R. Fossick, 'Roman Castleford, Excavations 1974–1985', *Yorkshire Archaeology* 5 (1999); the date 71 is always suspect, being derived from the arrival of Cerialis.
15. Ottaway, *Roman Yorkshire*, plan page 128.
16. Y. Boutwood, 'Roman fort and *vicus*, Newton Kyme, North Yorkshire', *Britannia* 27 (1996), pp. 340–344.
17. See the map in Hanson, *Agricola*, pp. 66–67.
18. Nick Higham, 'Rural Settlements West of the Pennines', in Branigan (ed), *Rome and the Brigantes*, pp. 41–47, map on p. 42.
19. Ottaway, *Roman Yorkshire*, pp. 124–134.
20. John Zant, in N. Hodgson (ed), *Hadrian's Wall 1999 – 2009* (Kendal, 2009), pp. 140–149.
21. *RIB* II.3, 2434.3.
22. Wacher, *Towns*, pp. 206 – 209.

23. Salway, *Roman Britain*, p. 138.
24. Wacher, *Towns* pp. 137–144.
25. Ramm, *Parisi*, pp. 35–36.
26. Tacitus, *Agricola*, makes Cerealis attack the Brigantes, and Frontinus the Silures; Agricola was to conquer the rest; it looks very much like a programme of imperial expansion spread over several governorships, organized by an emperor with some knowledge of the country.
27. Tacitus, *Agricola*, 17.
28. But there was an eastern example, in the network of cities founded in northern Syria between 300 and 280 BC by King Seleukos I with the primary aim of securing the area in the face of hostility from foreign rulers – but the aim was not primarily to control the population, which was thin on the ground.
29. Suetonius, *Nero*, 18.

Chapter 6: Frontinus on War
1. Frontinus' *Art of War* is referred to by Vegetius, *Epitome rei militaris* 1.8 and 2.3; he is also credited by Aelian (*Tactica*, 1.2) with a book on tactics in Homer which has also vanished; several items from Homer are in the *Stratagems*.
2. Book I, preface.
3. Birley, *Fasti*, 70, for example, with references.
4. Aelian, *Tactica*, preface.
5. Many of the compilers of military tactics had no experience of war – Onasander, for example, was best known as a commentator on Plato.
6. E.W. Marsden, *Greek and Roman Artillery*, 2 vols (Oxford, 1969–1971).
7. Cited twelve times in *Stratagems*.
8. I discount such men as the leaders of sets of mercenaries, who may have been expert but rarely commanded more than a small set of soldiers.
9. W.A. Oldfather *et al.* (ed. and trans.) *Aeneas Tacticus, Asclepiodotos, Onasander* (Loeb Library, Cambridge, 1928).
10. Addressed to Trajan, cf Brian Campbell, *Greek and Roman Military Writers* (London, 2004), p. 136; Campbell's book, a compilation of items from a dozen writers, including Frontinus, is essentially a new version of *Stratagems*.
11. Campbell, *Military Writers*, nos 280–282.
12. Arrian, *Tactics, Extaxis contra Alanos*, and *Anabasis*; see P.A. Stadter, *Arrian of Nicomedia* (Chapel Hill, NC, 1980).
13. R. Shepherd (trans.), *Polyaenus's Stratagems of War* (London, 1793, reprinted Chicago, 1974).
14. A. Grillone (ed.), *De Munitionibus Castrum* (Leipzig, 1977, ed. and trans. of Ps-Hyginus.)
15. Plutarch, *Aemilius Paullus*, 20.

Chapter 7: *Comes* in Germania
1. Levick, *Vespasian*, p. 178.
2. Brian W. Jones, *The Emperor Titus* (Beckenham, Kent, 1984), pp. 91–93.
3. Cassius Dio 66.23; Suetonius, *Titus* 8.3.
4. Cassius Dio 66.24.1–2; Suetonius, *Titus* 8.4.
5. *AE* (1954), p. 137, implies this completion.
6. Jones, *Titus*, pp. 149–150.

7. Paul McKendrick, *The North African Stones Speak* (London, 1980), ch 8.
8. Jones, *Titus*, p. 138, gives a suggested list of probable *consilium* members, based on Crook, *Consilium Principis*.
9. Cassius Dio 66.2 6.4; Suetonius, *Titus* 11.
10. Jones, *Titus*, pp. 154–155.
11. Cassius Dio 66.26.3; Suetonius, *Titus* 11; T.V. Buttrey, *Documentary Evidence for the Chronology of Flavian Titulature* (Meisenheim 1988), p. 20; Brian W. Jones, *Domitian* (London, 1992), pp. 20–21.
12. The evidence is a military diploma (*RMD* V, 327) which has to be heavily restored to produce Frontinus' name, though part of it is certainly visible; essentially what office he held is still not clear; the publisher of the fragment assumed it to be governor of Germania Inferior in '81–84', even though Domitian's main work, in which Frontinus was involved, was in Superior.
13. J.F. Drinkwater, *Roman Gaul* (Beckenham, Kent, 1983), Chapter 3: 'The Creation of the Germanies'; Albino Garzetti, *From Tiberias to the Antonines* (English edition, London, 1974), pp. 278–279.
14. *ILS* 5832; H. Schoenberger, 'The Roman Frontier in Germany: an Archaeological Survey', *JRS* (1969), pp. 156–157; questions of dating of these forts exist, but the name *Arae Flaviae* - 'altars of the Flavians' – should be a good fat clue, one would have thought.
15. Schoenberger, 'Roman Frontier', p. 154.
16. *CIL* XIII, 9082.
17. Schoenberger, 'Roman Frontier', p. 155.
18. E. Luttwak, *The Grand Strategy of the Roman Empire* (Baltimore, 1978), p. 86, says that 250 miles would be saved.
19. Tacitus, *Histories* 4.65; *Germania* 41.
20. Frontinus, *Stratagems* 1.1.6.
21. Frontinus was in Titus' *consilium*; Domitian was not – but, of course, as his brother Domitian would obviously have access to Titus which others would not have.
22. Tacitus, *Germania* 37; Suetonius, *Domitian* 6, only displays his lack of understanding of what was being achieved.
23. Jones, *Domitian*, has references in full, but not an account of the war; he lists the legions employed on p. 128.
24. Frontinus, *Strategems* 2.3.22.
25. *Ibid*, 2.11.7.
26. Luttwak, *Grand Strategy* 87.
27. Joachim von Elbe, *Roman Germany, a Guide to Sites and Museums*, 2nd ed. (Mainz, 1977), p. 248.

Chapter 8: Asia
1. Birley, *Fasti* 71.
2. *BMC*, Ionia p. 250, nos 133–137.
3. Tullia Ritti, *An Epigraphic Guide to Hierapolis*, trans. Paul R. Arthur (Istanbul, 2006); the arch is now being referred to as 'the Frontinus Arch'.
4. *ILS* 8828.
5. *IGRRP* IV, 847.
6. *SEG* 2009.
7. Pliny, *Epistles*, book 10.

8. Stephen Mitchell, *Anatolia*, vol. 1 (Oxford, 1993), pp. 170, 229–230, and map 7.
9. Pliny *Epistles*, book 10, illustrates such rivalries in Bithynia; see Roy K. Gibson, *Man of the Empire, the Life of Pliny the Younger* (Oxford, 2020), pp. 190–221.
10. Andrew Lintott, *Imperium Romanum, Politics and Administration* (London, 1993), pp. 27–31; the edict of Q. Mucius Scaevola, issued for Asia in 95 BC was taken as the model by the Senate, but there had been long enough for provinces to incorporate changes.
11. See Pliny's examples in Bithynia (note 9).
12. Richard J.A. Talbert, *The Senate of Imperial Rome* (Princeton NJ, 1984) pp. 55–56; the proviso was restated by Marcus Aurelius, implying that it had fallen out of use by then.
13. H. Halfmann, 'Die Senatoren aus dem ostlichen Teil der Imperium Romanum bis zum Ende der 2Jh n Chr.', *Hypomnemata* 58 (Gottingen, 1979).
14. S.R.F. Price, *Rituals and Power, the Roman Imperial Cult in Asia Minor* (Cambridge, 1984).
15. Joyce Reynolds, *Aphrodiseias and Rome* (The Society for the Promotion of Roman Studies, 1982); other volumes on the inscriptions from the city have been published since.
16. An early example is Ronald Syme, *The Provincial at Rome* (Oxford, 1999, but written in 1935 and 1936), and *Greeks Invading the Roman Government* (Brookline MA, 1982); Talbert, *Senate*, 31–33; for details see Halfmann, *Senatoren*.
17. G. W. Bowersock, *Fiction as History, Nero to Julian* (Berkeley and Los Angeles, 1994); *Augustus and the Greek World* (Oxford 1965), and *Greek Sophists in the Roman Empire* (Oxford, 1969).
18. Simon Swain, *Hellenism and Empire, Language, Classicism and Power in the Greek World, A.D. 50 – 250* (Oxford, 1996), p. 69.
19. M. McCrum and A.G. Woodhead, *Select Documents of the Principates of the Flavian Emperors, including the Year of Revolution, A.D. 68 – 69* (Cambridge, 1968) 27, no 63, lines 61–62, dated to 2 September, though this was when the news reached Rome, and the event must have happened some months earlier.
20. Jones, *Titus*, pp. 150–151.
21. Cassius Dio 66.19.
22. Suetonius, *Nero* 57.2; Tacitus, *Histories* 1.2.8; P.A. Gallivan, 'The "false-Neros", a re-examination', *Historia* 22 (1973), pp. 364–365; Brian Jones, *The Emperor Titus* (Beckenham, Kent, 1984), pp. 150–151; id, *Domitian*, pp. 158, 182–183.
23. Mitchell, *Anatolia*, vol. 1, map 7 and pp. 118–120.

Chapter 9: Nerva
1. Aelian, *Tactica*, preface 3.
2. Martial 10.58.1–2 and 5.
3. This date is a reasonable assumption by Christian Settipani, *Continuite Gentilice et Continuite Familiale dans les Familles Senatoriale Romaines a l'epoque Imperiale* (Oxford, 2006).
4. Pliny, *Epistles* 5.1.
5. Jorg Rupke, *Fasti Sacerdotum, a Prospography of Pagan, Jewish, and Christian Religious Officials in the City of Rome, 300 BC to AD 499*, trans. David M. B. Stevenson (Oxford, 2008), no. 2034, p. 740.
6. Pliny, *Epistles* 4.8.

7. Piny, *Epistles* 9.19.
8. Juvenal, *Satires* 4.
9. In Sir Ronald Syme's words, 'A man who had never seen an army or a province'; *Tacitus*, p. 1; Tacitus, *Annals* 15.72; *ILS* 273.
10. Rupke, *Fasti*, 1278; *PIR* V 1224–1227 for the outline of Nerva's career and those of his four ancestors – they held the consulship in each generation, except that of his father.
11. Note 8.
12. For a larger explanation of all this see John D. Grainger, *Nerva and the Roman Succession Crisis of 96 – 98* (London, 2003), pp. 22–25 and 112–116, which has full references.
13. W. Eck, *Die Statthalter der Germanischen Provinzen von 1 – 3 Jahrhundert* (Cologne, 1985); S. Dusanic and M.R. Vasic, 'An Upper Moesian Diploma of AD 96', *Chiron* 7, pp. 291–304; summarized in Grainger, *Nerva*, p. 23. For the careers of the legions see Nigel Pollard and Joanne Barry, *The Complete Roman Legions* (London, 2012).
14. Grainger, *Nerva*, Ch 3; Jones, *Domitian*, Ch 10, interprets the events as a 'palace plot', but it seems to me to be more extensive than that.
15. Suetonius, *Domitian* 16–17; Dio Cassius 67.1–17.2; Jones, *Domitian*, p. 193–196; B.W. Henderson, *Five Roman Emperors, Vespasian – Trajan A.D. 69 – 117* (Cambridge, 1927).

Chapter 10: The New Regime at Work

1. *Epitome de Caesaribus* 12.11; Syme, *Tacitus* 635, note 5.
2. Dio Cassius 68.3.3.
3. These measures are noted in Grainger, *Nerva*, Ch 5.
4. Dio Cassius 68.2.1.
5. R. Duncan-Jones, *Money and Government in the Roman Empire* (Cambridge, 1994), Ch 7; K.A. Woolf, 'Food, Property, and Patronage: the Significance of the Epigraphy of the Roman Alimentary Schemes in Early Imperial Italy', *PSBR* 58 (1990), pp. 197–221.
6. Pliny, *Epistles* 1.8.10 and 7.18.2; *ILS* 2927.
7. *ILS* 6675; Duncan-Jones, *Money and Government*, pp. 291–295.
8. Duncan-Jones, *Money and Government*, p. 291.
9. Pliny, *Epistles* 1.9; Pliny, *Panegyricus* 62.2; R. Syme, 'The Imperial Finances under Domitian, Nerva, and Trajan', *JRS* 20 (1930), pp. 55–70.
10. Dio Cassius 68.3.2; *Epitome de Caesaribus* 12.6.
11. Dio Cassius 68.2.3.
12. Grainger, *Nerva*, pp. 92–94; Birley, *Fasti*, pp. 235–237; E. Dabrowa, *The Governors of Roman Syria from Augustus to Septimius Severus* (Bonn, 1998), pp. 73–74.
13. Suetonius, *Domitian* 17.
14. Dio Cassius 68.2.3 – 4, and 3.3.
15. Anthony R. Birley, *Lives of the Later Caesars* (London, 1976); the 'biographies' of Nerva and Trajan were compiled from the available sources for their reigns; Trajan's succession is at pp. 36–37 (in 'Nerva'), and pp. 40–41 ('Trajan').

Chapter 11: Traianus Imperator

1. *Epitome de Caesaribus* 12.10 – 11.
2. Dio Cassius 68.5.4.

3. *PIR* A 1366.
4. For this appointment: *Epitome de Caesaribus* 13.9; *ILS* 5035.
5. Pliny, *Panegyricus* 21 and 84.6 – 8; Dio Cassius 68.3.
6. Pliny, *Panegyricus* 10.1 and 18.1.
7. Pliny, *Panegyricus* 12 and 16.2.
8. *PIR* S 777.
9. Pliny, *Panegyricus* 23.1 and 6.

Chapter 12: Water, and Another Book

1. The painting of the Forth Bridge comes to mind as an analogous matter.
2. Also called *The Aqueducts of Rome*, or versions thereof.
3. The most convenient editions of *de Aquis* are by Charles C. Bennett, in the Loeb series (Cambridge MA, 1925), the translation revised by Clemens Heschel and edited by Mary B. McIlwain, and by R.H. Rodgers, *The Aqueducts of Rome* (without translation), *Frontinus De Aqueductu urbis Romae*, with detailed notes (238 pages of notes from 52 pages of text) (Cambridge, 2004). Comments and discussion of the texts have been numerous, probably because large sections of the aqueducts remain. The most useful have been, since they are in English, Trevor Hodge, *Roman Aqueducts and Water Supply*, 2nd ed (London, 2002); Christer Bruun, *The Water Supply of Ancient Rome, a Study in Roman Imperial Administration* (Helsinki, 1991); Michael Peachin, *Frontinus and the curae of the curator aquarum* (Stuttgart, 2004); Dean R. Blackburn and A. Trevor Hodge, *Frontinus' Legacy, Essays on Frontinus' de aquis urbis Romae* (Ann Arbor, 2004); Thomas Ashby, *The Aqueducts of Ancient Rome* (Oxford, 1935); Harry Evans, *Water Distribution in Ancient Rome, the Evidence if Frontinus* (Ann Arbor, 1994), and an article by Barry Baldwin, 'Notes on the De Aquis of Frontinus', in C. Deroux, (ed), *Studies in Latin Literature and Roman History* VII, Collection Latomus (Brussels, 1994), pp. 484–506. These will be referred to, where necessary, by the authors' or editors' names.
4. Hodge, p. 347.
5. Hodge, pp. 174–174 and note 11.
6. See the extensive bibliographies in Hodge, Bruun, Peachin, and Blackburn/Hodge.
7. Rodgers, pp. 335–336.
8. Evans, quoted by Rodgers, p. 336.
9. Peachin, pp. 155 – 159; it is characteristic of the study of the book that whereas Peachin uses the passage to claim that Martial had a copy of the book with him and quoted Frontinus, Rodgers (p 249) reverses that, suggesting that Frontinus was quoting Martial.
10. Peachin p. 1; Hodge p. 16; Rogers, pp. 27–29, notes these discrepancies: Frontinus can be tedious at times, as in his list and figures, but he is thoroughly elegant when needed; he writes as required by his subject.
11. Hodge, p. 16.
12. *De Aquis* pp. 64, 87, 88.

Chapter 13: The Narbonesensian and Other Connections

1. Birley, *Fasti* p. 70, note 4.
2. Syme, *Tacitus*, Appendix 83.
3. Cassius Dio 59.18–20; Jerome, *Chronographia* 179H; A.L.F. Rivet, *Gallia Narbonensis, Southern Gaul in Roman Times* (London, 1988) p. 163; Syme, *Tacitus*, pp. 604–605.

4. *PIR* D 652, 667.
5. Rivet, *Gallia Narbonensis*, pp. 162–181.
6. *Ibid*, pp. 115–129.
7. *Ibid*, p. 136.
8. Possibly C. Memmius Regulus (cos 31) was the first, but his origin is unclear; see later in this chapter.
9. *PIR* V 44.
10. Rivet, *Gallia Narbonensis*, pp. 305–331.
11. Tacitus, Annals 24.5.
12. *PIR* V 44, 45; L 260.
13. *PIR* P 661, 662, 663.
14. Tacitus, *Annals* 68.
15. *PIR* S 625.
16. *PIR* B 97, 99, 101, 102; Settipani, *Continuite*, p. 476.
17. Settipani, *Continuite*, pp. 289–294.
18. Syme, *Tacitus*, pp. 604–605.
19. Syme, *Tacitus*, p. 597.
20. *PIR* M 468, 467; see also the genealogical chart of Spartans, including Memmii, in Settipani, *Continuite*, p. 496.
21. *PIR* I 344; Tacitus, *Agricola* 7.1.
22. *PIR* I 126.
23. Birley, *Fasti*, p. 75.
24. *PIR* V 1464.
25. *PIR* P 633.
26. *PIR* M 565, 566, 567, 572; Jones, *Domitian*, pp. 192–192; Rivet, *Gallia Narbonensis* 190–211.
27. *ILS* 979; *Inscriptions latines de la Gaule*, 206; Syme, *Tacitus* 591.
28. Syme, *Tacitus*, Ch XLV; note particularly pp. 622–623.
29. *PIR* A 1509.
30. *PIR* A 1086.
31. *PIR* M 223.
32. *PIR* C 84.
33. *PIR* I 241; The elder son's name is Ti. Iulius Candidus Marius Celsus, thus an adoptee.
34. *PIR* I 401.
35. For this connection see Grainger, *Nerva*, Ch 7 and tables 5a-c, with the references, and notably Halfmann, 'Senatoren', G.W. Bowersock, 'Roman Senators from the Near East', *Tituli* 5 (1972); S. Jamieson, 'Cornutus Tertullus and the Plancii of Perge,' *JRS* 55 (1965); and C.P. Jones, 'The Plancii of Perge and Diana Planciana', *HSCP* 80 (1976).
36. As Syme points out, *Tacitus*, p. 623.
37. The basic discussion here this still Syme, *Tacitus*, appendices 83 and 84.
38. Syme, *Tacitus*, p. 166.
39. *PIR* A 1509.
40. *PIR* U 864; M 296.
41. *PIR* V 502, P 600, R 248.
42. Dio Cassius 66.3.4; Suetonius, *Domitian* 1.3.

Chapter 14: The Man

1. The recent discussions include Eric Birley, 'The Enigma of Calvisius Ruso', *ZPE* 51 (1983), pp. 263–269; Sir Ronald Syme, 'P. Calvisius Ruso, One Person or Two?', *ZPE* 56 (1984), pp. 173–192; Bernard Remy, 'Le Carriere de P. Calvisius Ruso Julius Frontinus, Governeur de Cappadocia-Galatie, *MEFRA* 95 (1983), pp. 163–182; G. di Vita-Evrard, 'Des Calvisii Rusones a Licinius Sura', *MEFRA* 99 (1987), pp. 281–338.
2. Invented by Syme to explain the Ruso name, and utilized elsewhere; there is no record of her existence.
3. His existence was always shadowy, and especially since his consulship of 84 has been discarded he has receded into invisibility; no real record of him exists, except as an invention to bolster a theory.
4. *AE* (1914), 267, from Antioch-in-Pisidia; a second, briefer, inscription is at *AE* (1907), 54, from Kanna (now Genne or Genet), in Lycaonia.
5. Rupke, *Fasti Sacerdotum*, p. 1065, interprets the Antioch-in-Pisidia inscription, which gives the most detail of Ruso's career as showing him acting as *rex sacrorum* from 101; yet the *rex* was not permitted to leave the city, so he could not be both *rex* and governor of Cappadocia; the interpretation of him as *rex* is based on an incomplete word in the inscription, whose restoration is disputed; he must be discarded as *rex*.
6. *CIL* XII 1859 and 1860, from Vienna.
7. *RIB* I, 800. A third possible member of the family is L. Julius Lupercus, whose name appears as quaestor on a lead weight from Nicomedia in Bithynia in the 150s (*SEG* 2005, 1370); it is suggested that the cognomen is unusual enough to suggest a relationship, but it is less than proven.
8. *AE* (1914), 267.
9. W.C. McDermott, 'Stemmata quid faciunt: the Descendants of Frontinus', *Ancient Society* 7 (1976), pp. 229–261.
10. *ILS* 1105, and 8820.
11. *PIR* P 602; his full name is Q. Roscius Coelius Murena Silius Decianus Vibullius Pius Julius Eurycles Herclanus Pompeius Falco, which includes indications of descent from a variety of consular families and Greek royalty and Athenian wealth.
12. C.E. Stevens, *The Building of Hadrian's Wall* (Kendal, 1966).
13. *CIL* X 6231 = *ILS* 1035.
14. Birley, *Fasti*, pp. 95–100.
15. *PIR* P 639.
16. Fronto, *Ad Marcus Aurelius* 2.6.
17. Ronald Syme, 'Pliny's less Successful Friends', *Historia* 9 (1960).

Bibliography

Abbreviations
AE – Annee Epigraphique
BMC – British Museum Catalogue
CIL – Corpus Inscriptionum Latinarum
ILS – Inscriptionses Latinae Selectae
JRS – Journal of Roman Studies
PIR – Prosopograhia imperii Romanorum
PSBR – Papers of the British School at Rome
RIB – Roman Inscriptions of Britain
RMD – Roman Military Diplomas
SEG – Supplementum Epigraphicum Graecum
ZPE – Zeitschrift fur Papyrologie und Epigrafik

Bibliography
Abramson, P., D.S. Berg and M.R. Fossick, *Roman Castleford, Excavations 1974 – 1985*, Yorkshire Archaeology 5 (1999).
Ashby, Thomas, *The Aqueducts of Ancient Rome* (Oxford, 1935).
Baldwin, Barry, 'Notes on the De Aquis of Frontinus', in C. Deroux, (ed) *Studies in Latin Literature and Roman History*, VII, Collection Latomus (Brussels, 1994), pp. 484–506.
Bennett, G.E. (ed), *Frontinus, Stratagems and De Aquis*, Loeb Library (Cambridge, 1925).
Birley, Anthony R. 'The Governors of Roman Britain', *Epigraphische Studien* (1967), pp. 63–102.
Birley, Anthony R., *The Fasti of Roman Britain* (Oxford, 1981).
Birley, Anthony R., *Lives of the Later Caesars* (London, 1976).
Birley, Eric, 'The Enigma of Calvisius Ruso', *ZPE* 51 (1983), pp. 263–269.
Blackburn, Dean R., and A. Trevor Hodge, *Frontinus' Legacy, Essays on Frontinus' de aquis urbis Romae* (Ann Arbor, 2004).
Boutwood, Y., 'Roman fort and *vicus*, Newton Kyme, North Yorkshire', *Britannia* 27 (1996), pp. 340–344.
Bowersock, G.W., *Augustus and the Greek World* (Oxford, 1965).
Bowersock, G.W., *Greek Sophists in the Roman Empire* (Oxford, 1969).
Bowersock, G.W., *Fiction as History, Nero to Julian* (Berkeley and Los Angeles, 1994).
Bowersock, G.W., 'Roman Senators from the Near East', *Tituli* 5 (1972).
Branigan, Keith (ed), *Rome and the Brigantes; the Impact of Rome in Northern England* (Sheffield, 1980).
Bruun, Christer, *The Water Supply of Ancient Rome, a Study in Roman Imperial Administration* (Helsinki, 1991).
Burnham, Barry C., and Jeffrey L. Davies, *Roman Frontiers in Wales and the Marches* (Royal Commission on the Ancient and Historical Monuments of Wales, Aberystwyth, 2010).

Buttrey, T.V., *Documentary Evidence for the Chronology of Flavian Titulature* (Meisenheim, 1988).
Campbell, Brian, *The Writings of the Roman Land Surveyors* (Society for the Promotion of Roman Studies, monograph no. 9, London, 2000).
Campbell, Brian, *Greek and Roman Military Writers* (London, 2004).
Crook, J., *Consilium Principis: Imperial Councils and Counsellors from Augustus to Diocletian* (Cambridge, 1955).
Cuomo, Serafina, 'A Roman Engineer's Tales', *JRS* 101 (2011), pp. 143–165.
Dabrowa, E., *The Governors of Roman Syria from Augustus to Septimius Severus* (Bonn, 1998).
Dilke, O.A.W., *The Roman Land Surveyors, an Introduction to the Agrimensores* (Newton Abbot, 1971).
Drinkwater, J.F., *Roman Gaul* (Beckenham, Kent, 1983).
Duncan-Jones, R., *Money and Government in the Roman Empire* (Cambridge, 1994).
Dunn, Daisy, *In the Shadow of Vesuvius* (London, 2019).
Dusanic, S., and M.R. Vasic, 'An Upper Moesian Diploma of AD 96', *Chiron* 7, pp. 291–304.
Eck, W., *Die Statthalter der Germanischen Provinzen von 1 – 3 Jahrhundert* (Cologne, 1985).
Elbe, Joachim von, *Roman Germany, a Guide to Sites and Museums*, 2nd ed (Mainz, 1977).
Evans, Harry, *Water Distribution in Ancient Rome, the Evidence if Frontinus* (Ann Arbor, 1994).
Gallivan, P.A., 'The "false-Neros", a re-examination', *Historia* 22 (1973).
Garlick, Tom, *Roman Lancashire* (Whitehaven, 1977).
Garzetti, Albino *From Tiberias to the Antonines*, English edition (London, 1974).
Gibson, Roy K, *Man of High Empire* (Oxford, 2020).
Goguey, Rene, 'Legionnaires Romains chez les Lingons: la VIIIeme Augusta a Mirabeau (Cote d'Or)', *Revue Archeologique de l'Est*, 57 (2008), pp. 227–257.
Grainger, John D., *Nerva and the Roman Succession Crisis of 96 – 98* (London, 2003).
Grillone, A., (ed), *De Munitionibus Castrum*, (ed. and trans. of Ps-Hyginus.) (Leipzig 1977)
Haley, Evan W., *Baetica Felix, People and Prosperity in Southern Spain from Caesar to Septimius Severus* (Austin, TX, 2003).
Halfmann, H., 'Die Senatoren aus dem ostlichen Teil der Imperium Romanum bis zum Ende der 2Jh n Chr.', *Hypomnemata* 58 (Gottingen, 1979).
Halkon, Peter, *The Parisi, Britons and Romans in Eastern Yorkshire* (Stroud, 2013).
Hanson, W.S., *Agricola and the Conquest of the North*, (London, 1987).
Hanson, W.S., and D.B. Campbell, 'The Brigantes: from Clientage to Conquest', *Britannia* 17, pp. 73–89.
Henderson, B.W., *Civil War and Rebellion in the Roman Empire* (London, 1908).
Henderson, John, *A Roman Life, Rutilius Gallicus on Paper and in Stone* (Exeter, 1998).
Higham, Nick, 'Rural Settlements West of the Pennines', in Branigan (ed), *Rome and the Brigantes*, pp. 41–47.
Hodge, Trevor, *Roman Aqueducts and Water Supply*, 2nd ed, (London, 2002).
Hodgson, N., (ed), *Hadrian's Wall, 1999 – 2009* (Kendal, 2009).
Holder, P.A., *The Roman, Army in Britain* (London, 1982).
Houlder, Christopher, *Wales, an Archaeological Guide* (London, 1978).
Jamieson, S., 'Cornutus Tertullus and the Plancii of Perge,' *JRS* 55 (1965).

Jones, B.W., and R. Develin, 'M. Arrecinus Clemens', *Antichthon* 10 (1976), pp. 79–83.
Jones, Brian W., *The Emperor Titus* (Beckenham, Kent, 1984).
Jones, Brian W., *The Emperor Domitian* (London, 1992).
Jones, C.P., 'The Plancii of Perge and Diana Planciana', *HSCP* 80 (1976).
Konig, Alison, 'Frontinus' cameo role in Tacitus' Agricola', *Classical Quarterly*, 63 (2013), pp. 361–376.
Leunisson, Paul, 'Direct Promotion from Proconsul to Consul under the Principate', *ZPE* 89 (1991), p. 236.
Levick, Barbara, *Vespasian* (London, 1990).
Lintott, Andrew, *Imperium Romanum, Politics and Administration* (London, 1993).
Luttwak, E., *The Grand Strategy of the Roman Empire* (Baltimore, 1978).
MacKendrick, Paul, *The North African Stones Speak* (London, 1980).
Marsden, E.W., *Greek and Roman Artillery*, 2 vols (Oxford, 1969–1971).
McCrum, M., and A.G. Woodhead, *Select Documents of the Principates of the Flavian Emperors, including the Year of Revolution, A.D. 68 – 69* (Cambridge, 1968).
McDermott, W.C., 'Stemmata quid faciunt: the Descendants of Frontinus', *Ancient Society* 7, (1976) pp. 229–261.
Mitchell, Stephen, *Anatolia*, 2 vols (Oxford, 1993).
Mullen, Alex, *Southern Gaul and the Mediterranean, Multilingualism and Multiple Identities in the Iron Age and Roman Province* (Cambridge, 2013).
Nuttjens, Patrick (ed), *A History of York* (Pickering, 2007).
Oldfather, W.A., et al (ed and trans) *Aeneas Tacticus, Asclepiodotos, Onasander*, Loeb Library (Cambridge, 1928).
Ottaway, Patrick, *Roman Yorkshire* (Pickering, 2018).
Peachin, Michael, *Frontinus and the curae of the curator aquarum* (Stuttgart, 2004).
Picard, Gilbert Charles, *L'Ascension d'un dynastie Gauloise, la Gloire des Sedatii*, (Paris, 1990).
Pollard, Nigel and Joanne Barry, *The Complete Roman Legions* (London, 2012).
Price, S.R.F., *Rituals and Power, the Roman Imperial Cult in Asia Minor* (Cambridge, 1984).
Raepsaet-Charlier, M.-Th., *Prosopographie des Femmes de l'Ordre senatorial (Ie – IIe siecles)* (Louvain, 1987).
Ramm, Herman, *The Parisi* (London, 1978).
Remy, Bernard, 'Le Carriere de P. Calvisius Ruso Julius Frontinus, Governeur de Cappadocia-Galatie', *MEFRA* 95 (1983), pp. 163–182.
Reynolds, Joyce, *Aphrodiseias and Rome* (1982).
Ritti, Tullia, *An Epigraphic Guide to Hierapolis*, trans. Paul R. Arthur (Istanbul, 2006).
Rivet, A.L.F., *Gallia Narbonensis, Southern Gaul in Roman Times* (London, 1988).
Rivet, A.L.F., and Colin Smith, *The Place Names of Roman Britain* (London, 1979).
Rodgers, R.W. (ed), *Frontinus, De Aquis* (Cambridge, 2004).
Rupke, Jorg, *Fasti Sacerdotum, a Prospography of Pagan, Jewish, and Christian Religious Officials in the City of Rome, 300 BC to AD 499*, trans. David M. B. Stevenson (Oxford, 2008).
Salway, Peter, *Roman Britain* (Oxford, 1981).
Schoenberger, H., 'The Roman Frontier in Germany: an Archaeological Survey', *JRS* (1969), pp. 156–157.
Settipani, Christian, *Continuite Gentilice et Continuite Familiale dans les Familles Senatoriale Romaines a l'epoque Imperiale* (Oxford, 2006).

Shepherd, R. (trans), *Polyaenus's Stratagems of War* (London, 1793, reprinted Chicago, 1974).
Stadter, P.A., *Arrian of Nicomedia* (Chapel Hill NC, 1980).
Stevens, C.E., *The Building of Hadrian's Wall*, (Kendal, 1966).
Swain, Simon, *Hellenism and Empire, Language, Classicism and Power in the Greek World, A.D. 50–250* (Oxford, 1996).
Syme, R., 'The Imperial Finances under Domitian, Nerva, and Trajan', *JRS* 20 (1930), pp. 55–70.
Syme, Sir Ronald, *Tacitus* (Oxford, 1958).
Syme, Sir Ronald, *The Provincial at Rome* (Oxford, 1999).
Syme, Sir Ronald, *Greeks Invading the Roman Government* (Brookline, MA, 1982).
Syme, Sir Ronald, 'P. Calvisius Ruso, One Person or Two?', *ZPE* 56 (1984), pp. 173–192.
Syme, Sir Ronald, 'Pliny's Less Successful Friends', *Historia* 9 (1960).
Talbert, Richard J.A., *The Senate of Imperial Rome* (Princeton NJ, 1984).
Thulin, C. (ed), *Corpus Agrimensorum Romanorum* (Leipzig, 1913).
Townend, G.B., 'Some Flavian Connections', *JRS* 51 (1961), pp. 54–61.
Vita-Evrard, G. di, 'Des Calvisii Rusones a Licinius Sura', *MEFRA* 99 (1987), pp. 281–338.
Wacher, John, *The Towns of Roman Britain* (London, 1974).
Ward Perkins, J.B., 'The Career of Sex. Iulius Frontinus', *Classical Quarterly* (1937).
Webster, Graham, *The Roman Invasion of Britain*, revised ed (London, 1973).
Webster, Graham, *Boudica* (London, 1978).
Wellesley, Kenneth, *The Long Year, A.D. 69* 2nd ed (Bristol, 1989).
Wheeler, R.E.M., *The Stanwick Fortifications* (London, 1954).
White, Roger and Philip Barker, *Wroxeter, Life and Death of a Roman City* (Stroud, 1998).
Woolf, K.A., 'Food, Property, and Patronage: the Significance of the Epigraphy of the Roman Alimentary Schemes in Early Imperial Italy', *PSBR* 58 (1990), pp. 197–221.
Wikipedia entries on 'Centuriation', 'List of Roman Consuls', 'Sextus Julius Frontinus'.
'Roman Britain in 2014', *Britannia* 46 (2015).
'Roman Britain in 2017', *Britannia* 49 (2018).

Index

Abergavenny, ix, 65, 71
Achaia, 144, 195, 196, 199
Acilius Aviola, M., 165–6, 183
Ad Flexum, 152
Aedui, 34
Aegean Sea, 131
Aelian, 103, 108, 144, 146
Aelius Caesar, L., 210
Aelius Hadrianus Afer, P., 194, 198
Aelius Lamia Plautius Aemilianus, 200
Aemilius Paullus, 111
Aemilius Rufus, 7, 8
Aeneas Tacticus, 105
Afranius Burrus, Sex., 196, 198, 202
Africa, xiii, 2–4, 9, 11, 13, 16, 23–4, 38, 42, 46, 100, 130, 134, 216, 220
Agrennius Urbicus, 4
Ager Uritanus, 24
Agri Decumates, 110, 124, 150
Aire, river, 57
Alesia, 32
Alexander the Great, 107, 108
Alexandria-by-Egypt, 1, 17
Alexandria Troas, 136, 139
Alimenta, 163–4
Alpes Cottiae, 178
Alps, 13
Ambibulus, 145
Ammaedara, 134
Amorium, 142
Anatolia, 108
Anglesey, 54, 73, 75–6, 78
Ankyra, 142
Annia Faustina, 210
Annius Bassus, L., 41, 49
Annius Verus, 194
Antunnacum, 125
Antioch-in-Pisidia, 46
Antoninus Pius, emperor, 54, 196–7, 214
Antonine Limes, 128, 129, 149
Antonius Primus, M., 12, 17, 193
Antonius Saturninus, 128, 143
Anxur (Terracina), 144, 146, 210, 217
Apamaea Kelainai, 132, 142
Apennine Hills, 191

Aphrodisias, 137–9
Apollodoros of Damascus, 108, 180
aqueducts, Roman water system, 184–7
   Aqua Anio Nova, 186
   Aqua Anio Vetus 186
   Aqua Claudia, 185
   Aqua Julia, 185
   Aqua Marcia, 186
   Aqua Tepula, 185
   Aqua Traiana, 186, 189, 223
   Aqua Virgo, 185
Aquincum, 152
Arae Flaviae, 119–20, 151
Arcadian League, 105
Arelate, 196
Argentorate, 119–20, 123
Armenia, xiii, 5, 42–3, 49, 50, 200
Army, Roman:
   Legions:
      I Adiutrix, 123, 152
      I Augusta, 52, 60–4, 67, 91, 92, 95
      I Italica, 144, 153
      I Minervia, 145, 181
      II Adiutrix, 34, 35, 59, 79–80, 90, 93, 152
      III Augusta, 24, 114
      III Gallica, 7, 199
      IV Flavia, 152
      IV Scythica, 141
      V Alaudae, 47
      V Macedonica, 153, 209
      VI Ferrata, 7
      VI Victrix, 12
      VII Claudia, 152
      VII Galbiana, 200, 217
      VII Gallica, 17, 31
      VII Gemina, 152
      VIII Augusta, 34, 123
      IX Hispana, 51, 63, 69, 81–2, 89, 92–3
      X Fretensis, 12, 41, 152, 200, 209
      XI Claudia, 41, 123
      XIII Gemina, 152
      XIV Gemina, 54–5, 59, 64–5, 123, 152
      XV Apollinaris, 42, 152, 200

XX Valeria Victrix, 55, 59, 62–4, 81
XXII Primigenia, 34
Auxilia:
   ala Gallorum et Thracum Classiana, 60
   ala Gallorum Petriana, 60
   ala Gallorum Seposiana, 60
   I Hispanorum Equitata, 60
   II Asturum, 60
   II Lingones, 206
Arrecina Tertulla, 47
Arrecinus Clemens, L., 47, 49
Arrius Antoninus, Cn., 175, 194, 197, 199, 202
Arruntius Catellius Celer, C., 184
Artabanus IV, Parthian king, 141
Artaxata, 5, 7–8
Arval Brethren, 140
Asia, xiii, 42, 103, 130–43, 152, 195, 206, 208, 210
   aristocratic network, 48, 197, 199, 218
   Frontinus, governor of, 130–43, 217
Asklepiodotos, 106
Assyria, 100
Aswan, 110
Attius Suburanus Aemilianus, Sex., 178–9, 181
Augustus, emperor, 29, 38, 53, 109, 118, 130, 136–7, 153, 186
Aurelius Fulvus, T., 161, 168, 197–9
Aventicum, 114

Baetica, 12, 41–2, 152, 200, 216
Baiae, 144
Basel, 118
Batavians, auxiliaries, 59–60
Bavaria, 128
Bedriacum, 17, 55
Bellicius Natalis, C., 193–4, 197, 202
Berytus, 197, 199
Bithynia-and-Pontus, 133–4, 189
Biton, 106, 108
Black Mountains, 66
Black Sea, 118
Bohemia, 150, 174, 179–80
Bonna, 127, 145, 172, 181
Boudica, 51, 54, 60, 79, 94
Bowes, 61, 82, 87, 89
Brecon Beacons, 66, 70
Brecon Gaer, 71, 75, 77
Bremetenacum, 86–8, 92
Brigantes, 54, 56–8, 60–5, 69, 79–90, 92, 221
Brigetio, 152
Bristol Channel, 70

Britannia, xiii, 5, 24, 29, 31, 35–6, 41, 43, 50–1, 53–100, 104, 110, 117–18, 123, 144, 180, 202, 206, 209, 211, 217, 221, 223
Brithdir, ix, 75
Broxtowe, 81
Brough, 84, 88
Bryn y Gefelliau, ix, 75
Burrium, 63–5, 67, 69, 91

Caecilius Piso Crassus Frugi Licinanus, C., 165, 167–8, 170, 175, 181
Caecilius Simplex, Cn., 40, 197, 199, 202
Caecina Alienus, A., 41, 113
Caerau, 75
Caer Gai, 75
Caergwanaf, ix, 72
Caerhun, ix, 75, 77, 95
Caerleon, ix, 67, 70–2
Caernarfon, ix, 75, 95
Caersws, ix, 71, 74–5, 77
Calgacus, 97
Caligula, emperor, xii, 53, 114, 196
Calpetanus Rantius Quirinalis Valerius Festus, C., 46, 49
Calpurnius Piso, L., 13, 175
Calpurnius Piso Licinianus, 46
Calvisius Ruso, P., 195, 198, 207
Calvisius Ruso Julius Frontinus, P., 204–208
Calvisius Tullus Ruso, P., 206, 208, 210
Campania, 146, 158
Camulodunum (Colchester), 24, 95
Camulodunum (Slack), 86
Canon Frome, 65
Capitoline Temple, 43, 122, 140, 162
Cappadocia, 152, 167
Cappadocia-and-Galatia, 200, 206, 208
Caratacus, 54, 56
Cardiff, 65–6, 71
Carlisle, 80, 83, 85, 87
Carmarthen, 66, 71–2
Carnuntum, 17, 119, 121, 152
Carthage, 213
Cartimandua, queen, 54, 56–8, 89
Carvetii, 57–8, 61, 83, 87, 93
Casperius Aelianus, 161–2, 168, 169–71, 173, 178, 184
Castel Collen, 75
Castleford, x, 85–6
Castleford farm, 65
Castleshaw, 88
Castra Regina, 119
Cataractonium, 88
Catius Caesius Fronto, Ti., 154, 156–7
Cato the Elder, 214
Catuvellauni-Trinovantes, 53

Cawthorne, 84, 88, 93
Ceionia Fabia, 210
Celts, Celtic language, 15–16
centuriation, 22–4, 29
Chatti, 116, 120, 126–8, 131, 150, 222
Chepstow, 65
Cheriton, 139
Cheshire, 76
Chester, 70, 75, 77
Chesterfield, 82, 85
Chaereas and Callirhoe, 139
Cilicia, 145, 181
Civil War, 2, 11, 14, 31, 35–6, 38, 41, 53, 55, 98, 100, 105, 138, 141, 147, 193, 196, 202, 216, 218, 220–1
Claudia, 210
Claudia Ammiana Dryantilla, 211
Claudius, emperor, 14, 38–9, 42, 53, 155, 157, 194, 198
Cleveland Hills, 81, 84
Clifford, 65
Clodius Eprius Marcellus, T., 43–4, 49, 113
Coelbren, ix, 71
Colonia Agrippinensis, 177–9
Columella, 214
Commodus, emperor, 210–11
Comum, 154
Condate, 86
Constance, Lake, 119
consuls, Roman, 35–52
Conwy, 75
Corinium, 94
Corionototae, x, 57
Cornelius Lusio, L., 42
Cornelius Nigrinus Curiatius Maternus, P., 167, 175, 181
Cornelius Palma Frontonianus, A., 181
Cornelius Tacitus, 175, 196, 198
Cornovii, 54, 81
Corpus Agrimensorum, 3, 20–30
Cottius Paetus D. Valerius Asiaticus Saturninus, 194
Craven gap, 78
Cremona, 44
Cumbria, 57, 79, 81, 99
Curator aquarum, 44

Dacia, 153, 160, 174, 179–80, 182, 223
Dacian War, 141, 149–50
Dalmatia, 199
Danube river, 31, 78, 108, 118–19, 127, 141, 153, 160, 179, 180, 184
Dasumia, 208
Deceangli, 66, 72, 75, 76, 80, 93
Decebalus, 179–80

Dee, river, 54, 80
Demetae, 66, 71–2, 74–6, 93
Denmark, 153
Derbyshire, 85
Dere Street, 61, 80, 88
Derventio (Malton), 61, 82, 84, 89, 92, 97
Deva (Chester), 76, 86, 89–90, 92–3
  legionary fortress, 79–80
Didia Severina, 210
Didius Julianus, emperor, 210
Dio Chrysostom, 139
Dobunni, 53, 67, 69
Dolaucothi, 72, 99
Domitia Decidiana, 196
Domitia Lucilla, 194, 198, 206, 208
Domitian, emperor, 1, 5, 31, 33, 35–6, 38, 40–1, 50, 54, 59, 102, 104, 109–10, 112, 116–19, 130, 138, 141, 143, 147, 164, 169, 195, 212–13, 215, 217–19, 222–3
  accession, 115
  frontier policy, 149–53, 174–5
  German war, 122–4, 149–51
  murder of, 154–8, 160
  statues of, 163
Domitilla, 155
Domitius Afer, Cn., 192
Domitius Ahenobarbus, Cn., 15, 191–2
Domitius Corbulo, Cn., 5–8, 10, 14, 18, 22, 39, 42–3, 49, 50, 100, 102, 107, 191, 195, 198, 199–200, 202, 221, 224
Domitius Lucanus, 192, 198
Domitius Tullus, Cn., 47, 49, 174, 176, 192, 194, 197, 206
Don river, 25, 86
Doncaster, x, 85–6, 88
Dumnonii, 53
Durham, 58, 79, 81
Durocortum (Reims), 117
Durotriges, 53, 67, 69
Duvius Avitus, L., 196
Dyfed, 66, 75
Dyfi River, 73

Eboracum (York), 61, 82, 84, 87–9, 92–3
Eden Valley, 57–8, 61, 81–2, 88
Egypt, 161, 167, 196, 200
Elmet, 57
Emerita Augusta, 4, 23
Ems River, 125
England, North, 24
English Channel, 117
Epameinondas of Thebes, 106–107, 111
Ephesos, 131–2, 136–7
Erglodd, ix, 75
Etruria, 194, 198, 201

Etruscan surveying, 22, 213
Euphrates river, 140–1
Exeter, 53

Flavia Domitilla, 35
Flavius Fimbria, L., 47, 49
Flavius Sabinus, T., 43, 47–9
Fleetwood, 86
Forden Gaer, 74
Formiae, 103, 114, 144
forts, layout, 93–4
Forth-Clyde line, 99
Forum Iulii, 195, 197–8
Fosse way, 53
Frontinus, Sextus Julius,
  books by, 211–15
    Art of War, 100–105, 109, 146, 187, 218
    Commentum, 4, 20, 25–6, 28
    de Aquis, 184, 187–8, 223
    on Homeric tactics, 101, 103–104, 139
    on surveying, 28–30, 214, 222
    Practice of Agriculture, The, 213–14
    Stratagems, 5–6, 18, 24, 32, 100–106, 109, 116, 124, 185, 187, 190, 213, 222
  Career and offices, xii–xiii, 9–11, 21, 26–8, 205, 212, 216, 223–225
    an *eques*, 3–5, 21, 35
    augur, 145
    auxilia officer, 8
    comes in exercitus Germania, 116–18, 218
    consul, 10, 36, 49–52, 144, 146, 176, 219
    curator aquarum, 103, 116, 165, 168, 180, 182–90
    family and descendants, 126, 204–11
    founder of legionary fortresses, 89–90, 94
    governor of Asia, 103, 104, 116, 130–44, 158
    governor of Britannia, 36, 51–2, 62–99, 100, 104
    governor of Germania, 104, 113–29
    in Imperial *consilium*, 115, 146, 150–1, 164, 217
    network of friends, 145, 191
    organizer of fort network, 92–3, 96, 99, 221
    origin, 13–16
    praetor urbanus, 1–3, 18, 31, 35, 41
    and the Senate, 181
    senatorial financial commission, 165, 218
    surveyor, 9, 20–30
    travels, 148

Gades, 42
Galatia, 42, 48
Galba, emperor, 12–13, 16–17, 30–1, 35, 37, 39, 42, 48–50, 138, 148, 152, 160, 175, 199, 200, 202, 216–17, 224
Gallia Belgica, 32, 117, 127, 178, 181
Gallia, Gaul, 5, 9, 14, 24, 31–2, 53, 69, 83, 104, 117, 119, 122, 124, 144, 191–2
Gargani, 5, 76
Gavius Atticus, 48
Gelligaer, 71
Germania, Germany, xiii, 31, 37, 63, 78, 104, 109, 111–12, 116, 128, 132, 144, 149–51, 176, 212, 215, 217
Germania Inferior, 116, 127, 177, 179, 218, 222
Germania Superior, 116, 127, 152, 177, 179, 181
German war, 5, 41, 59, 122–4
Glevum, 56, 63, 65–7, 69–70, 82, 91, 94
Gower, 66
Greece, 48, 199
Greek language, 16
Grinario, 125, 127

Hadrian, emperor, 54, 177, 194, 198, 208–209
Hadrian's Wall, 209, 222
Hadrumetum, 4
Hafan, 74
Halikarnassos, 132
Hamilcar Barca, 107
Hannibal, 6, 15, 107, 193
Hasdrubal, 15
Hayton, 84
Heddenberg, 121
Heideberg, 120
Herculanium, 113, 121–2, 128, 150–1
Hermunduri, 122, 128, 150–1, 179
Herodotus, 105
Heron of Alexandria, 106, 108
Hierapolis, 132, 139, 145
Hindwell Farm, ix, 65
Hispania Citerior, 43, 46
Hofheim, 121
Humber river, 53–4, 56, 61, 65, 81–2, 84

Iazyges, 153
Iceni, 53
Inheiden, 125
'Initia', 7
Intimilia, 196
Isca Dumnoniorum, 56, 60, 65, 94
Isca Silurum, 67, 75, 80–1, 89, 91, 94–5
Italy, 23, 107, 136, 192
Iunius Q. Vibius Crispus, L., 44, 49

Jerusalem, 152, 209
Jewish War, 10, 38, 216
Judaea, 151–2, 199–200
Julia Frontina, 126, 144, 204, 209
Julius Agricola, Cn., 14, 16, 67, 73–6, 78, 88–9, 97, 100, 109–10, 114, 118, 129, 180, 195, 197–8, 212, 221–2
Julius Caesar, C., 192, 214
Julius Cordinus Cn. Rutilius Gallicus, Q., 42, 47, 49, 200
Julius Erucius Clarus Vibianus, C., 211
Julius Marinus, L., 197, 199, 201
Julius Montanus, T., 136
Julius Verus, emperor, 110
Julius Vestinus Atticus, M., 193–5, 198
Julius Vindex, 13, 33, 193
Juvenal, 44–5

Kemel, 125
Kent, 53
Kidda river, 121
Kirkham, 92
Kos, 132
Kyzikos, 132

Ladenberg, 120
Laecanius Bassus Caecina Paetus, C., 41, 48–9
Lake District, 87
Lambaesis, 24, 114
Lancashire, 57–8, 64, 79, 80–1, 85, 92
Lancaster, 88
Laodikeia-ad-Lykon, 132, 139, 209
Leas Rigg, 84, 88
Legenda, 6
Lesbos, 136
lex Mamilia, 27, 213
Liber Coloniarum, 25–6
Licinius Crassus, M., 6
Licinius Mucianus, C., 2, 18, 32–4, 41, 43, 47, 50, 148, 200
Lincolnshire, 89
Lindum Colonia, 24, 56, 63, 82, 84, 88
Lingones, 31–6, 50–1, 92, 108, 117–18, 128, 217–18, 220–1
Livy, 5, 105
Llandeilo, 71
Llandovery, ix, 71–2, 75
Llanfair Caereinion, ix, 74
Llanfor, ix, 75, 77
Llanio, ix, 75
Llanmelin, 68
Lleyn Peninsula, 66, 75
Londinium, 95
Lugdunum, 15, 32–5, 193

Lugii, 151
Luguvallium (Carlisle), 57, 61–2, 79–80, 82, 87–8, 90, 92–3
Lune river, 86
Lusitania, 4, 12
Lycia-and-Pamphylia, 47–8, 196, 209, 211
Lykia, 131, 143

Macedonia, 195, 199
Main river, 121, 125, 150
Mamucium (Manchester), 86, 88, 92
Manlius Patruinus, L., 48
Manlius Valens, 182
Marcius Priscus, Sex., 47–49
Marcomanni, 150–1, 160, 174, 177, 179
Marcus Aurelius, emperor, 54, 108–109, 112, 194, 197–8, 208, 210
Maridunum (Carmarthen), 70, 74
Marius Celsus, P., 197, 199–202
Martial, 30, 144–6, 158, 189
Massalia, 15–16, 198
Mattiaci, 124
Mauretania, 110, 114
Maxentius, 155
Mediolanum (Whitchurch), 76
Memmius Regulus, P., 193, 195, 199
Menai Strait, 73
Mersey river, 54–5, 58, 66, 80, 86, 88
Mesopotamia, 111
Mettius Modestus, M., 196
Mettius Rufus, 196
Mirabeau-sur-Beze legionary fortress, 34, 36, 50, 89
Moesia, 151–3, 195, 198, 209
Mogontiacum, 116–17, 119–21, 123, 143
Monmouth, 65
Mons Graupius, 110
Moravia, 150
Morecambe Bay, 99
Moselle river, 31–2
Mursa, 152
Musellae, 152
Mycenae, 213–14

Nabataea, 209
Naples, Bay of, 114
Narbo Martius, 15, 191
Narbonensis, viii, 11, 13–18, 23, 30, 32, 47–8, 100, 138, 191–203, 207–208
Neckar river, 119, 125, 127
Nemausus, 192–4, 197–8, 201
Nero, emperor, xii, 12, 16, 22, 38, 40, 42, 64, 136, 138–48, 160, 194, 198, 202, 216
Nero-pretenders, 140–2, 151

Nerva, emperor, 44–5, 49, 103, 136, 146–69, 183–4, 189, 197, 218–19, 223
  death, 174
  legislation, 162–4
  plots against, 165–72
  successor, 173–5, 177
  and taxation, 156–72
Newton Kyme, 86
Newton-on-Trent, 81
Nijmegen, 90
Nile river, 110
Norbanus, 161
North Sea, 87, 117–18
Northumbria, 57
Northwich, 86, 88
Nottinghamshire, 85
Novae, 144, 153

Octopitae, 66, 75
Oescus, 153
Offenberg, 120
Okaben, 121
Onasander, 108, 110
Oppenheim, 116, 126
Ordovices, 56, 64, 66, 69, 73–8, 80, 82, 84, 88, 91, 93, 98–9, 221
Osmanthorpe, x, 81
Ostorius Scapula, P., 54
Otho, emperor, 12, 16, 31, 41–3, 48–9, 55, 138, 148, 166, 196–7, 200, 216–17, 224
Ouse river, 61, 82, 84

Palestine, 41, 45, 139, 167
Pallantia, 4, 23
Pandeteria, 153
Pannonia, 17, 46, 109, 150, 151, 171–3, 177, 181, 200
Parisi, x, 57–8, 61–2, 81–5, 87–9, 91–3
Parthenius, 154–6, 169–70
Parthian War, 1–2, 5–6, 27, 64, 109, 111–12, 140–2, 209
Patmos, 139
Peak District, 54
Pedius Casca., L., 46
Pennal, ix, 74, 75
Pennines, 61, 79, 81, 86–8, 92, 99
Penlleyn, 75
Pen Llystyn, ix, 75
Pentrehyling, 74
Pen y Crocbren, ix, 74
Penydarren, ix, 71
Pen y Gaer, ix, 71
Petillius Cerialis Caesius Rufus, Q., 31–3, 35–6, 41, 43, 47, 49, 51, 59–62, 69, 78, 81–5, 89, 98, 220–1

Petriana, 60–1, 84, 88
Petronius Secundus, Ti., 158, 161, 170
Philip II, 107, 111
Philon of Byzantion, 106, 108
Phrygia, 132, 142, 145
Phyllis, 169
Pinarius Aemilius Cicatricula Pompeius Longinus, Cn., 151, 153, 177, 173
Pinarius Cornelius Clemens, Cn., 119–23, 151
Plautius, A., 54, 98
Plautius Silvanus Aelianus, T., 43, 49
Plautus, 29
Pliny the Younger, 30, 47, 133, 145–6, 158, 164, 180, 189
Plotius Grypus, 2, 50
Plutarch, 145
Poetovio, 152
Polyainos, 108–109
Polybius, 5, 105
Pompeia Falconilla, 210
Pompeia Paullina, 196
Pompeia Plotina, 14, 194, 198
Pompeii, 113
Pompeius Collega, Cn., 49, 200
Pompeius Falco, Q., 132, 209–10, 214
Pompeius Magnus, Cn., 107, 109, 136
Pompeius Silvanus Staberius Flavinus, M., 41
Pompeius Sosius Priscus Q., 210
Pompeius Sosius Priscus Falco, Q., 210
Pompeius Vopiscus, L., 193–4, 199, 202
Pomponius, C., 48
Pontius Laelianus, M., 210
Pontus, 199
Poppaea, 166
Portus Gaditanus, 42
Praetorian Guard, 151, 161, 169–71, 174, 178, 219
Propontis, 131–2
'Pseudo-Hyginus', 109
Ptolemy I, 18
Pumsaint, ix, 72, 75
Punic Wars, 107
Pydna, 11
Pyrenees, 13, 15, 192–3

Quadi, 150–1, 160, 174, 179
Quinctilius Valerius Maximus, Aex., 136
Quinctius Atticus, C., 40.

Raetia, 117, 150, 161
Regalianus, emperor, 211
Regni, 53
Revelation, 139

Rhine frontier, 117, 124–9, 220
Rhine river, 31–2, 34, 47, 118, 120–1, 127, 129
Rhineland, 59, 64, 116, 152
Rhone river, 32, 193
Rhoxolani, 199
Ribble river, 57–8, 80, 86–8, 90, 221
Ribblesdale, 88
Ribchester, x, 86, 88
Roecliffe, 61–2, 82, 87, 89
Roman surveying, 22
Rome, fire of, 114
  governing system, xii
  pomerium extension, 67, 77–8, 97
  water supplies, 23, 212
Roscius Coelius, 37–8, 46, 55, 209
Rossington bridge, 81
Ruscino, 192, 195, 199, 201

Sagur, 155
St John, 139
Salmantica, 4, 23
Salvius Otho Cocceianus, M., 166,
Scarborough, 81
Scipio Africanus, 107
Scotland, 110, 129, 222
Scottish Highlands, 79, 97, 110, 222
Sebaste, 142
'Second sophistic', 139
Seleukeia Zeugma, 140, 141
Selgovae, 81
Semnonae, 151
Senate, Roman Senators, 1, 4, 30, 36–7, 44, 179
Seneca, 189, 196, 201–202
Septimius Severus, emperor, 55, 111–12, 211
Sequani, 32–4
Sergius Octavius Laenas, P., 166
Sergius Paullus, L., 48–9
Setantii, x, 57–8, 81, 83, 86–7, 93
Setantium Portus, 51
Severn river, 54, 56, 65–6, 68, 74, 77, 80, 84, 88, 91
siegecraft, 105–106
Sigellius, 155
Silius Italicus, 138, 156
Silures, 56, 62, 64, 66–74, 81, 84, 88, 90–1, 99, 108, 120, 125, 221
Singidunum, 152
Slack, 86, 88
Smyrna, 131–2
Snowdonia, 73–4, 80, 91
Soane river, 32
Solway river, 57–8, 80
Sosia Frontina, 209

Sosia Polla, 132, 209–10
Sosius, C., 145
Sosius Senecio, Q., 144–6, 172, 181, 204, 209, 219
Spain, 3–4, 9, 11, 16, 23, 37, 100, 138, 143, 189, 192, 216–17, 220, 224
Stainmore Pass, 61, 80, 88
Stamford Bridge, 84, 88
Stanwick, 57–8, 82–3, 87
Statilia Messalina, 194
Stephanus, 155–6, 169
Sudbrook, 18
Suessa Aurunca, 23–4
Suetonius Paullinus, 54, 62, 79–80
Sulpicia Agrippina, 211
Sulpicius Galba, Ser., 12
Sulpicius Pollio, C., 211
Surveying methods, Roman, 22
Syria, 1, 7, 37, 41–2, 63, 78, 142, 152, 168, 200

Tacitus, 3, 32, 45
  Annals, 6
Tai Cothinau, 75
Tarentum, 165, 168
Tarraconensis, 4, 12
Taunus Hills, 120–1, 124
Tawe river, 70
Tectoverdi, 57
Tees river, 57–8, 81, 83, 87, 90, 99, 221
Templeborough, x, 82, 85
Terentius Maximus, 140–1
Terracina (Anxur), 11, 114, 144, 210
Thrace, 199
Thucydides, 5, 105
Thysdrus, 4, 134
Tiberius, emperor, 38, 116, 149, 153, 191, 216
Tigranocerta, 6–8
Tiridates, Parthian king, 7
Titus, emperor, 1, 36, 38, 44, 109, 113–15, 122, 141, 147, 216, 219
Tolosa, 193
Towy river, 66, 70
Trajan, emperor, xiii, 4, 14, 54, 103, 108, 110, 112, 136, 143, 146, 152, 159, 160, 184–9, 194, 197, 199, 208–209, 213, 216, 218, 220–1
  nominated emperor, 172–3, 175–7
  frontier policy, 179–80
  and Rome, 180, 184
Transpadana, 42, 45
Trawscoed, 75
Trebellius Maximus, 54–6, 62–4, 209

Trebonius Proculus Mettius Modestus, C., 196, 201
Trent river, 64, 81
Trent Vale, 82
Treveri, 31–4
Troy/Ilion, 139
Tyne river, 57
Tyne-Solway line, 87, 89, 99

Ulpius Traianus, M., 12, 41, 49, 152, 200
Urban colonists, 157
Usk, 70

Vadandrus, 6
Valerius Asiaticus, D., 193–5, 198, 201
Valerius Catullus, M., l., 45
Valerius Lupercus, Q., 204
Valerius Lupercus Julius Frontinus, Q., 204–207
Valerius Paulinus, Q., 196–7, 201
Vasio, 196–8
Vegetia, 214
Veleia, 164
Venedoti, 66, 75, 76, 93
Venta Silurum (Caerwent), 68, 90–1, 94
Venutius, 56–8, 65–6, 79, 81, 83, 87
Verginius Rufus, L., 13, 165, 175
Verona, 45
Verulamium, 94–5
Veranius, Q., 108
Vespasian, Emperor, 1–2, 5, 10, 13, 16–18, 35–52, 59, 63, 77–8, 97, 109, 113–14, 117, 121–3, 128, 130, 136, 138, 142, 147–8, 183, 193, 196, 199–200, 202, 206, 208–209, 216–17, 219–20
Vestini, 191, 195, 198
Vestricius Spurinna, T., 48–9, 165
Vesuvius, Mount, 113
Vetera, 116

Vettius Bolanus, M., 56–7, 58–60, 62, 79, 81, 87, 110
Vettulenus Civica Cerialis, C., 141–3, 200
Via Domitia, 192
Vienna, 193–4, 197–8, 202, 206–208, 210–11
Viminacium, 152
Vindobona, 152
Vindonissa (Windisch), 120, 123
Viroconium, 56, 62–4, 73–4, 80, 82, 89
Vistula river, 153
Vitellius, Emperor, 16–17, 31, 40–1, 46, 54–5, 96–7, 138, 148, 223
Vitruvius, 214
Volcae Arecomici, 192
Vologaeses, Parthian king, 7
Volsinii, 194
Votadini, 81

Wales, 24, 54, 63, 69–78, 90, 97–9, 110, 153, 180
   North, 56, 64, 67, 212, 221–2
   Roman fort network, 70–3, 80
   South, 56, 62, 67
Walton-le-Dale, x, 86, 88, 92
Wensleydale, 88
Wetterau, 120–2, 124–5, 129, 150
Wharfe river, 57
Whitchurch, ix–x, 76, 82
Wigan, 86, 92
Wiston, 72, 74
Wye river, 66, 70

Xenophon, 5, 105

York, 61–2, 85–6
Yorkshire, 57, 61, 79
Yorkshire Wolds, 82, 84
Y Pigwn, 71